THE IRAQI MARSHLANDS AND THE MARSH ARABS

THE IRAQI MARSHLANDS AND THE MARSH ARABS

The Ma'dan, their Culture and the Environment

SAM KUBBA

THE IRAQI MARSHLANDS AND THE MARSH ARABS
The Ma'dan, their Culture and the Environment

Published by
Ithaca Press
8 Southern Court
South Street
Reading
RG1 4QS
UK

www.ithacapress.co.uk

Ithaca Press is an imprint of Garnet Publishing Limited.

First Edition

ISBN: 978-0-86372-333-9

British Library Cataloguing-in-Publication Data
A catalogue record for this book is available from the British Library

Jacket design by Garnet Publishing

Printed in Great Britain by the MPG Books Group,
Bodmin and King's Lynn

DEDICATION

This book is dedicated to the Iraqi Marsh Arabs and the Ma'dan who witnessed, endured and survived the ruthless desiccation of their homeland. It is also dedicated to a dear friend, the late Ms Nada al-Jaboori, who was one of the book's contributing authors but who was sadly killed in a recent assassination attempt on the Iraqi Vice President. She will always be in our prayers and our hearts. May the Lord watch over her.

ACKNOWLEDGEMENTS

A book of this scope would not have been possible without the active and passive support of many friends, colleagues and scholars who have contributed greatly to my thinking and insights during the writing of this book, and have been instrumental in the crystallization and formulation of my thoughts on many of the subjects and issues discussed within. To them I am heavily indebted, as I am to the innumerable people, NGOs and organizations that have contributed ideas, comments, photographs, illustrations and other items that have helped make this book a reality.

I must also confess that without the enthusiasm of Garnet Publishing & Ithaca Press, this book may never have seen the light of day. My special thanks to Dan Nunn and Arash Hejazi, Editorial Managers, for their support and advice and for proofing much of this book. I would also like to express my deepest appreciation to Nadia Khayat, Projects Manager, Pamela Park, Production Manager and Christine Hart, Office Manager, who together managed to carry me through the final stretch. To these wonderful professionals, I can only say, thank you.

I wish to thank Mr Hassan Partow of UNEP for his constructive comments and permission to use some UNEP photographs. I am also indebted to Professor Barry Warner, Project Director of CIMI, for his assistance and permission to use some of the many photographs CIMI has of the Iraqi Marshlands. In this respect, I also wish to thank Mudhaffar Salim, Jasim al-Asadi and Dr Faris Kubba for permission to use some of the excellent marshland-related photographs they took.

The information for Chapter 10 is based on experience and information gathered during the Canada-Iraq Marshlands Initiative. Keith Holmes, University of Victoria, compiled Figure 10.1. I thank the innumerable scientists, students, assistants and logisticians in Iraq from the Universities of Babylon, Baghdad, Basra, Kufa and Thi Qar, and from the Ministry of Water Resources for their participation without whose collaboration CIMI would not have been possible. The Iraq Ministry of Higher Education and Research and the Canadian International Development Agency provided financial support. Dr T. Asada provided useful comments on the draft of chapter 10.

I especially wish to express a deep appreciation to the Iraqi Ministry of Water Resources and to H. E. Dr Latif Jamal Rashid for writing the Foreword and who went out of his way to be helpful.

Finally, I wish to thank the many people who mean so much to me and who kept me going with their enthusiasm and knowledge. I relied upon them in so many ways: for advice, support and motivation. Without them, I could not have completed this book.

CONTENTS

FOREWORD

The Mesopotamian Marshlands, located in southern Iraq, constitute the largest wetland ecosystem in the Middle East and Western Eurasia. The wetlands are the locale in which human civilization began with the Sumerian culture more than 5,000 years ago, and have made great contributions to humanity in all aspects of life. The marshlands are considered by many as the cradle of civilizations and are often referred to as the site of the biblical "Garden of Eden".

Until the 1970s, the marshlands were once the permanent habitat for various types of endemic species of mammals, birds and fish and an intercontinental flyway for millions of migratory birds. They play a key role in the support of endangered species and sustaining freshwater fisheries. In addition to these important ecological benefits, these marshlands represent a unique element of the global heritage and resources.

The marshes were associated with periods of flooding due to their location in the sedimentary plain which exposed them to inundation during the flooding of the Tigris and Euphrates. For this reason, they were known to the Chaldeans as a "Land of Water".

The world of the marshes in southern Iraq has drawn the attention of many Iraqi and foreign scientists and scholars as it is considered a fertile ground for various types of science and research and its life is of a unique nature.

Since the 1970s and after reading the history books that talk about the Iraqi marshes and their environment, I personally have started to focus on this subject and have found that this 5,000-year-old cultural heritage represents a link from the modern world to the roots of its civilization and ancient history.

The unique ecosystem of the Mesopotamian Marshlands has maintained its environmental and economic integration as well as its cultural and heritage importance for thousands of years until this integral ecosystem was deliberately destroyed and transformed into a man-made desert by the former regime (Saddam's regime). The attack that was launched on the marshes was so severe that less than 10 per cent global change of the original area has miraculously survived. Indeed, the attack exposed the 5,000-year-old continuous civilization to the danger of a permanent disappearance.

As a result of destructive policies, wars and mismanagement of the National Water, the ecological and natural balance had faced massive destruction and this turned the beautiful landscape and thousands of square kilometers of seasonal and permanent lakes as well as vast areas of reeds into desert. Extinction of several endemic animal and botanical species and the displacement of thousands of the Marsh Arab population who were forced to flee the marshes were also a result of those destructive policies.

After the end of military operations, the desiccation process and displacement of Marsh Arabs, my great concern when I was outside Iraq was to stop the destruction and devastation that hit the marsh area and so I worked as an active member in restoring normalcy to the marsh area and launched a number of campaigns, conferences and symposia to mobilize world public opinion against the desiccation and genocide of the population of the marshes. The draining of marshlands in southern Iraq was another humanitarian tragedy just like the bombing of the Kurdish village of Halabja with mustard gas. Indeed, the process led to a humanitarian, cultural and environmental catastrophe in the area.

After the downfall of the former regime in April 2003, I had the honor of taking responsibility as Minister of Water Resources and had the opportunity to achieve the goal of effective restoration of the marsh area. Thus, a number of field trips and frequent visits to the marshes were made in order to prepare necessary plans and studies for this purpose. Reviving the marshes ecosystem and focusing on the development of the region in accordance with scientific bases to conserve the biological diversity and improve the environmental situation were all part of planned objectives. Accordingly, 75 per cent of the total area included in the inundation was flooded and restored at the end of 2007.

There are several factors that control the process of re-flooding and restoring the marshlands with water, the most important one being the climate change represented by increasing or decreasing the amount of rain, snow as well as water inflows to the Tigris and Euphrates Rivers and their tributaries.

The other factor is the actions and policies of riparian countries. Such actions are: the construction of storage dams and irrigation projects, and the use of operational plans to control large quantities of water reaching Iraq. Not to mention that the construction of structures and other irrigation projects which control water inflows to the marshes have negatively affected water management and water quality and quantity in the marshes.

The Iraqi Marshes have provoked great interest from a number of states such as the United States, Italy, the United Kingdom, Japan and Canada. A number of governmental and non-governmental organizations, including the World Bank and UN organizations, particularly the UNEP, have all contributed to the restoration of the marshes through financing several projects to protect the marsh environment and maintain its history and heritage of civilization.

The restoration of the Iraqi Marshlands is an official policy and activity of the Ministry of Water Resources and one of its priorities. The main objective behind bringing back life to the marshes is to create an intact ecosystem, sustain the ecological integrity socially and culturally, preserve archaeological sites and heritage as well as improve and develop basic services for residents in coordination with the relevant ministries in the areas of housing, health, education, environment, roads, communications and others.

The Ministry of Water Resources has achieved a lot in the area of marshland re-flooding and restoration and is continuing to implement works and projects that will provide the marshes with economic prosperity and sustainability. It will also develop restoration plans for more areas in accordance with the overall strategy of the Ministry of Water Resources in water management which is based upon the available water inflows. Unfortunately, Iraq during the past two years witnessed a severe shortage of water due to lack of rain, snow and low water inflows of the Tigris and Euphrates and their tributaries which have not allowed us to fully re-flood the areas planned to be inundated. Our hope is to continue to improve the quality and quantity of water in the marsh area and to expand the rehabilitation programmes according to the plans prepared by the Ministry.

Dr Latif Jamal Rashid, Minister of Water Resources, Baghdad, Iraq – January 2010

INTRODUCTION

Sam A.A. Kubba

Art and architecture ultimately tend to reflect the society we live in, its values, its customs and the aspirations of its people. This book illuminates the rich cultural and architectural heritage of the Iraqi marshlands and its people as well as a wildlife environment spanning over five thousand years. The book further attempts to reflect the opulent legacy of these communities rooted in the dawn of human history, as seen through centuries of almost uninterrupted cultural development and progress. The current marsh dwellers are our only remaining visible link with this rich cultural past.

It is here, on the shores of the ancient marshlands, that the legendary *Epic of Gilgamesh* was enacted. The site is also considered by many religious scholars to be the inspiration for the biblical Garden of Eden in the Bible and the Koran. Likewise, many archeologists believe this was the Eden alluded to in the Old Testament and earlier texts of the ancient Near East. Scholars also regard the marshes as the birthplace of the patriarch Abraham. The Iraqi marshlands are therefore an area of major significance in the history of the three monotheistic religions: Christianity, Islam and Judaism.

Fed by the Tigris and Euphrates Rivers, this giant wetlands originally covered an estimated area of 15,000 to 20,000 square kilometers (equivalent to 5,800 to 7,700 square miles). The Mesopotamian marshlands formed one of the largest wetlands in the world and an aquatic ecosystem that has supported unique human communities for five millennia. Their global significance stems primarily from their impact in the intercontinental migration of birds, and for sustaining rare and native flora and fauna, as well as being a valuable habitat for wildlife including several endangered species.

This book is divided into twelve chapters providing the reader with a rare insight into the Marsh Arabs and the Ma'dan, and their habitat from ancient times to the present day. Chapter 1 deals with the history of southern Mesopotamia, including the biblical "Garden of Eden", and the Gilgamesh epic. It then discusses Ottoman and British rule, the Hashemite Monarchy and the decimation of the marshes by Saddam, and ends with the restoration efforts that are now in place. Chapter 2 describes the social and tribal culture of the marshland inhabitants, including religion, marriage, etc. Chapter 3 throws light on the richness of the arts and crafts of the marsh inhabitants and highlights this with numerous photographs. Chapter 4 discusses the physical environment of the area, including its topography and terrain, geology, soil conditions, climate, etc. In Chapter 5, the agriculture of the region from the earliest times to the present is discussed and in Chapter 6, the wetland's wildlife and ecosystem, including its plants, animals, birds, endangered species, etc. is covered.

As we go through Chapters 7 through 9, an outline is given of the design principles used by the ancient Sumerians and marsh dwellers as well as the building materials available at the time to these ancient people and the materials available to the Marsh Arabs today. Ancient tools and construction methods, etc., are also discussed. Chapter 10 consists of an overview of restoration efforts that are in place since the fall of the Saddam regime, and Chapter 11 talks about sustainable housing proposals. In the final chapter, the Hammar, Central and Huwaiza Marshes are investigated as well as the future of the marshlands, and how damming projects, drought and transboundary issues are impacting restoration efforts and the region. In this respect, the United Nations Environmental Program (UNEP) has put as one of its main objectives an attempt to try and broker an agreement among the countries involved in the damming projects along the Tigris and Euphrates Rivers in addition to discussing water management issues affecting the region, and to work together to try and resolve them.

The Mesopotamian marshlands, the Marsh Arabs and the Ma'adan have already been celebrated in several awe-inspiring books by writers such as Dame Freya Stark, Wilfred Thesiger, Gavin Maxwell, Gavin Young and Edward Ochsenschlager. Justifiably so; some of the world's earliest records of civilization, including Ur, Uruk (Warka), Eridu, Larsa, Lagash and Nina, existed on the fringes of the marshlands. Its people are therefore proud heirs to a culture that can be traced back thousands of years to the dawn of written history.

The demise of the marshlands began when Saddam Hussein seized power in the early 1970s. One of his first actions was the ordering of sections of the wetland to be drained to make room for military factories, chemical plants and other industries. In 1980, during the Iran–Iraq War, they were drained still further because of the land's perceived tactical value. But the greatest impact in their demise came upon the conclusion of the Gulf War in 1991 when Hussein gave the order to drain the marshes completely in retribution for the Shia uprising against his regime. The tremendous cost of draining the marshes put a heavy burden on Iraq's economy as well as having a disastrous impact on the marshes' environmental ecosystem. The reed beds were burned and the waters poisoned. By the time Saddam's regime collapsed, roughly 93 per cent of the marshes had been desiccated.

Baroness Emma Nicholson of Winterbourne, founder of a non-government relief group called Assisting Marsh Arab Refugees (AMAR), is one of many outspoken advocates for restoring the Iraqi marshes to their original splendour. But much of the credit for restoring the Iraqi marshes must go to environmental activists who initiated the Eden Again Project. Many international agencies also came to the rescue to restore the Iraqi wetlands including the United Nations Environmental Program (UNEP), the US Agency for International Development (USAID), the Canadian International Development Agency (CIDA), Canadian Iraqi Marshlands Initiation (CIMI), Italy's Ministry of the Environment and Territory (IMET) and the Government of Japan.

Good progress is now being made on several fronts in the overall effort to restore the social, economic and environmental systems for Iraq's marsh dwellers and to revive the link between the ancient past and the present. Iraq's Ministry of Water Resources (MoWR), formerly known as the Ministry of Irrigation, is the lead agency for restoration of the Iraqi Marshlands and has declared this to be its highest priority. The Ministry has already acted to restore water flow to portions of the marshlands, as requested by local marsh dwellers. The Eden Again Project is working closely with the MoWR and The Center for Restoration of the Iraqi marshlands (CRIM). RKBT, a Canadian firm of architects of Iraqi origin won an architectural competition organized by the Iraqi Ministry of Culture for a research center and museums to be built in the Iraqi marshes. UNEP has recently taken further action in restoring the environment and providing clean water and sanitation services to about 85,000 inhabitants of the southern Iraqi marshlands. Many other projects are also underway or in the preliminary stage.

Figure 1 A Marsh Arab and a Marsh woman and son (Photos: Jasim al-Asadi).

1

HISTORY OF THE IRAQI MARSHES

Sam A.A. Kubba
Abbas F. Jamali

FORMATION OF THE MARSHES

Most scholars conclude that the Iraqi marshlands are geologically modern, and probably originated some time during the Holocene era following the end of the last glacial maximum. About 18,000 years ago, the global sea level is estimated to have been about 120–130 metres (approx 394–427 feet) lower than at present, in which case the Gulf would have been completely dry, and the Shatt al-Arab would have flowed directly into the Gulf of Oman. Paul Sanlaville concludes that because the ground water level was very low it is unlikely that the marshes existed at the time and that "the first cities must have been settled on the lower valley-sides, close to the rivers and clearly below the present level of the plain".

Sea level began to rise in the Gulf Basin from about 12,000 BC and the rise was particularly rapid between 9,000 and 6,000 years ago (towards the end of the Ubaid period). Over the centuries there appeared to be continuous changes caused by the variable flow of water, climate change and developments in irrigation patterns. Some researchers opine that at about 5,000 to 4,000 BC, the Mesopotamian marshlands were covered by a lagoon-type marine environment, likely having saline waters (Sanlaville, 2002). As the sea level rose, the rivers began to deposit sediment and create large raised deltas, causing the shoreline to move to its current location, possibly some time between 3,000 and 1,000 BC (Sanlaville, 2002).

Having a clear understanding of how the marshlands of lower Mesopotamia were formed historically greatly facilitates the grasping of how they have been affected by water management projects. One of the distinguishing topographical features of the lower Tigris–Euphrates valley is its extremely flat alluvial plain. In fact, the Euphrates reportedly falls only 4 cm/ km (1.575 in/3281 ft.) over the last 300 km (186.4 miles), and the slope of the Tigris is about 8 cm/km which roughly equals 3.15 in/3281 ft. (Scott, 1995). Because of the level terrain, both rivers (but particularly the Euphrates) have deviated from a straight course, drifting in various loops that finally separate and become distributaries that dissipate into an enormous inland delta. The Euphrates velocity decreases rapidly due to its lack of tributaries along its lengthy course; the river then dissolves into the marshes but re-emerges just prior to its confluence with the Tigris River at Qurna. The Tigris on the other hand displays a comparatively stronger hydraulic force that enables it to retain a more constant course. However, it should be noted that in its lower areas around the city of Amarah, the Tigris also swiftly starts to lose its velocity and erupts into an array of distributaries feeding directly into the marshes.

Another important factor contributing to the formation of the marshlands is that the lower Mesopotamian plain considerably narrows as it approaches the Gulf. This formulation is the result of the large alluvial fan of Wadi Batin and the Al Dibdibah plain drawing in from the Nejid towards the west, and the Karkheh and Karun rivers descending from the Zagros Mountains eastwards. The Karkheh River discharges into the marshes on the eastern flank of the Tigris River, whose waters ultimately overflow into the Shatt-al-Arab via the Suwaib River. For its part, the Karun joins the Tigris–Euphrates Rivers below their convergence point in the lower section of the Shatt-al-Arab, at the port city of Khorramshahr 72 km (44.74 miles) from the Gulf. By spreading out at the head of the Gulf, the Wadi Batin/al Dibdibah, the Karkheh and Karun are able to suppress the width of the lower Mesopotamian valley to less than 45 km (28 miles) and thwart the twin rivers from flowing directly into the sea (Rzóska, 1980). This impedes the natural drainage of the Tigris and Euphrates, forcing them to deposit their sediment loads inland, thus resulting in the formation of a double delta consisting of a marshland complex and marine estuary.

Throughout history the large fluctuation in the water discharge volumes of both the Tigris and Euphrates Rivers has been one of their primary characteristics. Spring floods generally occurred between February and May, and were caused by snowmelt in the headwater region in Turkey and the Zagros Mountains. These short-lived but intense seasonal floods have formerly been about 1.5 to 3 meters (4.9 to 9.8 feet), but in 1954 the Tigris reached a record 9 meters (nearly 30 feet) causing large-scale inundations (Scott, 1995). Due to the flat topography of the plain, the flood pulses are able to maintain a vast complex of interconnected shallow lakes, back swamps and marshlands in the lower Mesopotamian plain. The marshlands are a highly dynamic ecosystem that is primarily dependent on spring floods for its replenishment and existence, and the high summer heat may cause the shallower areas to completely dry up leaving salt flats and reverting back to desert conditions.

ANCIENT HISTORY: THE SUMERIANS, GARDEN OF EDEN AND THE *EPIC OF GILGAMESH*

Although little archaeological exploration has been conducted within the marshes themselves, many of the earliest records of history and civilization can be found on the fringes of the marshlands, including the ancient towns of Ubaid, Eridu, Uruk, Isin, Kish, Larsa, Lagash and Nippur. Moreover, many mounds or "tells" can be found that rise above the marsh waters and that are believed to be sites of ancient cities such as Agar, Dibin, Qubab, Ishan and Waquf (Roux, 1993). Most of the ancient sites relate to various periods in Iraq's ancient history such as the Ubaid Period (4500–3800 BC), the Uruk Period (3800–3500 BC), and the Jamdat Naser Period (3500–3200 BC).

Over millennia the southern Iraqi marshlands have been pivotal in the socio-economic and cultural lives of marsh dwellers, and have been instrumental in providing ecological services and biodiversity benefits that extend beyond their geographic limits. Indeed, many scholars feel that the wetlands area has a special place in ancient Iraqi history and characterized it as the cradle of civilization by the coming together of powerful intellectual, social, economic and political forces. Not only has it been home to ancient human communities for more than five millennia, but the Marsh Arabs are considered by many to be heirs of the Sumerians and Babylonians and act as a continuous link to the peoples of ancient Mesopotamia, although their numbers have over the centuries been augmented by immigration and intermarriages with the Persians on the east and the Bedouins on the west (Salim, 1962). Figure 1.1 is an example of a traditional *mudhif* (guest house). Examples of *mudhifs* can also be found on numerous cylinder seals and other artefacts.

The Iraqi marshes and its people are inevitably linked to the country's water or lack of it. Like oil in the present day, water can be seen as either a blessing or curse. In a part of the world where water is limited it can mean the difference between life and death; but since the time of Noah or the similar Sumerian legend recorded in the *Epic of Gilgamesh* (legendary King of Uruk *c.* 27th century BC), too much water in the form of uncontrolled floods has also been a threat to man and other living creatures. Just as in our day, the ability to use natural resources can lead to peoples' prosperity and the rise of civilizations which the covetous and more powerful seek to destroy.

Iraq's wetlands are created by the confluence of the two great rivers, the Tigris and Euphrates, along with their tributaries. Some of the waters originate in the mountains of present-day Iraq but much of the water comes from Iraq's neighbors, Iran to the east for the Tigris tributaries, Turkey to the north for the Tigris and Turkey via Syria for the Euphrates from the north-west.

Figure 1.1 An example of a traditional Marsh Arab *mudhif* (guest house) which is similar to that built in ancient times (Photo: Mudhafar Salim).

The availability of water in an otherwise arid land provided the basis for life in the marshes, i.e., fishing, hunting and the raising of water buffalo. The reeds were used to make mats, and build houses and boats. This availability of food resources made for the romantic idea that the marshes were once the Garden of Eden. A suggested location and even the tree of Adam and Eve was claimed to be at Qurna where the Tigris and Euphrates Rivers unite to form the Shatt al-Arab or Arab River. The Sumerians, Akkadians and Babylonians of southern Iraq also used the river waters for irrigation. Agriculture flourished and was the basis for the rise of city states where the first writing, the first codes of law and the wheel were invented. Carving, music and metalwork also flourished. Trade reached Egypt and the Indian subcontinent, and while there were land routes for trade, sea routes were also used. Thor Hyerdahl, the famous Scandinavian writer and seaman, journeyed to southern Iraq and had a boat made from local papyrus. He named it *Tigris* (a National Geographic film was made of *The Tigris Expedition*) and sailed it to the port of Karachi in Pakistan and thence back past what was then the South Yemen island of Soccotra to Djibouti at the mouth of the Red Sea. He proved that the sea routes could have been used in ancient trade between southern Iraq, India and elsewhere. The blue lapis lazuli found in the jewels of the royal grave in Ur was thought to have been mined in the Badakhshan region of Afghanistan.

In the Sumerian city state of Uruk (Erech), which is located on the southern banks of the Euphrates, lived the mythological Sumerian hero-king Gilgamesh (*c*. 2700–2650 BC) of the epic poem named after him (Figure 1.2). The epic of Gilgamesh, as recorded in cuneiform script on clay tablets, tells among other things, the story of its hero who, after his beloved friend Enkidu dies, sets out to discover the secret of eternal life. He seeks the secret from the Noah-like Utnapishtin who has become godlike (immortal) through following the god's command to build a boat for his wife and himself and thus survive the flood that kills other creatures. It is interesting to note here that the flood story in Gilgamesh was a close analogue of the flood story in the Hebrew Bible.

On his way to Utnapishtin, Gilgamesh braves poisonous scorpions and meets Sidure, a female who directs him to Urshanabi, a ferryman. He builds a raft and sails on the sea of death in search of Utnapishtin. After much hardship he arrives. To reward his efforts Utnapishtin shares with Gilgamesh a special secret that only the gods know; that there is a plant that hides among the rocks that thirsts and thrusts itself deep in the earth, with thistles that sting. This plant contains eternal life for Gilgamesh. Gilgamesh searches, dives beneath the cold waters, finds the plant and, though it stings him, brings it back to the surface. With a feeling of gratitude and in a generous spirit Gilgamesh intended to take it back home to Uruk for the aged to eat, and for himself as well that he may remain young forever. But a snake eats the plant and it is the snake that becomes young. The philosophical conclusion is that one might as well enjoy life while it lasts.

What is interesting is that in the *Epic of Gilgamesh*, the world's first epic poem to be written, Gilgamesh makes mention of the marshlands: "Ever the river has risen and brought us the flood" and "A reed has not come forth... all the lands were sea, then Eridu was made." The Iraqi Museum possesses several artefacts representing Gilgamesh with water buffaloes in the Tigris and Euphrates. Moreover, the boats used by today's Marsh Arabs are almost identical to those found at the Royal Cemetery of Ur (Figure 1.3). Clay tablets from the Sumerian period document the marsh environment alive with wildlife.

Figure 1.2 Gilgamesh, the Sumerian hero-king of Uruk (*c*. 2700–2650 BC), (Louvre Museum).

Figure 1.3 A model of an ancient *mashuf* (canoe), discovered at the Sumerian city of Ur in southern Iraq.

According to a noted British archeologist who worked in Iraq, M. E. L. Mallowan, also noted for being the husband of mystery writer Agatha Christie, unlike their Iranian neighbors, the early Sumerian inhabitants of lower Mesopotamia (who included but were by no means exclusively marsh dwellers) lacked raw materials and so traded their agricultural produce in exchange for gold, semi-precious stones, the copper from the upper Euphrates and elsewhere. According to Mallowan, the Sumerian decline, as evidenced by a switch from growing wheat to growing barley, was due to increasing soil salinity due to poor drainage. Barley is a crop known to be more tolerant of salt than wheat. To this day salinity continues to be not only a major agricultural problem in southern Iraq but also a cause of the decreased water quality of the remaining marshes.

Several of the world's first records of civilization lie on the fringes of the marshlands, including Ur, Uruk, Eridu, Larsa, Lagash and Nina. While archaeological exploration has been minimal within the marshes themselves, there are numerous mounds, or "tells", which rise above the marsh waters and which are believed to be sites of ancient cities (Roux, 1993). Many of these areas were used as platforms upon which today's marsh inhabitants built their homes and communities. Artefacts such as flint-stone tools, pottery and earthenware found in Tell Al Ubaid (8 km north of Ur) date back to civilizations of the Ubaid period (4500–3800 BC), the Warka era (3800–3500 BC) and the Jamdat Naser period (3500–3200 BC). Likewise, the fact that reeds were found mixed with the artefacts, alongside indications of their use in home construction for these civilizations, strongly suggests that the marshes truly existed at that time.

The power of the Sumerians began to decline and by the 23rd century BC the Sumerians found themselves too weak to defend themselves against foreign invasion. The Semitic ruler Sargon I who reigned from about 2335–2279 BC succeeded in conquering the entire country and founded a new capital for his dynasty north of Sumer called Agade. The Akkadian dynasty lasted about a century, during which time the area became very prosperous.

Another period of great prosperity was during the reign of Ur-Nammu (2113–2095 BC) who founded the 3rd Dynasty of Ur (Figure 1.4, 1.5) and

Figure 1.4 Cylinder seal impression showing Ur-Nammu, King of Ur (2113–2095 BC). (British Museum).

who created a law code that antedates that of the Babylonian king Hammurabi by about three centuries. Some scholars consider Hammurabi's ascension to the throne as sole ruler of Sumer and Akkad as marking the end of the Sumerian state even though the Sumerian civilization was adopted almost in its entirety by Babylonia. The Sumerian civilization was followed by the Babylonian and Assyrian Empires.

The Assyrians called the marshes Narmrtu which meant "the bitter water" or Tamdu Shamatu Kildi, which meant "the sea of the city of Kildah". Historically, the dense reed beds which only small boats were able to penetrate created a safe haven for Chaldeans, who defeated the Assyrian ruler Sargon in the 7th century BC. In 703 BC, it was written that the King of Babylon "fled like a bird to the swampland" and the King of Assyria "sent ...warriors into the midst of the swamps... and they searched for five days" but the King of Babylon could not be found (Roux, 1993). The Assyrian Empire was followed by the Chaldean, Persian and Greek Empires.

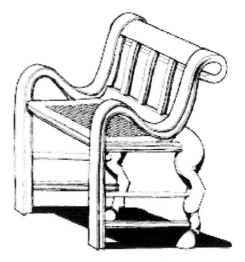

Figure 1.5 A tentative reconstruction of the throne (with backrest) that Ur-Nammu is shown seated on.

THE MARSHLANDS DURING THE ARAB AND OTTOMAN EMPIRES

From the Abbasid era (750–1258 AD) onwards, inhabitants of the marshlands were outside the control of the central government. The thick reed beds, waterways, wildlife and independent nature of the people made the region resistant to any external control while at the same time providing a place of refuge for bandits, rebels and smugglers. During this period, the Tigris–Euphrates delta had become discarded marshland as a result of peasant migration and repeated flooding that could only be reclaimed through intensive labor. Even the Ottoman Turks failed to incorporate the rigorously independent Ma'dan people who had inhabited the vast wetlands since prehistory into their empire.

Most historical sources seem to indicate that the marshlands were not very significant before the coming of the Arabs to Iraq, primarily because the first rulers of the area took great pains to drain the water accumulated in the lands around Babylon. They dug canals and built drainage systems in large areas to cultivate the lands, and converted them into fields. The areas between Kufa, Wasit and Basrah were generally well-populated. According to Arab historians, the Zanj (black slaves of east African origin), a rebellious slave army led by Ali bin Mohammed, were among those that took refuge in this vast wetland during the Abbasid period, from where they plagued the Abbasid central government. The Zanj Uprising took place near Basrah over a period of about fifteen years (869–883 AD) which at its zenith was reportedly about 500,000 strong and which was one of the few revolts where women played an active role in the struggle.

With war on the horizon and the marshland areas expanding due to degraded flood control and reduced irrigation, some people were forced to escape to higher ground. When the Arab (Islamic) Empire stabilized, the rulers lacked any knowledge regarding cultivation of the land. Neglecting the dams and failing to block the gaps further increased the flooded lands. However, during the Umayyad Caliphate only part of this area was cultivated.

Descriptions of the Iraqi marshlands can be found in various Arab books and accounts of journeys. Some Arab geographers opined that the marshlands had existed since the creation of the world. Al Masudi (943 AD), a well-known Arab historian and geographer born in Baghdad, states that when the Tigris changed its course towards Wasit it split up into several rivers culminating in the lands between Wasit and Basrah. The Euphrates also fed into the marshlands, which in historic times had been named the Babylonian marshes and in the Islamic Age, the Kufa marshes. This period saw the marsh area shrink or increase in size depending on the intensity of the floods of the two rivers and according to the ability of the central government to control the water of the rivers.

The state and area of the marshes remained unchanged during the Ottoman reign. This was because they neglected agricultural and drainage works in the area. The Ottomans were also weak in their administration, controlling only the main cities such as Baghdad, Basrah and Mosul. Most of the authority devolved to regional tribal chieftains.

During early Ottoman rule little was done of any consequence to instigate repairs on the ageing irrigation system which was in place during the Abbasid rule. The city of Baghdad and other areas had bunds or embankments built on the riverbanks to protect the city and crops from the destructive floods. The Ottoman *wali* (governor) Nadhim Pasha had a bund built east of Risafah (east Baghdad; Baghdad being divided by the Tigris River) in addition to the bund on the riverbank. Thus, if the narrow course of the river passing through Baghdad could not hold the flow they could break the bund north of Baghdad resulting in east Baghdad becoming an island, but reducing the height of the waters and thus preventing the city from being flooded. This was usually good enough but in 1954 the Diyala tributary river, which usually took the excess water south of Baghdad back to the Tigris, was itself in flood so the water around Baghdad rose to the top of the bund and would have drowned the city had there been a strong wind to make waves or had it not been for the army and volunteers who used protective sandbags to raise the bund height. Elsewhere and in other times flood waters did break the bund and destroy the crops, especially on the Tigris. Tribesmen were therefore regularly drafted in to maintain the bunds and dredge the irrigation canals.

During Ottoman rule, flood waters came in abundance to replenish the marshes with good quality fresh water of moderate salt content, which would drain back into the rivers and eventually to the gulf of Basrah. We assume there was no problem of salinity in the marshes. The Marsh Arabs during this period lived as the marsh dwellers of old must have at the time of the Sumerians but without the brilliant culture. Even their tribal chiefs were illiterate and relied on the *mullahs* trained in the city of Najaf to teach and handle any correspondence.

It should be noted that the Ottoman Turks with all their power were unable to impose even a semblance of authority over the marsh dwellers during their rule and between 1625 and 1668 and between 1694 and 1701, it was the local sheikhs that ruled the marsh area and Basrah and completely ignored the Ottoman governor of Baghdad.

Saddat al-Hindiyah (Indian Barrage)

Both the Tigris and the Euphrates have been known to change course. Cities that were once on the banks of the Euphrates such as Ur and Babylon are now some distance from the river. Rivers would also branch out, giving more water to one branch than to the other. One branch of the Euphrates which used to end up completely dry much of the time was the tributary going to the city of Hilla, close to the ancient city of Babylon. During the late Ottoman rule in Iraq a princely family in India made a will bequeathing their wealth to certain heirs and, in case of their demise, to a charitable cause in Iraq. The heirs all died and it was decided to use the inheritance to build a barrage to regulate the flow of water in the Euphrates. Thus it was that the flow of water to the western marshes was regulated by an "Indian" (*Hindiya* in Arabic) barrage. It was built according to a design by a British engineer and had as a witness a young man from Hilla, descendent of a very prominent Arab Jewish family, named Nessim Sousa. The young Nessim attended the celebrations of the Hindiyah barrage inauguration then rode his beloved horse in a race with the water that started to flow in the previously dry Hilla River. The Hilla River continues to flow, providing a livelihood for the region's farmers but reducing the quantity and quality of water going to the western marshes.

BRITISH AND HASHEMITE MONARCHY RULE

By the beginning of the twentieth century, most of the Ottoman territories had become the prime focus of European power politics. Prior to the outbreak of the First World War in 1914, the marsh dwellers were almost totally isolated from the outside world. However, when in 1914 the British discovered that Turkey had decided to enter the war on the side of the Germans, British forces were brought in from India and landed at al-Faw on the Shatt al-Arab; they then moved rapidly toward Basrah. However, after the First World War ended, the League of Nations was formed and in 1920 Iraq was formally placed under a League of Nations Class A mandate, administered by the British whose forces had occupied most of the country during this period.

In 1921 a conference was held in Cairo in which the British set specific parameters for Iraqi political life which were destined to continue until the 1958 revolution. The British chose the Hashemite Emir Faisal ibn Hussain, brother of Abdullah, the recently declared ruler of neighboring Jordan, to be Iraq's first king. To legitimize Faisal as Iraq's first monarch, the British decided to conduct a one-question plebiscite that was meticulously prepared and which gave a return of 96 per cent in Faisal's favor. In 1932 Iraq achieved independence and established an indigenous Iraqi army, although British forces had to intervene in 1941 to thwart a pro-Nazi coup, withdrawing again in 1947. Also, to counter the monarch's nationalistic aspirations and as a means of ensuring the king's dependence, the British cultivated the tribal sheikhs, whose power had for many years been on the wane.

One of the major goals of British policy was to divide and rule and to ensure that the monarchy was stronger than any single tribe but remained weaker than a coalition of tribes. This would allow British power to be decisive in ultimately arbitrating potential disputes between the two. In fact, in March 1924, the elected Constituent Assembly met for the first time and formally ratified the Anglo–Iraqi treaty despite considerable opposition from many of those present.

By the time independence was achieved, many Marsh Arabs had already joined the mass rural migration to the cities. Many gradually drifted and ended up in shantytowns around the cities of Baghdad, Basrah, al-Amarah, al-Nasiriyah and Kirkuk, while others sought waged labor in neighboring agricultural farms and in the oilfields. A series of poor rainfalls in the 1950s accelerated this drift to the urban areas.

Dr Shakir M. Salim's anthropological field investigation of the marshlands (for the Iraqi government) was conducted mainly in the town of Chibayish and was considered to be the first of its kind by an Iraqi national. The area's native inhabitants are commonly known as Ma'dan or Marsh Arabs although Dr Salim prefers to use the generic term "Marsh Dwellers". Prior to the early 1990s the area's population was estimated to range between 350,000 and 500,000.

In 1958 the Hashemite Dynasty was overthrown by a group of army officers led by Brigadier Abdul al-Karim Kassem, who was himself overthrown in 1963 by Colonel Abdul Salem Arif. The last coup to take place prior to removing Saddam from power was the one in August 1968 that brought the Ba'ath Party to power under the banner of pan-Arabism and socialism. In July 1979, after a brief power struggle within the Iraqi Ba'ath Party, Saddam emerged victorious and became President and undisputed party leader (having summarily executed most of his opponents). Between the overthrow of King Faisal II and Saddam's rise to the presidency, little of consequence took place with regard to the marshlands.

DESTRUCTION OF THE MARSHES DURING THE SADDAM ERA

The greatest devastation to the marshlands occurred years prior to Iraq's invasion of Kuwait. Saddam Hussein, as president of Iraq, destroyed roughly 90 per cent of the 20,000 sq. km of marshland (7,722 square miles).

Most ecological scientists agree that the destruction of the marshes was a catastrophe of global significance and certainly one of the most grievous ecological crimes of the twentieth century. Saddam Hussein deliberately and methodically managed to drain, reportedly poison with herbicides and desiccate the lush wetlands that were home to over 250,000 Marsh Arabs, as well as a crucial stopover for birds migrating from Europe to Africa. The marshlands also served a critical function to the entire Arabian Gulf by filtering out toxins while contributing organic matter to fish breeding in the region.

Saddam was frustrated by the continuous Shia opposition which was largely disorganized but which eluded his army by retreating into the marshlands. He decided to punish them by launching a punitive assault in 1991 that brought desertification to one of the world's most valuable delta regions. Saddam worked his engineers around the clock for nine months to build a canal to divert agricultural drainage water that once flowed into the Gulf's Hammar marsh. The 350-mile Saddam River canal project (also known as the Third River) was based on a major British-designed municipal project that commenced in 1953 and was designed to carry water from the central Euphrates agricultural region and irrigate the land between the Tigris and the Euphrates for farming. Saddam co-opted the project and drained the marshlands, destroying the livelihoods of the Arabs who lived there. Saddam's purpose in drying the marshes was primarily to flush out Shia rebels hiding in the fairly safe haven of the inaccessible reed marshes and at the same time to get at rich oil reserves.

This was followed in 1994 by the building of another canal, the Mother of Battles River, which channeled fresh water from the Euphrates into a salt water marsh. The Mother of Battles River essentially removed large quantities of water from the Euphrates and conveyed it around the Hammar to the Arabian Gulf. Diversion of the Euphrates water into the canal was implemented by constructing a large dam across the Euphrates River. To the south of the Saddam River and running parallel to it, a large pipeline was built called the Loyalty to the Leader Canal, which also takes water from the Euphrates River.

Drainage canals were also constructed on the central marshes (such as the Prosperity River and the Crown of Battles River) to drain the Huwaiza Marsh. In 1997, another lethal blow to the marshes was the building of the Fidelity to the Leader Canal, which diverted water from the Hammar Marsh.

Saddam capped his crimes by poisoning whatever water remained after the non-stop erection of locks, dykes, earth embankments and massive canals. This is verified by amateur videotapes recorded by Iraqi refugees showing the use of toxins to kill fish and water buffalo.

Human casualties caused by the first Gulf War, whether combat or collateral, were not significant. The widespread pillage that followed, especially in urban areas, caused much greater harm. And the insurgency that came shortly after the pillaging was worse yet. But it too was confined mostly to urban areas.

In 1991, following the Gulf War, the Marsh Arabs, commonly referred to as Ma'dan, joined the failed Shiite uprising. Although for all practical purposes the revolt was easily crushed by Saddam's troops, the "disloyal" Ma'dan retreated to the marshes and remained largely elusive and out of reach. The marshes had always provided the ultimate sanctuary and it was the marshes that had bestowed cover on its inhabitants thus allowing them to avoid their enemies and survive for thousands of years. Whenever an enemy approached, the marsh dwellers retreated deep within the marshes and surrounded themselves by water and near-impenetrable beds of reeds, patiently waiting for their attackers to give up and depart.

But from the First Gulf War onwards until the adoption of a southern "No Fly Zone" in 1992, the strategy changed and Iraqi forces pursued the rebels mercilessly, strafing them from helicopter gunships. After that, Saddam implemented a deliberate policy of uprooting and exterminating the marsh inhabitants and anyone else seeking refuge among them. The regime used heavy artillery and chemical weapons such as napalm and phosphorous to clear the villagers. It then instituted an economic blockade of the marshlands, denying all access to medicines and medical care. Survivors were often removed at gunpoint.

In many cases the marsh dwellers were falsely accused of being members of opposition parties and participating in anti-government activities. A former Iraqi intelligence officer recently admitted that two thousand prisoners, mostly Marsh Arabs, were executed in a single day. The ex-captain claims that many were buried in a special section of a nearby cemetery where numbers were the only means of identification. Although some of the bodies were returned to their families for burial, the regime was reluctant to do this across the board to prevent exposure of its actions. Moreover, most victims' families assumed that court hearings would be held for the public record prior to any executions. However, in most cases this did not happen, especially for the Ma'dan who were arbitrarily arrested and murdered.

Even after the Saddam regime quashed the revolt and slaughtered thousands of Ma'dan and attacked their villages, Saddam continued the retribution process. Using the guise of increasing agricultural acreage, he ordered the marshes to be drained. To do this, as we have seen, a massive network of canals, pipelines and dams were constructed. State-owned businesses and private firms were employed to work on the projects and were required to dispatch all their earth-moving equipment to the region. The regime provided financial inducements to Sunnis from Saddam's strongholds in the Anbar province, such as Tikrit and Fallujah, to encourage them to travel south to participate in these projects.

From the regime's standpoint, the engineering feat was an outstanding success. The Euphrates River, which had previously flowed entirely into the southern half of the marshes, was now diverted into a wide newly built canal which the regime called the Mother of All Battles River and which stretched more than 100 miles around the former wetlands. Higher up the Euphrates, billions of gallons of water were redirected into a depression in the desert. This draining of the marshes was classified by environmentalists as a major ecological calamity and lacking any rational justification. What remained after the land was drained has been characterized as mostly barren desert with large salt-encrusted areas (Figure 1.6).

Although estimates vary, the Brookings Institution estimates that by 1999 all but a handful of the 250,000 Marsh Arab inhabitants had been driven into exile or killed. On the other hand, according to a 2001 United Nations estimate, "40,000 had made it into Iran as refugees, 20–40,000 still inhabited the remaining part of the marshes and 170,000 to 190,000 Marsh Arabs were either dead or displaced".

In 1994, Joseph Dellapenna, a professor at Villanova University Law School and an expert on international water rights, said Saddam Hussein, in addition to his other crimes, is "also guilty of genocide against the Marsh Arabs". Dellapenna also noted that while Saddam had ostensibly drained the marshes for agricultural purposes, nothing was ever done to develop the reclaimed land, and instead it was left to turn into a barren and salt-covered desert. This, perhaps more than anything else, revealed the true intentions of the Iraqi dictator. Dellapenna told Radio Free Europe/Radio Liberty, "What makes this a crime under international law was its purpose. And I think the purpose was fairly clear, which was to destroy a culture and to destroy a people. And that's genocide. And genocide is an international crime. It's a crime against humanity". Dellapenna also said it was an ecological crime, which he termed *ecocide*, but noted that sadly there is no legal instrument in place under international law to prosecute anyone for the destruction of a unique ecological system.

By the end of the twentieth century, Iraq's marshlands were almost completely destroyed, mainly through upstream dam construction and drainage. The extent of wetland destruction becomes evident by comparing maps of the marshland region from 1973 to 2000. The wetland area in southern Iraq covered over 20,000 square kilometers in 1973. This area had shrunk to cover just over

800 square kilometers (309 square miles) in 2000. The Mesopotamian marshes of southern Iraq had been all but destroyed by Saddam Hussein's regime by the year 2000 and the Marsh Arabs who inhabited this region while it flourished became refugees in Iran, Iraq and other parts of the Middle East as a result of the desiccation of the area.

Initial assessments by various organizations and NGOs suggested that poor water quality, in addition to the presence of toxic materials and high saline soil conditions in the drained marshes, would prohibit their ecological restoration and frustrate attempts to reestablish the Marsh Arab culture of fishing and agriculture. However, by September 2005 the unexpected high volume of good-quality water entering the marshes from the Tigris and Euphrates Rivers allowed an estimated 39 per cent of the former marshes to be reflooded. But while reflooding does not necessarily guarantee that the restoration process will be successful, recent field surveys have observed an admirable rate of reestablishment of native macroinvertebrates, macrophytes, fish and birds in the reflooded marshes. The main concern is whether the future availability of water for restoration is adequate or whether only a portion of the former marshes may be restored. Also, the significant reduction in landscape connectivity between marshes was a cause of great concern, particularly with relation to potential extinctions of local species and lower diversity in isolated wetlands.

As mentioned earlier, the drainage of the marshes in the 1990s led to a massive migration of the marsh dweller population, either to urban locations within Iraq or to neighboring countries such as Iran. Reliable estimates of the marsh dweller population prior to the 1990s are not available, but a 1988 estimate puts the number of marsh dwellers at about 500,000. It is further estimated that by 1997 only 192,000 marsh dwellers remained in southern Iraq (although not necessarily in the former marsh area). However, findings of a recent USAID-funded demographic census and public health survey suggest the presence of about 85,000 marsh dwellers still inhabiting in or residing on the fringes of the marshes. The number is roughly twice that which most people generally believed to be still in the area and a third of the population of two decades ago. A 2003 United Nations Environment Program (UNEP) *Desk Study on the Environment in Iraq* states that there are approximately 40,000 Marsh Arabs living in refugee camps in Khuzestan province, Iran.

Prior to the wholesale destruction and desiccation of the Saddam era, the social and economic life of the marsh dwellers had evolved in a manner that was completely integrated with the marsh environment. Water buffalo fed on young reed shoots and were one of the backbones of the wetlands economy, providing milk, yogurt, butter, meat and fuel dung. Reeds provided critical construction material for the *sarifa* huts and *mudhifs*. Fishing in the wetlands once accounted for over 60 per cent of the inland fish catch in Iraq, and waterfowl hunting was another local livelihood source. Agriculture in the areas adjacent to and impacted by the hydrological patterns of the marshes thrived through the cultivation of rice, cereals, vegetables, dates and sugar cane. In addition to this, the marshes helped prevent saltwater intrusion and erosion control among other things.

Figure 1.6 A reed village near Chibayish, Iraq, was surrounded by water before the drought began; now it is totally dry (Raheem Salman/Los Angeles Times).

Impact of Recent Conflicts

The UNEP 2003 *Desk Study on the Environment in Iraq* states that the Middle East in general, and Iraq in particular, have found themselves throughout history in the middle of warring influences from all sides. A detailed analysis of impacts of all historical wars is beyond the scope of this book, but a brief synopsis of impacts during the last five conflicts may be warranted. Much of the following information is based upon the above study.

The Saddam regime used the Huwayza Marsh as a military tool during the Iran–Iraq War, to their advantage e.g., as a shield against an advancing army. Many fierce battles were fought here during this time and much damage was inflicted. The area was generally drained and flooded according to military needs. The military usage caused extensive physical damage to the surface vegetation and soils, including the digging of trenches, bunkers and movement of military vehicles. Likewise, the presence of unexploded ordnance poses a very real danger here. And while dispersed chemical agents used during the Iran–Iraq War may not currently pose a threat, there nevertheless remains a potential threat from intact canisters to local inhabitants, scientific personnel, and/or wildlife.

The records also show that during the Iran–Iraq War, a road was built across the Qurnah Marshes parallel to the west bank of the Tigris, essentially bisecting the marshes from north to south. The road was to allow for troop transport and military access. Unfortunately, the elevated road also cut off the water supply to the central marshes between the road and the Tigris River, thereby effectively desiccating a huge area. In addition to this, the once extensive date palm forests along the Shatt al-Arab River estuary were destroyed during this time period, also largely due to the Iran–Iraq War.

The first Gulf War was swift and the fighting did not have a very significant direct effect on the marshlands themselves. However, at the end of the Gulf War in 1991, as the Iraqi army retreated, it did so sabotaging more than 700 oil wells in Kuwait, leaving them gushing oil and burning. This created a black soot that was up to 2 centimeters thick which was deposited over a 1,000 sq. km (approx. 386 sq. miles) of desert as a result of atmospheric fallout, depositing a total of 320,000 tons of burnt debris (Literathy, 1993). The atmospheric fallout was predominantly deposited downwind, and caused damage to the wetland vegetation in the Khuzestan lowlands of neighboring southwestern Iran by acidic "black rain" from the burning Kuwaiti oilwell-fields. It is probable that the wetlands around Basrah were similarly affected since it is only a short distance to the west.

Following the first Gulf War, there was a widespread civil uprising in southern Iraq and particularly around the marsh areas. The marshlands were used by the rebels as a safe haven or refuge, which the Iraqi army could not effectively control. Mainly to address this problem, Saddam without hesitation decided to implement the marshlands drainage program during the 1990s which is described above. Following the complete desiccation of the marshlands, the dried reed beds and villages constructed of reeds were burned by the Iraqi regime.

United Nations economic sanctions between the two Gulf Wars caused further damage to the marshlands. Sewage treatment plants destroyed during the first Gulf War remained unrepaired, and untreated waste flowed downstream to their final resting point which in many cases was the marshlands. Moreover, enormous logistical difficulties often prevented humanitarian aid from reaching the area. And although active resistance within Iraq persisted it was mostly confined to the main population centers. The most obvious impact resulting from this instability has been the inability to reconstruct the area's infrastructure and obtain reliable scientific data for the region.

During the second Gulf War of 2003, the marshlands managed to avoid suffering any significant direct impact. This is partially because the route of the coalition forces towards Baghdad did not pass through the marshlands. And although some fires at the Rumayllah oilfield erupted, these were rapidly extinguished. Also, during the early days of the conflict, hydraulic facilities including major dams on Iraq's rivers, along with petroleum production facilities, were secured which prevented any significant adverse impacts as a result of flooding or petroleum burning. Officials within the Ministry of Water Resources and local citizens took action to re-flood various portions of the marshlands shortly after the commencement of the second Gulf War.

THE STATUS OF THE IRAQI MARSHLANDS TODAY

Even with the burden of sanctions, the twentieth century saw a relative social stabilization and relative economic prosperity. Iraq's oil wealth induced many changes. For example the majority of those that inhabited the marshlands drifted to the urban cities of Basrah, Baghdad, Mosul and Kirkuk. But today, the marsh dwellers face many challenges that go well beyond undoing the devastation and destruction that Saddam brought upon the inhabitants of the marshes. What has to be corrected are the many dams that have been built in Turkey, Syria and Iraq which have reduced the historical flow of the Tigris and Euphrates Rivers that merge and feed the marshes. Another thorny problem is the presence of oilfields that lie beneath some of the former marshes.

Since Sumerian times, the traditional occupation of the Marsh Arabs has been fishing and today over 80 per cent of those that have returned to reflooded areas are engaged in the fishing industry. Iraq's coastline is relatively short, and the freshwater fishing industry of the marshlands which once accounted for roughly two-thirds of Iraq's annual catch is thought today to stand below 10 per cent. Moreover, today's marshland returnees continue to face the problem of a total lack of the infrastructure required to support normal everyday life, including a lack of adequate safe drinking water, electricity, sewage treatment facilities, refuse collection and schools, clinics and other public facilities.

For many, life in the marshes was one of survival. The daily struggle with high temperatures, high humidity and seasonal flooding, in addition to trying to cope with a variety of insects, poisonous snakes, lack of drinking water and potential wild boar attacks turned the life of the marsh dweller into a scramble to stay alive. Government presence hardly existed and tribal laws ruled supreme. Marsh dwellers avoided paying any taxes and they did not anticipate receiving any government services. Medical services, for example, were minimal and marsh dwellers often resorted to herbs to treat ailments, as is often found in traditional societies. Likewise, schools were difficult to build due to the dispersion of the marsh dwellers in large areas separated by bodies of water and lack of government assistance, and electricity was more a pipe dream than a reality.

Also, historically these wetlands were considered to be a main source of fresh water for human consumption, supplying communities living in and surrounding the marshes. This source gradually became contaminated until it was no longer suitable for human consumption. And since potable water was not available, the marsh dwellers were forced to drink the polluted marsh water. The destruction of the marshes has thus had severe human health consequences as a result of the loss of clean water and degradation of sanitation standards.

It is not surprising therefore that many of the marsh dwellers were afflicted with dysentery, diarrhea and bilharzia. To address the problem of providing clean drinking water, six pilot sites were selected to supply drinking water and sanitation facilities as per the scope of works outlined in a UNEP Program which is discussed in greater detail in Chapter 10. The six sites chosen to implement the pilot project are:

1. Al-Kirmashiya, Thi-Qar Governorate (Figure 1.7A)
2. Al-Sewelmat, Missan Governorate (Figure 1.7B)
3. Badir al-Rumaidh, Thi-Qar Governorate (Figure 1.7C)
4. Al-Mashab, Basrah Governorate (Figure 1.7D)
5. Al-Hadam, Missan Governorate (Figure 1.7E)
6. Al-Jeweber, Thi-Qar Governorate (Figure 1.7F)

Figure 1.7A Al-Kirmashiya pilot site in Thi-Qar Governorate showing a marsh dweller with his pan receiving potable water provided by UNEP (Photo: Dr Faris Kubba).

Figure 1.7B Pilot sites of al-Sewelmat in Missan Governorate showing piping connections of UNEP water equipment (Photo: Dr Faris Kubba).

Figure 1.7C Pilot site of Badir al-Rumaidh in Thi-Qar Governorate. The second picture shows an inspector working controls (Photo: Dr Faris Kubba).

Figure 1.7D, E Pilot sites of al-Mashab in Thi-Qar Governorate depicting UNEP equipment, and al-Haddam pilot site in Missan Governorate showing a young girl getting water from the UNEP outlet (Photo: Dr Faris Kubba).

Figure 1.7F Pilot site of al-Jeweber in Thi-Qar Governorate, showing UNEP monitor discussing commissioning of project (Photo: Dr Faris Kubba).

Among the most significant developments that adversely impacted the marshes of southern Iraq were the establishment of modern controls in Turkey, Syria, Iran and Iraq of the waters of the Tigris and the Euphrates. These controls led to a substantial decrease in the great floodwaters that affected the marsh areas of southern Iraq. Additionally, the irrigation projects that were implemented during the Saddam era and before played an active role in determining the courses of the Tigris and Euphrates and their branches, making future changes more difficult.

Since the demise of the Iraqi regime in 2003, previous inhabitants of the wetlands have started to gradually return to the former marshes and residents have made ad hoc efforts to return water to some of the drained areas. The extent of the reflooding since 2003 varies and the effects of such actions remain unclear. As noted by the Eden Again project, "For the long-term viability of this vital marsh area and other marshes, there needs to be a systematic management program that would replicate the natural flooding of the marsh and the hydrodynamic period. Further, in order to understand the natural healing process, there is a need to monitor the progress of the restoration, including quality of water and water level". In 2004 The Iraq Marshlands Restoration Program Action Plan prepared under the auspices of USAID reached the same conclusion.

As reflooding is essentially a recent phenomenon, its effect and impact on the return of aquatic and emergent plants, fish and wildlife and how the latter will adapt to the wetlands environment remains unclear and how the ecosystem will change over time also remains unknown. By May 2003, we start seeing an increase in water supply to the marshes in part as a result of the opening of control structures and breaking of levees by mechanical diggers and in part due to exceptionally high rainfall. The Iraq Ministry of Water Resources stated that by May 2004 up to 40 per cent of the original marshes had been reflooded, but that the state of recovery varied according to location.

By 2005 there were still over 250,000 Marsh Arab refugees who had failed to return to their former home and lifestyle which despite its independence was characterized by extreme poverty and hardship. Furthermore, many of these displaced persons have since settled in urban centers where they have lived for years whether in Iraq, Iran, Syria or Saudi Arabia. Although some marsh dwellers have chosen to return (especially to the Hammar Marsh), the majority have chosen not to. This is mainly because there is little incentive to do so; why return to villages that lack essential utilities, sanitation, drinking water, healthcare and modern schools? Moreover, with the reduction in wildlife stock, it is even harder to merely survive through hunting or fishing. However, many of those that have resettled in the marshes have managed to gain representation through various organizations and political parties.

2

PEOPLE AND CULTURE

Sam A.A. Kubba

GENERAL OVERVIEW

There is often a sharp divide that characterizes rural and urban communities; this is particularly true of Iraqi society which started to break down as a result of policies instituted by the previous Iraqi government. The indigenous Marsh Arabs and Ma'dan however have despite all kinds of losses and uncertainties tried to resist these policies and remain in the marshes and conserve their ancient way of life, culture and daily needs. For five thousand years they have learned to master their inhospitable habitat while retaining a homage and respect for the aquatic environment that houses them. Most marsh dwellers are primarily cultivators, reed gatherers (Figure 2.1), skilled fishermen (Figure 2.2) or buffalo breeders (Figure 2.3) and their society and economy has over the millennia been supported largely by reed-associated crafts in addition to fishing and buffalo breeding. Traditionally the Marsh Arabs and Ma'dan lived in villages that consisted of island settlements, floating platforms or manmade reed islands.

Tragically, the Iraqi regime refused to allow them to pursue their distinctive way of life and showed their disapproval by poisoning the marsh waters with large amounts of chemicals, depriving the besieged Marsh Arabs of any type of food or water. This process was accelerated by the Iran–Iraq War, and the continuous conflicts that followed have devastated large areas of the rural south, triggering a large-scale rural exodus to the capital and other urban centers. These migrations had a fundamental impact on the marsh dwellers' social customs, tribal culture and way of life. The marshes of southern Iraq, which Professor Hamid Ahmed describes as *The Eastern Venice* or *The Arab Venice*, ceased to exist.

For centuries the marsh dwellers were largely oblivious to the outside world, and vice versa, until 1824, when Baillie Fraser, a Scottish traveler and novelist (1783–1856) brought them to the attention of the Western world when he described them as the "stoutest fairest and comeliest of all Arabs" and admired their openness, frankness and civility. They were again forgotten until the well-known British explorer Wilfred Thesiger chronicled the seven years he spent with them in his famous 1964 book *The Marsh Arabs*. This was followed by others and culminated in the emergence of Saddam Hussein on the stage; during his brutal reign the marshes were systematically desiccated, leaving its inhabitants with no way to fish or farm, no reeds or birds, and thus forcing them to leave the only place they considered home since ancient times. Tragically, a land that once proudly supported a unique biodiverse aquatic ecosystem has now become a fractured, crusty and barren landscape. It was only after the Saddam regime was toppled that strenuous efforts were made to revive the marshes. These efforts are now bearing fruit although some complications are being encountered due to drought and dam-building.

It should be noted that with all the progress that the twentieth and twenty-first centuries brought to Iraq – the advent of the automobile and computers, of television and telephones – it all failed to significantly permeate the dense reed beds and narrow waterways that protected the marsh areas. But devotion to the traditional ways also left settlements without sanitation or modern healthcare. Traditionally, women collected polluted water from rivers and streams and filtered it in ceramic vessels packed with charcoal to make it potable. Villagers would normally dig pits to bury the little garbage they generated. And when grazing for the buffaloes became short and sparse, the tribe would move still deeper into the marshes (Figure 2.3). Southern Iraq is once again experiencing a devastating drought which is sadly threatening the livelihood of these brave people.

SOCIAL CUSTOMS

According to Fulanain, "Hospitality among the Arabs of the desert has become a byword" (Fulanain, 1927). In describing a newlywed bride Fulanain says, "She was a pretty girl, sturdily built, barely fifteen; a deep fringe of black hair hid her forehead, a silver ring set with blue stones was in her nose, and her chin was decorated with indigo tattooing." (Fulanain, 1927: p. 15). Later in the book he describes one of Haji Rikkan's nephews as wearing "a thick silver ring, and his nails were dyed with henna (a cosmetic dye), two forms of adornment scorned by the elder twin…" (Fulanain, 1927: p. 26).

Some of the customs would be considered inappropriate by Western standards, for example, Marsh Arab men and women typically eat separately, and rarely speak during a meal. All chatting usually takes place before or after a meal. The Haji said, "We sleep in the same bed as our womenfolk", "but eat with them? No, that were too great a disgrace." (Fulanain, 1927: p. 18). Fulanain also describes the typical *mudhif*, according to Fulanain, a *mudhif* is a guest-hall which among the bani Lam tribe consisted of a hair tent, and among the Albu Mohammad comprised of a reed hut.

Figure 2.1 Marsh Arabs transporting reeds by boat (Photo: Jasim al-Asadi).

Figure 2.2 Marsh Arabs preparing nets for fishing (Photo: Jasim al-Asadi).

Marriage and Divorce

In Islam a man is allowed to have up to four wives at any particular time, and in the Shia sect of Islam this number can be increased through the institution of *mit'a* (which is particularly popular in Iran). The *mit'a* is essentially a legally contractual marriage of limited duration. While polygamy *mit'a* are permitted in Islam, they are not often practiced in Iraq. Marriages are traditionally arranged by the parents, though the children have some choice in the matter. In arranged marriages the father usually has authority over the choice of spouse although members of the family can also influence the choice. Premarital chastity cannot be overemphasized, which is one reason why early marriages are encouraged. Additonally, marriage among cousins is still common and in many cases the father would look first to his brothers' children or close relatives for potential mates. In fact, a man has first claim to a first cousin on his father's side – a right that only the woman's father can bestow upon another suitor. Marriage within a family lineage boasts several advantages and in this respect, Professor Edward Ochsenschlager who conducted extensive field work at al-Hiba near the marshes says, "Such marriages have the benefit of (1) costing less to arrange because the bride price and dowry can be kept to a minimum, (2) aiding the patrilineal kinship organization by keeping this distributed property in the family unit, (3) providing the comfort of a familiar environment for both marriage partners who know their in-laws well and have been brought up in

Figure 2.3 A buffalo breeder is forced to move deeper into the marshes to feed his stock (Photo: Hassan Partow – UNEP).

much the same way. For the father, the fact that he accepts a low bride price for his daughters is offset by the fact that he can acquire wives for his sons at the same reduced rate." (Ochsenschlager, E, 2004: pp. 19–21).

The bride price is typically paid in cash (usually in advance) although in some cases, with the bride's parents' agreement, it may be paid in cattle, or furniture, etc. While a father is certainly entitled to seek a greater dowry for his daughter by marrying her outside the lineage, by doing so he may be subject to severe criticism, although in urban areas such as Baghdad this may not necessarily be the case. In any case the matchmaking process is frequently conducted with the active assistance of an older woman in the village who will seek out a suitable mate, in conjunction with the mother and sister who also play crucial roles, particularly in checking up on the potential bride's lineage and character. According to a survey conducted by Dr Salim in the 1950s among 120 families which contained 118 men in al-Chibayish, he found that 85 of them (72 per cent) were monogamous and the rest, 33 (28 per cent) were polygamous. Of the latter the majority of polygamous men had only two wives while a few had three (Salim, 1962).

During weddings, people of the village would normally bring in one or more gypsy families from the surrounding areas, and the gypsy girls would dress in brightly colored clothes, and they would loosen their hair and display their bodily charms as they sang and danced into the late hours of the night to the rhythmic beats of drums and the music of *rebecs* (traditional pear-shaped, three-stringed fiddles played with a bow), as the men of their families play it for them. During these celebrations men often seized this opportunity to drink *arrack* (a traditional alcoholic drink that is popular in the Middle East and the Far East, usually distilled from fermented palm sap, rice or molasses).

In many of the towns surrounding the wetlands and on rare occasions within the marshlands themselves, the *dhakar binta* ("male girls") entertain at marriage feasts and other social occasions. These are generally young boys who essentially follow the profession of dancer/male prostitute. On some occasions local singing groups were brought in that consisted of only men and instead of playing the *rebec* and drums they used large tambourines (*tayaran*) and large drums to produce melodious music. Most of those groups were black or had dark complexions, and some of them wore women's dancing costumes, while others performed acrobatic moves. In this respect, Thesiger describing the dancing at a wedding celebration he attended where a *dhakar binta* was hired says, "For some time we had heard the distant sounds of singing and drumming. The boy wore a scarlet gown with ropes of imitation pearls and heavy gold ear-rings. His hair, combed and scented, hung round his shoulders; his breasts were padded and his face was made up. He looked like an affected girl and behaved with the mincing mannerisms of a female prostitute, but he certainly could dance. He used a pair of castanets in each hand, the mark of the professional since no village lad used them. Strangely enough, his gestures were far less erotic than those of the boys I had watched at Awaidiya. Much of his dancing was a gymnastic display of a high order." (Wilfred Thesiger, 1964: p. 125).

One may also come across a *mustarjil* who is actually born a woman, but who has the heart of a man and basically lives like a man. Thesiger says that they are equally accepted and enjoy considerable respect from their fellow Ma'dans; they dress like men and are treated accordingly although they sleep with the women. Marsh Arabs also accept men who dress and live as women.

Salim confirms the tradition in many Islamic countries that a husband can divorce his wife at any time and for any reason. However, the main grounds for requesting the return of the bride price from the bride's family would be adultery, or if she is found not to be a virgin. Bad behavior can also sometimes be grounds for divorce. In traditional Iraqi society such as is the case in the marshlands, adultery by women is often punishable by death at the hands of her kin or by divorce from the husband. Divorcees usually end up with their natal families and have little prospect of remarrying. Salim concludes that the inhabitants of Chibayish "prefer widows to divorcees as there is always a presupposition of the latter's bad conduct. A divorcee who remarries is usually worth about half the usual brideprice." Salim also says that widows are shown considerable respect and are "helped both by her own kin and that of her husband. If she has children she has a chance of being remarried in her deceased husband's lineage. Otherwise, she may either remain in her husband's home or live near a brother-in-law. Childless widows often return to their kin and have greater chances of remarriage.' As for adulterous wives, it is not infrequent that they are secretly killed by family members upon return. This is considered an 'honor killing" (Salim, 1962).

Salim also notes, "There is another type of extra-lineage marriage in which no brideprice is paid: marriage by exchange (*sidiq*). Sisters, and more rarely daughters and brother's daughters, may be exchanged in marriage." In a similar vein Salim observes that "After the death of the wife, the husband may marry her sister. There is no obligation or right on the part of the husband to claim his deceased wife's sister, but if the deceased wife has left small children, it is thought that their mother's sister would look after them better than a stranger stepmother would do. Similarly there is no obligation for levirate marriage, but many men marry their brother's widows if the brothers have left children for whose upbringing they are responsible."

One doesn't have to look too closely to recognize numerous parallels between the modern and ancient marsh dwellers. The characteristic arched reed buildings and mat impressions are amply represented in the archaeological record (Figure 2.4, 2.5). There are numerous artifacts in the Iraq Museum and elsewhere displaying impressions left in sediment showing how Sumerians wove their baskets from reeds. The patterns closely resembled that of modern weavers. Likewise, fragments of sun-dried mud pottery exhibited similar styles to jars produced by today's traditional potters. Terracotta models of ancient boats can also be found in the Iraq Museum that closely resemble the modern, bitumen-coated wooden boats that the Ma'dan pole through the water and which are discussed in greater detail in Chapter 3.

A.   **B.**

Figure 2.4 Sumerian seal impressions of ancient reed huts.

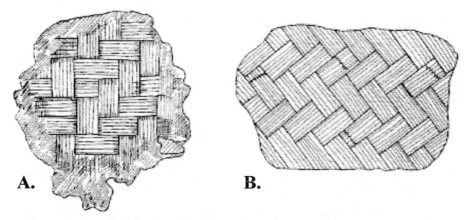

A.   **B.**

Figure 2.5   Ancient clay impressions of reed mats depicting two types of patterns which closely resemble those of today's modern weavers .

Ochsenschlager's ethno-archaeological fieldwork was based largely on a study near the large mound of Hiba (ancient Lagash) in the marshes of southern Iraq. He examined the material culture of three tribes living near Hiba to arrive at informed speculation on how the ancient Sumerians may have lived and worked here, particularly since it is believed that the Sumerians lived over 5,000 years ago in a similar ecological setting. For example, Ochsenschlager observed the amount of time and effort it took a weaver to finish a particular kind of basket, from which he would estimate the economic value of such an artifact in ancient Sumer.

Language

Although Arabic is the main language today the Ma'dan's dialect differs from that of say people from Baghdad or Mosul. Some speakers of Iraqi Arabic tend to consider the Ma'dan Arabic an inferior form of the language. Moreover, there are many local dialects so distinctive that people in one community may not fully understand speakers a few hundred miles away (e.g., can be compared with the Cockney dialect and its Scottish counterpart). The common language for literate Arabs among the many millions of speakers is modern standard Arabic, which is used in conjunction with a person's local dialect and which is often corrupted with a large amount of "slang". It should also be remembered that some of the marsh dwellers may be of non-Semitic origin. For example, it is probable that some of the marsh dwellers are descendents of the ancient Sumerians and of the other people who have made the marshes their homeland. In ancient times, the Sumerian language emerged as the prevailing speech for the region. The Sumerians developed a cuneiform script which was a system used for writing on clay and which for two millennia remained the primary means of written communication in the region.

A large number of people inhabited the marshes during the Iran–Iraq War when large numbers of Iraqis who were military deserters or who opposed the war fled to the wetlands for refuge. There are various estimates of how many of the estimated 500,000 original indigenous inhabitants of the marshes remained after the marshlands were desiccated, although several scholars now put the number at less than 10,000. Some are known to have fled to Iran, while others became political refugees and part of the world's diaspora. In such cases, cultural customs are usually downplayed and social interaction is avoided.

TRIBAL CULTURE

The Iraqi Marshes are inhabited by genuine Arab tribes, including Malik, Tamin and Assad, who emigrated from the Arabian Peninsula and settled in these fertile regions many centuries ago, but the birthright of the Marsh Arabs is an ancient one. Marsh Arab society is basically comprised of clans or groups of families of shared lineage, headed by a leader known as a "sheikh". A "tribe", on the other hand, consists of a political federation of clans based on local perceptions of kinship, whether real or fictive. Pastoral nomads in much of the Middle East typically organized themselves by tribe. Some settled villagers also organize themselves by tribe. Urban populations, however, even when they had a rural or tribal background, often failed to maintain strong kinship affiliations, and although tribes played a central role in different eras of Iraq's rich history, their influence began to wane during the twentieth and twentiy first centuries, partly due to the impact of urbanization, nationalism and associated processes that sometimes caused a relative shift from ingrained tribal and clan loyalties towards organized political parties such as the Istiqlal, Ba'ath, Da'wa and Communist parties.

As with the majority of tribes in southern Iraq, the main authority remains the tribal sheikh who to this day continues to collect a tribute from his tribe in order to sustain and maintain the tribal *mudhif* or guest house, which acts as the social, political, judicial and religious center of Marsh Arab life and which is used to display hospitality and settle disputes as well as to conduct diplomacy with other tribes and religious festivities.

The wetlands are inhabited by different Shia Arab tribes and tribal confederations including the Albu Muhammad, Albu-Hassan, Feraigat, Shaghanba, Malik, Bani Tamin and Bani Assad, and Bani Lam, most of whom emigrated from the Arabian Peninsula and settled in these fertile regions hundreds of years ago. Salim says that the village of Chibayish, which was the focus of his Ph.D. thesis, is mainly occupied by an ancient tribe called Beni Isad which in the marshlands consisted of nearly 11,000 persons (census of 1947 plus laborers working outside Chibayish when the census was taken). The Chibayish village population consists of nine main clans (each of which contains several lineages) living in the area at the time: Ahl ish-Shaikh, Ahl Ghrij, al-Hadadiyin, Ahl Khatir, Beni Aschiri, Ahl Anaisi, Ahl Wnais, Ahl li-Mabir and Ahl Wais. Salim says that according to tradition, Beni Isad is a Bedouin tribe that migrated from Arabia more than thirteen centuries ago. But accurate estimates of population size will vary, largely due to the paucity of official government data and the relative inaccessibility of the region, which left sections of the Marsh Arabs and Ma'dan population unaccounted for in population censuses. Moreover, prior to the abolition of the sheikhdom in 1924, the tribe was a political and military unit under the authority and control of the sheikh. However, today, the tribe has lost its political identity and clout and has come under the direct control of the central government.

Marsh dwellers, however, still consider the family as the basis of the social structure, the general characteristics of which are:

- The concept of family is more private than in many other cultures. Female relatives must be protected from outside influences and are taken care of at all times. It is inappropriate to ask questions about a Marsh Arab's wife or other female relatives.
- Family loyalty is very important and precedes other social relationships, including business. Nepotism among traditional society is considered a positive trait, and implies that employing people one knows and trusts such as relatives carries great weight.

- Marsh dwellers (as is the case with most traditional Iraqi families) take their family responsibilities very seriously.
- Extended families are typically much closer than extended families of other cultures and often consist of many members.
- In times of need the individual can normally look to a social network and assistance from his/her family.
- Elderly relatives are normally kept at home and looked after by the family and not as in Western cultures placed in a nursing home.

According to the author and Middle East observer Jane Chanaa, "Kinship groups are the fundamental social units, regulating many activities. Rights and obligations centre on the extended family and the lineage. The family remains the primary focus of loyalty; and it is in this context, rather than the broader one of corporate loyalties defined by sectarian, ethnic, or economic considerations, that the majority of Iraqis find the common denominators of their everyday lives. A mutually protective attitude among relatives is taken as a matter of course. Relatives tend to be preferred as business partners since they are believed to be more reliable than persons over whom one does not have the hold of kinship ties."

RELIGIOUS BELIEFS AND ETHNICITY

Ethnically, the Marsh Arab population composition has changed over the centuries and is heavily influenced by immigrations and intermarriage with the Persians to the east and Arab Bedouins to the west (Thesiger, 1964). Many of the non-Muslim tribes that inhabited the wetlands are thought to have converted to Shiite Islam in the late eighteenth through the nineteenth centuries. Among these were the southern tribes of the Ma'dan, including the powerful Albu Muhammad which consisted of numerous clans. And although today the vast majority of marsh dwellers are Shia Muslims, anthropologist Salim maintains that they are not "strict in the religious observance". Salim points out that they have "abandoned many tenets of Islam and concentrate on their devotion to Imams", meaning devotion to Ali, Mohammad's cousin and son-in-law, and his sons Hassan and Hussein. The consequence of this is that the few who can afford it prefer making a pilgrimage to the holy centers of Shiite Islam, Najaf and Karbala, where the Imams are buried and, unlike Sunni Muslims pilgrimage to Mecca is consider by some as having only a second priority. Thesiger, a well-known observer of marshland life, was quoted as saying that during his many years with the Marsh Arabs he had met more people on their way to the Shi'ite shrine in Meshed, Iran (which earns them the title *Zair* or visitor) than to Mecca (which earns the title *Hajji*), although the distance between the two cities is roughly the same. Also, families that can claim descent from the prophet Muhammad earn the title of *Sayyid*.

The month of Ramadan is considered holy by all Muslims, during which they are required to fast from dawn to dusk. Moreover, they are permitted to work only six hours a day. Fasting includes no eating, drinking or cigarette smoking. And although expatriates are not required to fast, they must not eat, drink or smoke in public. After the breaking of the fast (*iftar*) at sunset, families and friends usually gather together to celebrate. These festivities may continue well into the night. Generally speaking, life and business take on a slower pace during Ramadan, and many businesses operate on a reduced schedule, and shops may stay open for longer hours to accommodate fasting Muslims.

Perhaps ironically, some marshland dwellers were known to visit the tomb of the Jewish prophet Ezra the Scribe, known in Arabic as al-Uzair, located on the Tigris River, some 50 miles north of Basrah. The grave lies under a blue, rather than the characteristic green, Muslim dome and for the most part its walls are covered with Hebrew letters. If one needs a possible explanation for this pilgrimage, it may be due to the absence of mosques in much of the marshes and al-Uzair tomb provides a solid building for the marsh dwellers for spiritual experience. Another possible explanation is the belief that al-Uzair responds to prayers for relief from a variety of ailments and personal problems. The old Jewish community in Iraq shared these beliefs, and it was not uncommon for parents to take their sickly child to the tomb to seek the prophet's blessings to achieve a quick recovery for the child. It should also be noted that there remain small communities of other denominations and minorities such as Mandaeans (Subba) who often work as boat builders, blacksmiths and craftsmen. Sabeans are people of African descent who in the past sought refuge and freedom in the wilderness of the marshes. The number of native Subba families gradually decreased due to being treated harshly by the local inhabitants and also due to the imposition of heavy taxes placed upon them, etc.

For some Ma'dan marsh dwellers heaven is an island called Hufaidh which is rumored to lie somewhere in the southwest stretches of the marshes, although nobody really knows precisely where it is. Thesiger describes it as "the legendary island, which no man may look on and keep his senses". It is said to contain palaces, palm trees and gardens of pomegranates, and huge water buffalo. It is also said that the *Jinn* which in Muslim legend is a spirit that can assume human or animal form and exercise supernatural influence over people, can hide the island from anyone who comes near it (Thesiger, 1964: pp. 23;84–85).

The Marsh Arabs have over the millennia developed a unique subsistence lifestyle that is firmly rooted in their history, their culture and their aquatic environment. Most of the marsh dwellers are semi-nomadic, but some have settled in villages typically built on the edges of the marshlands, or standing on artificial floating islands that can only be accessed by boat and which have to be regularly reinforced with reeds and mud. Floating villages usually comprise a group of separate islands, each housing an individual household.

WAY OF LIFE, ETC., OF MARSH DWELLERS

The traditional way of life of the marsh dwellers as recorded by Wilfred Thesiger, Gavin Maxwell, Robert A Fernea, Shakir Salim and Edward Ochsenschlager in the middle of the twentieth century, had changed little since Sumerian times.

The main income-generating activity of the Marsh Arabs and Ma'dan is reed mat weaving; this is exported to various markets throughout Iraq (Figure 2.6). The primary means of transport that the Marsh Arabs rely on are long bitumen-covered wooden canoes (although reed which requires greater maintenance is also used) called *mashuf*. This is really another relic of ancient Sumer as can be seen from the cylinder seals of Figure 2.7. Traditionally, as a courtesy, the marsh dwellers in canoes will greet all people on the shore and hail boats coming in the opposite direction. This courtesy is returned by the Marsh Arabs onshore.

Some of the earliest Mesopotamian settlements in "*the land between two rivers*" (in Greek) or "*the gift of the two rivers*" were built on floating islands built up of reed in these very same wetlands (Figure 2.8). It is here where writing was invented, where human beings developed agriculture, and worshipped a pantheon of deities (Hammer, Joshua, 2006: p. 46). The aquatic vegetation in the marshlands once provided nourishment for almost two thirds of the wintering waterfowl in the Middle Eastern region.

Marsh dwellers generally have few possessions – perhaps a small herd of water buffalo, a gun for hunting, sport and protection against wild boar attacks, some cooking utensils, blankets and a tar-coated reed canoe (*mashuf*) which they punt with a long reed pole. Even young children have their own reed *mashufs*, which they are taught to navigate at a very early age. But while the reed *mashufs* are inexpensive and materials are readily available to make them, they nevertheless need to be replaced annually. This has prompted some Marsh Arabs to start using the more durable wood and bitumen to make their canoes. In traditional reed houses, mud floors are covered with reed mats which serve as the basic floor surface.

Due to lack of sanitation facilities, the marshes often serve as the marsh dwellers' latrines or public lavatory. Because the drinking water source is normally the same source as that used as latrines, the Marsh Arabs and Ma'dan suffer from various endemic diseases such as bilharzia which is the scourge of the

Figure 2.6 Reed mats ready to be transported to different locations for use as flooring or in building construction (Photo: Jasim al-Asadi).

marshes. It is a disease of the bladder caused by minute flatworms passing from snails to humans and which the Ma'dan people consider it to be an inevitable consequence of the marsh way of life. Kidney stones and dysentery are other common ailments, although dysentery and similar diseases are not as widespread as one might expect which suggests that the local inhabitants may have acquired some immunity to such diseases.

As previously mentioned, the Marsh Arabs once constituted a society of about 500,000 or more people who have inhabited areas in and around an enormous freshwater wetland ecosystem that survived for thousands of years. However, following the first Gulf War (August 1990), the Marsh Arabs witnessed a total desiccation of their economy, their culture and their habitat by the Saddam regime. The destruction of the marshlands through land degradation and

Figure 2.7 Seal impressions of an ancient *mashuf* (canoe) used in Sumerian and Babylonian times.

desertification served both as a punishment and reminder for all who dared rebel against his regime. The draining and destruction of the marshes also prevented rebels and army deserters from seeking refuge there. It was the main catalyst that effectively devastated their way of life, as well as the culture and social cohesion of the marsh dwellers. Almost immediately after the fall of the Saddam regime, many of the remaining native marsh inhabitants took the initiative and spontaneously began to breach the dykes which had deprived the marsh area of much-needed water and bring back the water into the drained areas. Local observers indicate that more than 100 dams and embankments were destroyed during the first exciting days of freedom when optimism filled the air. Moreover, following the fall of Saddam's regime, much national and international interest was revived to help restore them and definitive steps were taken to facilitate the process. Today the marshes are benefiting from these intensive restoration efforts and are now slowly recovering. Assisting this process are various government organizations and international NGOs such as the United Nations Environment Program (UNEP) and the AMAR International Charitable Foundation.

Jane Chanaa believes that the sharp cleavage between the rural and urban communities that formerly characterized Iraqi society began to break down before the Iran–Iraq War,as a result of policies instituted by the government. The war accelerated this process. Continuous fighting has devastated large areas of the rural south, which triggered a massive rural migration to Baghdad. There have been many complaints that the British troops that occupy Basrah and the surrounding region have done little to fill the vacuum of authority that was created

Figure 2.8 Many marsh dwellers' homes consist of settlements built on floating islands consisting of reed and mud (Source: Jasim al-Asadi).

after Saddam's demise. Even tribal codes that were previously in place and used to settled disputes started to break down in the confusion.

The sex roles are clearly defined among the Ma'dans. Traditionally, the responsibility of the men is to milk the water-buffaloes and herd the animals. They also bear the responsibility for all the hunting and fishing. The womenfolk, who must sit behind the men in the canoes, cook all the meals, fetch the water and grind the grain. Cooking is usually done over fires fueled by the buffalo-dung cakes that they have made. The vast majority of male marsh dwellers have short moustaches which are considered to be a symbol of manhood.

Daily Life of the Marsh Dwellers

People of the marshes have built their lives around its unique aquatic ecosystem for thousands of years, fishing, raising water buffaloes for milk, cheese and yogurt, and living in huts woven from marsh reeds. Buffaloes also provide energy and crop fertilizer in the form of fuel dung and manure. Among those that have studied the Marsh Arabs and their way of life is Dr Shakir Salim, who studied the wetlands, particularly the inhabitants of Chibayish, during the middle of the last century, and who prefers to use the term "marsh dwellers" to describe all the inhabitants of the wetlands in southern Iraq, irrespective of their origin or type of economy. This term also avoids the indiscriminate use of Marsh Arab and Ma'dan to describe the marsh inhabitants. Salim says that the "marsh dwellers cannot be differentiated on a linguistic basis because there are only small local changes in dialect. To attempt to distinguish between Bedouin and Ma'dan is useless, since many of the immigrant Bedouin tribes have taken to buffalo-breeding, and have long since severed any connection with Bedouin life." (Salim, 1962: p. 9).

The primary cultural and physical Bedouin traits among the marsh dwellers of the Euphrates region which distinguish them from the eastern marsh dwellers of the Tigris reflect their long contact with the Arabian Desert. Moreover, Salim believes that it is more beneficial to classify today's marsh dwellers on an occupational basis. For example, cultivators, reed-gatherers and buffalo-breeders (Salim, 1962: p.9). It should be noted that Salim's study was conducted during the early 1950s and focused mainly on the Lower Euphrates area which was inhabited mainly by tribes displaying predominantly cultural and physical Bedouin traits as opposed to the eastern marsh dwellers of the Tigris which probably had for many years been in close contact with their Persian neighbor. This may also explain why the fishing industry is not mentioned in Salim's categorizations.

Prior to Saddam's desiccation of the wetlands, the Ma'dan depended largely on their herds of water buffalo for survival. The buffalo were to the Ma'dan what camels were to Arab Bedouin. However, there are several discrepancies between Salim and Thesiger's accounts. For example Salim states that a "rich" family usually owns between seven and ten beasts, whereas in Thesiger's "*The Marsh Arabs*" an ordinary nomad family owns between twenty and thirty and possibly far more. Water buffaloes are highly valued by the Ma'dan for their dairy products and are rarely sold or killed, particularly once they have fully grown and become productive. Among the main daily activities of the marsh dwellers are fishing, waterfowl hunting and, when possible, rice and millet cultivation. Curdled water-buffalo milk and fish are the normal staples of the Ma'dan diet; it may also contain some rice in families that grow it. Women cook bread in a round clay platter over an open fire, and when available wild boar and waterfowl are welcome meat on the table.

By 2005 there remained more than 250,000 Marsh Arab refugees who had not returned to their homeland. The traditional occupation of many marsh dwellers, particularly the Marsh Arabs, is fishing, and prior to the desiccation of the marshes, accounted for about two thirds of Iraq's annual catch. Today, however, although approximately 90 per cent of the returnees to reflooded areas are engaged in the fishing industry their total share of Iraq's annual catch is now thought to stand below 10 per cent.

The majority of Iraqis are anxious for the marshes to be restored to their former state. However, a recent opinion poll carried out by USAID to determine the specific hopes and aspirations of the populace, concluded the presence of something of a generational gap regarding life and work in the southern marshlands. The USAID survey indicated that people in the forties age group or older and who were born and raised in the wetlands, are more eager and enthusiastic to see the marshes restored, than for example the under-25 generation which has been mainly involved in agriculture and which is keen to see further agricultural development. This is because this younger generation grew up during a period when the marshes were being drained by the Saddam regime and therefore lack the traditional life experience of fishing, etc., that the wetlands once offered. There is also the generation in between these two groups that would like to see the marshlands restored, but would also have hopes for agriculture becoming a means for earning a sustainable livelihood.

There are several problems that face marshland returnees. The most significant is perhaps the total absence of an infrastructure that can support normal everyday life such as a lack of adequate safe drinking water, power supply, sewage treatment facilities, refuse collection, sanitation, medical and education facilities and clinics, among other things. The quality of life of marsh dwellers has deteriorated to such an extent in the last two decades, especially in the 1990s when hostilities were launched, that many had to migrate to other areas inside and outside Iraq. Witnesses note that the deteriorated situation made some of the marsh inhabitants think about emigration to Iran, Saudi Arabia and other parts of Iraq. This had a depressive impact in general on the way of life, including economic activity. In its turn, this adversely affected living standards and manifested itself in lower incomes, inferior quality of nourishment and medical aid, degradation of the environment, further decrease of potable water, etc. Upon the fall of Saddam's regime, however, a number of amelioration programs were developed and are being implemented for the region.

In attempting to describe the marsh dwellers' condition and predicament in the 1990s, international observers note that, on the whole, the UN sanctions deteriorated the Iraqis' overall quality of life, but an additional burden was imposed by the Iraqi authorities on the regions inhabited by ethnic minorities, including the southern regions. Furthermore, the hyperinflation of the 1990s, which was partly caused by the UN sanctions, depreciated the fixed incomes of many Iraqis.

During the early 1990s, the GDP decreased more than three times and prices increased dramatically, whereas the state employees' purchase capacity significantly decreased. This was particularly painful for the poorest strata including most of the marsh dwellers, who may have suffered more than other strata of Iraqi society. The continuous rise in food and pharmaceutical prices, combined with restrictions on the import of many of these articles, deprived the marsh dwellers of access to many basic needs such as important food items, home utensils, and even basic forms of medical care. This is further aggravated by the knowledge that the estimated annual income per capita of a marsh dweller was not very different from that of the world's poorest – less than one dollar per day.

As mentioned earlier, there were rarely safe or viable washing or toilet facilities. The inhabitants drank from, washed in and defecated into the same water source. Human and animal pollution was simply a dangerous fact of life in the marshes. These and other facts testify to the primitive and difficult living conditions that the marsh dwellers had to endure, particularly during winter. Summer conditions were just as grim with the onslaught of mosquitoes and flies, adding to the gravity of the already hazardous health conditions. Various NGOs were able to supply some food items, clothes and shoes on an irregular basis. This was in addition to foodstuffs provided by the authorities. The marsh dwellers were also able to catch fish from the marshes and draw water from its deeper reaches, which were less contaminated than that at the water's edge.

Impact of External Economic Development on the Marshlands Economy
The expansion of Iraq's southern provinces was part of the general expansion that Iraq witnessed in its urban population and urban economy. This expansion had an increasing impact upon the economic activities of the Marsh Arabs and

their traditional way of life. This impact became increasingly evident after the dramatic increase in oil prices during the mid-1970s and the economic boom that followed in Iraq and other oil-producing countries. Among the economic and social consequences of the economic boom is the acceleration of marsh dwellers' migration to cities and shanty townships in central and southern Iraq in search of permanent employment. Likewise, the marsh dwellers had strengthened existing ties between their traditional economy and the economy of neighboring provinces, which resulted in an expansion of trade between them. The military operations in the wetlands interrupted the improved way of life which augmented the marsh dwellers' system of seasonal work and temporary employment.

The mass migration from the marshlands' villages in the 1990s increased with the increase in military operations in the region; other factors that impacted the rise in migration were the deliberate and continuous drainage of marshes and lakes and the salination of the soil. Most current assessments put the number of all marsh dwellers at the beginning of the twenty first century in the wetlands' rural area at only between 10 per cent and 15 per cent of the number that inhabited the marshlands prior to the 1970s. The majority of the marsh population had migrated to large urban centers in addition to a great number that migrated to townships on the banks of the remaining lakes.

The dramatic rise in world oil prices in 1973 to 1974 had an immediate impact on the proceeds of oil exports which increased by almost fourfold. This provided a tremendous boost and impetus to the economy and development of the southern provinces, as well as of the country as a whole prior to the Iran–Iraq War. This increase of oil production capacity in the oil-producing regions, including the southern provinces, much of it in the south along the Iranian border, resulted in the accelerated development of numerous industrial projects. An accelerated development of transport infrastructure was also witnessed. Additionally, the country witnessed an increase in investments into agriculture and large scale irrigation projects.

It should be noted that there are some 33 major oilfields based in southern Iraq, of which 19 are located within vicinities where the majority of the native populations are marsh dwellers, including the four giant oilfields of Halfaya, Bin Umr, Majnun and West Qurna. Thus, increased oil production in the southern provinces, and a corresponding increase in construction of petroleum refining capacities, brought considerable wealth to the country which had a dramatic effect on its economy and prospects.

This meant that any substantial restoration and development of energy resources will, for the most part, be centered near or in the general area of the marsh dwellers' natural habitat, and are expected therefore to exert a powerful impact on their economic activities and day-to-day living habits. It is also likely to reinforce the general trends that were initially observed during the period after the oil boom of the mid-1970s when Iraq witnessed a rapid expansion of its urban economy.

This sudden and unexpected availability of wealth had a profound impact on the entire economic outlook of the country and its priorities. It also precipitated a concerted effort towards modernizing and upgrading traditional activities, and urbanization, in addition to an unprecedented wave of labor migration from the rural areas, including the marshlands, to urban centers. The modernization of the traditional activities associated with the marsh arabs and the Ma'dan and which dominated the marsh economy, essentially consisted of handicraft production, agriculture, fisheries and hunting. Jasim al-Asadi of Nature Iraq says that people who used to supplement their incomes by selling milk, cheese, reed mats and baskets are really hurting.

By the 1970s some marsh dwellers recognized that their traditional activities were no longer their main sources of life support which were either mixed with or replaced by elements of modern and semi-modern kinds of activities. Many marsh dwellers now found themselves traveling outside their native habitat in search of seasonal work and additional earnings. There was also a marsh dweller exodus to the cities of southern Iraq, including Basrah, Khor az Zubair, Qurna and Amarah and further north towards Baghdad in the search for employment to support their families.

Nevertheless, the adaptation of the marsh dwellers' economic life to the possible changes has been complicated by a number of circumstances, of which drought is the overriding factor in the Marsh Arabs' plight, but which also includes the mass migration during the previous period and the difficulty of the environmental rehabilitation and restoration of the wetlands. Turkey, Syria and Iran are often blamed as these countries have stemmed the flow of the Euphrates and Tigris into Iraq by the use of dams, etc. Another important factor complicating restoration is the lack of security and fierce ongoing inter-tribal feuding and firefights. Examples of this are the ttwenty-year-old feud between the Karamishah and the Shaghanba tribes of the Ma'dan, the tribal feuds between the Marsh Arab al-Bait Sa'idah tribe and the Banu Mansur, and the firefights between Banu Ammar and al-Ashur tribes, all of which have to this day proved extremely difficult to settle.

Most Marsh Arabs and Ma'dan have now come to face the reality that the marshes will most likely never recover completely. Prior to the 1950s the Tigris and Euphrates overflowed with snowmelt from the Turkish mountains that flooded their banks with seasonal regularity. These floods flushed out the saline water while simultaneously breathing new life into the environment. Today, a proud people who for thousands of years lived off the land must now buy food and bottled water to survive.

3

ARTS AND CRAFTS

Hamed T. Haykal

GENERAL

The marshes represent a world of charm, beauty and nature at its finest. It is a unique world of folklore, craftsmanship and impressive reed architecture, a world of perpetual life that formed itself over the course of thousands of years.

A large segment of the population of this region consists of people who are urbanites residing in cities, and rural people who reside in the villages that are scattered along the shores of the Tigris and the Euphrates Rivers and their tributaries; those people are peasants who practice farming and raising cattle and sheep as a profession, and nomads (Bedouins) who shepherd their sheep and cattle in the neighboring grazing lands or in the desert, in addition to the marsh inhabitants.

Salim classifies the inhabitants of the marshes into three broad divisions based on their occupation. These are: 1. Cultivators 2. Reed-gatherers and 3. Buffalo-breeders (Salim, 1970: p. 21). The cultivators comprise the largest single segment of marsh dwellers. And despite the social and economical differences among those three groups, they are nevertheless socially and economically integrated. Moreover, it is unlikely that the marsh inhabitants would have survived to this day had it not been for their having access to the markets of neighboring villages and towns to sell their products. In ancient times, most cities were surrounded by rural areas that supplied fresh fruit, vegetables and other perishable goods.

All these groups today share a common language (Arabic), culture and traditions, including farthest from the Arabian deserts, i.e., the Ma'dan. Arab codes were the ideal which governed the Ma'dans' lives and shaped the whole pattern of their behavior, from blood feuds to table manners (Thesiger, 1964: p. 101).

This chapter will describe a small agricultural village on the borders of the marshes which reflects an important segment of the marsh inhabitants. The choice of this agricultural village readily illustrates the strong interaction and cultural diversity of all the above-mentioned groups in an environment that allows them to meet and exchange goods and services. This mixture cannot be found in most marshland villages, or in most urban environments, or in a gathering of traveling nomads in the heart of the western desert.

The Village of Khdhaboh

The place I am about to describe is a typical agricultural village that lies on a small waterway which is a tributary of Shatt al-Arab and which is located between the city of Basrah to the south and Gourna, a smaller city to the north, within a thin strip of palm plantations that are infiltrated by other small waterways. To the east of this strip flows the Shatt al-Arab separating this section from the plain that flows to the Huwaiza Marsh. To the west there is a main highway linking Basrah to Baghdad and which passes through this area. Also to the west of this main highway are wide plains and meadows that spread out to the horizon, and which are sometimes planted with wheat or barley, and at other times overflow with floods. The Hammar Marsh lies to the west and north of Khdhaboh village. Thus, the village and the thin plantation strip that existed between Shatt al-Arab and the main highway constituted a long narrow island between Hammar Marsh and Shatt al-Arab. Every year numerous marsh families would visit this village and remain for two months or longer.

The Khdhaboh River (it is said that its name is derived from the word *khudhab* which is a dye that Arabs used to color their hair) proceeds along like other similar waterways, to the west to water the thick palm plantations, and from which numerous rivulets branch out to form smaller streams that end with "fingers" or channels, which were dug by humans.

In Khdhaboh Village there were two or three "mansions", built of gold-colored facing bricks; each "mansion" contained several rooms, *iewans*, kitchen, entrance foyer, *hibb* house, salt house, supply room, bathroom and guest room (*dewan*), similar to styles traditionally found in Baghdad and Basrah at that time, except that the Khdhaboh houses consisted of only one storey. The walls have a thickness of one meter and have arched openings topped with a squared ornament of protruding brick in the shape of triangles.

The few ordinary houses that existed were roofed with palm trunks containing bands of reed on them, and a layer of reed mats which were finished with a mixture of mud mixed with hay or straw. The doors and windows were made of wood, each with two paneled leaves, but without glass. The rooms surrounded a central courtyard, paved with squared yellow bricks called *farshi*; this was used throughout the house as well as for the stairs leading to the roof.

As for the roofs, they contained a low parapet facing the courtyard, and a high brick wall buttressed at regular intervals and topped with a cylinder-like cowl plastered with *juss* (gypsum). The brick wall was permeated with down-headed gaps enabling the observer to see the surrounding land. These were constructed to allow observation and also visual ability to shoot when necessary to drive potential thieves away, although no thieves appeared during the course of the past fifty years. Most of these houses were built during the previous century between the beginning of the 1930s and 1980s.

A distance of approximately one hundred meters to the west, and on the north bank of the Khdhaboh River, there is a hodgepodge collection of cottages, huts (*sarifas*), and guest houses (*mudhifs*) belonging to a large family that are the descendants of a single grandfather and his four sons over a period of less than fifty years, and which in the 1960s comprised of several hundred people. This simple village cluster consisted of four basic corner locations, each containing a guest house *(mudhif)* belonging to one of the four sons.

Houses in this compound essentially comprise of rooms constructed of pisé with high ceilings and covered with reed or date-palm trunks, and plastered with a mixture of mud and straw. The compound contains other types of construction, such as *sobat* which is a horizontal shed that is braced on four poles and is used for sleeping during summer nights. It is usually provided with a ladder of palm trunks as well. There is also another simple type called *kubar* that is used mostly as a shelter for animals. Randomly organized courtyards are filled with bags of dried grass that is used as fodder for cows in winter, in addition to providing shelter for cows, chickens, ducks and perhaps some sheep.

A sheltered conical kiln (*tannur*) is an oven used by the marsh dwellers for baking bread and measures between 80 and 100 cm high and gradually narrows towards the top which contains an opening of about 30 cm (12 inches). It is usually heated by dung patties and reeds. The baking process consists basically of spreading the dough over the heated surface until the bread is baked. The area also usually contains counters and workbenches when it is part of the main cooking area (Figure 3.1). The *tannur* is usually used to bake flat wheat bread. Sometimes as an alternative, a kitchen hearth is built in a lean-to or as a separated structure (Ochsenschlager, 2004: p. 100).

This compound also contains a number of clay cylinders made by women using a combination of mud and straw in the shape of a kiln. These cylinders were used to store grains like rice and wheat and unpressed dates often mixed with aromatic herbs like nutmeg or mint. Other formations are formed in the shape of solid domed cylinders with dark green colors; these are used for the storage of dung cakes (*mattal*). Thesiger calls these dung cakes (Thesiger, 1964: p. 55), while Gavin Young and others call them biscuit-like pats of buffalo-dung (Young, 1977: p. 125), and Ochsenschlager describes them as "conical stacks of dung patties that look like buildings in the courtyard" (Ochsenschlager, 2004: p. 108). *Mattal* is cow or buffalo manure mixed with straw and formed as disks and kept in the sun before being stacked up to make up those cylinders that are usually plastered with a layer of manure to protect them from rain and prepare them for use as dried disks for fuel. It is mostly used in the summer to form a chimney to drive away the relentless mosquitoes that are merciless when it comes to both humans and cows.

No obvious borders between the houses of this compound, which has four entrances, are evident, and most rooms and spaces are intertwined together. Compound entrances do not have doors, but are open narrow alleyways that allow people and animals to enter the compound and move around to their allocated rooms and lodgings. This seems to be a common characteristic in all rural settlements in the region, as described by Thesiger who wrote, "I soon found that these peoplehad no privacy in their lives and never expected any" (Thesiger, 1964: pp. 35; 88). Actually, privacy is a cultural attribute that varies from people to people and culture to culture. Thesiger probably reached his conclusion by observing the Ma'dan's privacy customs and comparing it with his own Western culture. Ochsenschlager wrote years later, describing this issue differently, saying: "Despite close living, the privacy of each family was strictly protected except in the courtyard which was a communal activity area" (Ochsenschlager, 2004: p. 100).

It is important to mention here that these guest houses (*mudhifs*) differed from the ones of the clan sheikhs in the marshes that have become known to many readers through the writings of Wilfred Thesiger, Gavin Young and others, and the term guest house started to take on a new meaning – a special form of structure having an oval section and built of reed bundles. Guest houses in Khdhaboh, on the other hand, are long structures with a triangular roof. The typical reed bows were exchanged with palm trunk-pillars supporting wooden plant-stems. Each two bows cross each other at the top of the structure and braced on the *hardi* which is the horizontal element, and on the horizontal *hutter* (plural of *httar*) along with reed bundles and water-soaked palm branches to increase its solidity which, in turn, hold the reed mats (*bouari*). If the guest house was long, then the *hardi* would contain several pieces of wooden stems with their tops fastened together with ropes, with the knots resting on wooden poles located in the middle of the space. In this case, the used poles are slender and set in a manner that does not block the view. The poles are also used to support shelves that hold copies of the Qur'an or clay disks (usually from Karbala) that people use to pray on. These praying tablets were typically kept in little packets that hung on the wall (Thesiger, 1964: p. 88).

Guest houses typically have one entrance in their long walls near one of the corners, and have a burning stove to make coffee (*wijagh*) besides a *hibb* for water, that sits on a wooden stand. The guest houses typically have a platform that is used for Housaini memorials in Muharram and Ramadan, and is covered with a black fabric during the other months of the year.

To the north of this compound lies another group that resides around a mansion that is smaller. In addition there are several cottages that belong to other small families. As one moves further along, another residence compound becomes visible which belongs to a family that is

Figure 3.1 The traditional *tannur* is a conical clay oven that had been a feature of Babylonia and today can be found in many parts of sourthern Iraq and the Middle East. The traditional *tannur* is used for baking bread and other foods. (Photo: Haydar Auda, 2008).

also descendant of the same grandfather. In the southern part of the compound one finds several cottages and huts belonging to various other families that lead to a small mansion located on the land of another wealthy family.

This area's economy relied solely on dates, despite the fact that other vegetables were planted in a limited range. These were used for domestic consumption and rarely sold. Yet, in the sixties, some people started growing tomatos, okra, cucumber, melon and peas, but it remained on a small scale and very primitive. The villagers also raised cows and some sheep, while women raised chickens and ducks (Figure 3.2).

What attracts the attention to this small village near Basrah is the diversity of the families that live in it when it comes to religion and dogma. It is also noticeable that the inhabitants of the village lack strong clan ties, for the people here belong to families that lack a strong tribal presence as is the case of the majority of villages in northern Basrah and the marshes. This may be due partially to the special economic relationships and type of production which depended on date production in an economy that needed landowners and farmers rather than tribal leaders and tribesmen. But this gradually changed as people were compelled to come together under clan formations with the spreading of political chaos and lack of security.

The families that lived in this region have all migrated to it from various places – mostly from the south, but also from other parts of the country. This is distinguishable by the different accents of the migrating families, although everyone speaks Arabic. Some of the families migrated here from areas east of Shatt al-Arab, while others came from the southern part.

The people of Khdhaboh know that this palm planted strip has gone through a recent reclamation and until fairly recently was immersed in water and inhabited by wild boars, and was created by the precipitations of Shatt al-Arab by years of seasonal floods. However, a number of current external elements have caused it to appear much as it did in the 1930s. These include the increasing international demand for dates, the tranquility that spread after the establishment of the modern nation and the revitalization it went through assisted by British investors. It is also said that a man from the city of Mosul designed the plantations and defined the distances between streams and rivulets and their straightness and points of intersection, and the distances between the trees themselves, using geometrical surveying methods. To this day, we are still able to see the remains of that old Mosul house.

Many Arab tribes migrated to the village of Khdhaboh in the form of families from the towns of Amarah and Bazun and the Albu-Shama tribes to build cottages or tents, exchanging their work for dates. The women work in transporting or gathering the scattered dates, or cleaning the dates

Figure 3.2 Photo depicting the breeding of cows, which is common in marsh villages (Photo: Dr Faris Kubba).

by separating the good ones from the defected ones in seasonal stores where the dates are collected *jouakheen*. Each woman gets a *wazna* for her effort, and a *wazna* is a palm-leaf basket that weighs about 30 kilograms of dates.

As for the men, they work as guards or on cleaning the water channels, which is important to guarantee two things; firstly increasing the height of the farms' land by providing it with good soil filled with organic materials, and secondly ensuring the adequacy of the work of the rivulets as they water the plantations under the effect of ebb and flow.

During the months of August and September of each year, the river gets filled with *mashhoofs* and *balams* (canoes and boats) that come from deep within the marsh interior and from the villages of Amarah. Those boats come filled with a variety of goods that are to be bartered for dates, pottery vessels of all kinds, salt extracted from the salt wells of Chibayish and *masfout* fish (a sort of river fish that marsh people capture in large quantities). However, due to the lack of means of suitable transportation, the fish are cleaned and salted to keep them from molding, and then stored in tin cans or in tar *guffa* vessels. Other agricultural products include pumpkin and melon. Exchange here depends on swapping a measure of the goods with the same weight in dates; this is called *addallah*, meaning "same amount", or with double the weight of dates, and this is called *addal nussah* which means "half the amount". Each boat carries a family, and each family carries its belongings of flour, rice, tea, sugar, bread kiln and a clay-disk for baking bread (Thesiger, 1964: p. 173; Salim, 1970: p. 373).

The village women knit baskets, hand fans, floor sweepers, bread dishes, table pieces and reed mats. They also make large and small baskets for use in transporting items like dates, or for cleaning rice. As for the men, they work together in making *khassaph* which is a form of fronds-baskets that are used to press dates in order to export them or use them domestically.

Some families that live in the village work on weaving textiles like rugs, mats and *adil* which is put on riding animals such as donkeys after being filled with grain and is used as a big sack.

As the village women weave their beautifully colored baskets utilizing new white palm fronds, they dye the fronds by soaking them in a crimson dye which is typically bought from markets in Basrah, while the

Bedouin women make other baskets using colored woolen strings and yarn, and which are called *safat*. The unusual thing about both kinds of baskets is that they are both made of *nisil* which is a wild plant that exist in large numbers and grow in the shape of needles, or from palm branches after soaking and grinding them to transform them into long supple fibers capable of being bent, twisted and formed easily. The color formations for both the yarn and frond baskets and their patterns are all similar, mainly using red, yellow, orange and blue.

While some people come to the village in boats, others come on donkeys, horses and camels. And at the time when some marsh inhabitants may sing sad songs at night, the Bedouins prefer to recite long poems in their assemblies and where the men gather around to listen to these long poems that tell tales of heroism, love or exile. Although the children do not understand much of what is said here and there, they nevertheless enjoy this magnificent variance. Gold and silver merchants roam the village during these months as well. They are usually of the Subba sect, and can be identified by their long beards and loose moustaches. They also usually wear red *kufics* (head cover). The village women know these merchants well and they know the honest ones from the dishonest ones; they also know who has the best merchandise. These merchants used to wander around the farms freely selling their gold and silver jewelry.

The village people of Khdhaboh are comprised of a number of different ethnic groups, from Bedouins to Ma'dan, desert inhabitants to marsh dwellers (Figure 3.3). At this time of year the village becomes a cultural and commercial festival, where everybody exchanges goods, stories, rumors, poetry and songs, and each wears their own dress and special tattoos, and talks in their mother accent, and peace, tranquility and amicable living encompasses the village. When October comes, everyone returns to their place of origin, and the farms hibernate for several months in mud and cold winter rain.

All this variance and similarity, the perfumes that women wear, and faces that reflect varying shapes because of tattoos and different head covers and head ropes that range between thin fine ropes to thick coarse ones, all add appeal and charm to the people and make them more joyful. One of

Figure 3.3 Marsh Arab and Ma'dan woman with child (Photos: Jasim al-Asadi).

the things that caught everyone's attention was the brilliant colors of women's costumes that ranged from yellow to red to turquoise, blue and pink, all brocaded with shiny golden strings, whereas the elderly women generally wore black.

The year of 1969 was a decisive year in the life of the region, having had a detrimental and lasting impact on it. That year the region faced a devastating flood that destroyed the area's economic system and the spatial distribution of existing human settlements. This period also witnessed a fundamental change to the political system that instigated major economic and social changes leading to the collapse of the traditional way of life. Numerous factories mushroomed, like the paper factory to the north of this village, and the electricity-generating station to the south of it, all mustering people to work in those enterprises and encouraging them to desert their old agricultural lifestyle. Agricultural associations were established, and irrigation canals were constructed to encourage the inhabitants to remain in towns like Amarah. But the villagers preferred not to migrate any more due to the weakness in date production on the one hand, and the presence of job opportunities in their areas on the other hand. That same year, factional organizations increased in the village, and tension and fear spread among the people, forcing them to leave their guest houses and causeries. During this upheaval many of the old traditions simply disappeared. And since 1979, colonial and domestic changes have also taken place, driving the country and the whole region into an era of sorrow and despair.

ARTS AND CRAFTS

Cultures are distinguished from one another by certain qualities that reflect their individuality, the way it expresses its beliefs and the way it responds to the environmental elements of its surroundings. Among the most distinguishing landmarks of a nation's culture, in addition to its architecture, are its clothes, tools, crafts and arts, with music at its forefront. If we examine Mesopotamian engravings, sculptures and bas-reliefs, in Mesopotamian culture, we discover a number of tools, clothes, head covers and other components that were coincidental in those paintings, engravings and sculptures and in which the ancient Iraqi artist endeavored to embody the spirit of important political or religious events. It is noticeable too that some of those factors vanished completely while others remained.

This resulted in cultural differences that continued to accompany the rise and decline of the various rulers that dominated Mesopotamia throughout its long history. Certain items like clothes and head covers, for example, whether for women or men, have fundamentally changed, whereas items like boats and agricultural tools remained substantially unchanged. This is largely explained by the fact that some elements had strong cultural ties with the nations that took turns in running the country; it is unreasonable therefore to expect the Arabs, who were the last nation to dominate this region, to renounce their traditional garments and head covers that they considered to be among the prime symbols reflecting honor and authenticity. Moreover, the inhabitants of the region continued their use of scythes and plows which experience has shown to be totally appropriate and effective when it came to performing works that were related to Iraq's environment. Furthermore, the occupiers also did not find it inconvenient to continue in the use of canoes (*mashuf*) which the local inhabitants had considerable expertise in constructing, and which have proven to be well suited to their function.

These facets of culture have two main aspects, the first is identity, and the other is pragmatism. Many cultural identity-related factors often disappear with the decline of nations and are replaced with new traits that exemplify the traditions of the dominant nations. Nevertheless, many vital traits related to work, transportation and construction, as well as other elements that the local environment and climate proved to be pivotal, have remained essentially unchanged. This may explain the dynamics of the strong cultural interaction that took place over the course of thousands of years, a phenomenon that went largely unnoticed in many other regions.

The migration of peoples from the Arabian Desert (al-Jazeera al-Arabia) was gradual, and made by races that interspersed with and eventually absorbed the cultures of the existent inhabitants. They also looked upon the Iraqi civilization with considerable respect and admiration, and they did not resist adopting some of their religious beliefs, legends, arts and crafts. Some names have been changed to suit the new language, just like introducing new techniques, and developing old ones to meet new and emerging challenges. It may be said, however, that in southern Iraq, building materials may have had the biggest role in the continuity of many traditional elements. The environment in southern Iraq, particularly in the marshes, provided and continues to provide much of the essential raw materials used in building construction and folk crafts since ancient times. Reed, cane, palm fronds and leafs, tree and palm trunks, sheep yarn, clay and tar are some of the raw materials used in construction as well as to produce various tools and supplies. At the time when camel hair was used to make the Bedouin tents that accompany the Bedouin's traveling lifestyle, materials like reed and canes were used to build Marsh Arabs' huts and guest houses (*mudhifs*) as shown in Figure 3.4. For some, water sometimes appeared to be a thorny problem for roaming nomads living in a barren desert, forcing them to use sheep - or goatskins to store the water and lessen its evaporation. However, water was rarely a problem for the marsh inhabitants.

1. Reed Mats

Reed mats are one of the principal crafts of the ancient marsh inhabitants, which was later picked up and mastered by other tribes that also lived in the wetlands by virtue of the increased demand for this material, particularly following the British occupation at the beginning of the twentieth

Figure 3.4 Guest house (*mudhif*) of Sayid Salh al-Battat on the southern edge of the Central Marshes (Photo: Dr Hamed Haykal, 2005).

century. The industry continues to flourish in Iraq to this day, and in many Iraqi cities the demand for it remains strong (Figure 3.5). Dr Shakir Salim describes the reed mat industry in considerable detail in his Ph.D. thesis "*ech-Chibayish*" (Salim, 1970: p. 326).

In describing the mat-making process, Ochsenschlager states, "Men harvest the reeds with a sickle-shaped, toothed knife and cut off the tops and bottoms. Wives, sons, or daughters tie bundles of reeds together and either bring them to the edge of the marsh or load them aboard a boat in which they will be transported to shore. On the shore each reed is skinned, split with a short, curved knife, and peeled. Women then lay ten to twenty sections flat on the ground and pound them with mallets, heavy wooden sticks, or even bitumen-covered pestles until they are pliable." He adds, "When enough material is collected, both men and women plait the mats (Figure 3.6). They lay out the requisite number of flattened reed strands next to each other on the ground and plait a weft of the same material across them at right angles in a twill pattern of either over two, under two or over three, under three." (Ochsenschlager, 2004: pp. 130–131).

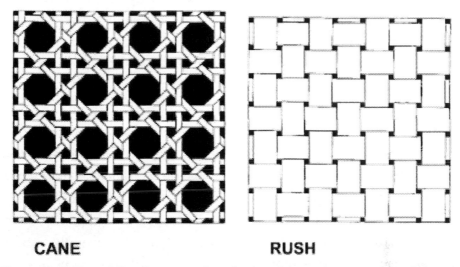

CANE   **RUSH**

Figure 3.5 Example of cane and rush weaving patterns used by the marsh dwellers (Source: Dr Sam Kubba).

Reed mats are used in several ways; their main use is in building and ceiling construction, and as a floor finish by basically spreading it over the mud floor (Figure 3.7). Reeds are also used to build temporary huts that can be easily dismantled and moved from one location to another. By placing them on bundles of palm fronds, they are sometimes used to create a base for placing dates on to protect them from the earth's humidity.

Figure 3.7 Baria reed mats are available in local markets (Photo: Dr Hamed Haykal, 2005).

Figure 3.6 Photo of Marsh Arab plaiting mats for use in building construction or as a floor finish (Photo: Mudhafar Salim).

[57]

Reed mats come in various sizes for reed mats ranging from the large, skillfully weaved mats in which all four edges are folded, to small ones which are folded from two sides only. The size, color and quality level of the mat depends on its function, and this essentially defines their price. Commercial sizes usually measure roughly 1 m (3' 4") x 2–3 m (6'6"–10' 0") and take two to three hours to make. Women also plait mats from *chulan* stems, which is a plant like *berdi* but it is shorter and thicker. *Chulan* grows on the shallow shores of the marsh and on riverbanks. *Chulan* mats are made with the use of calyx (*sutli*) strings in a horizontal line that is parallel to the long axis of the mat weft. *Chulan* makes up the mats' woof and is approximately 40 cm to 90 cm wide. Colors are usually used to ornament them; this being done by soaking some *chulan* sticks in water after melting crimson *cirmiz* dye using several colors, particularly red, green and blue.

Besides reed mats, there are different kinds of mats sewn by using different materials such as *chulan, husan* and palm fronds. Their dimensions, colors and quality depend on their function and usage.

2. Carpets

Carpets are considered an important furnishing element in a guest house, although this might not always be apparent as they are often kept aside. And even the owners of small houses that do not possess a guest house usually keep some carpets to spread out when guests are expected. Greeting guests by spreading out a carpet for the guest is considered a sign of respect and welcome (Thesiger, 1964: p. 49). However, laying out a carpet in front of a guest is considered inappropriate and offensive.

Previously, traditional carpet manufacture was a well-known and widespread craft of which most families were familiar. However, due to several factors (e.g., more efficient communications, better transport and increased competition from imported and government-manufactured products) the industry gradually slipped into decline and was largely replaced by the cheaper mass produced carpets. It wasn't long before only a limited number of families and their descendents continued to specialize in its manufacture. It should be noted that many carpets are named after the place they were weaved in.

Carpets are characterized by not being wide, with each carpet not being more than one meter wide (3' 4"). Carpet lengths, on the other hand, differ; some carpets are very long (*madda*) and are used in *mudhifs*, while others do not exceed 3–4 meters (approx. 10' 0"–13' 4"). There are also many types of carpets, some of them are expertly made and have detailed adornments and luminous colors which are typically used in *mudhifs*. Other kinds of carpets are of inferior quality and are called *adil*. These are put on the donkey's back or are used as sacks to store grains and transport them. Between the top quality and inferior qualities there exists a different grade of rugs (*bisat*) that is lighter and cheaper, and *izaar* which is a form of blanket. In addition there is a scattered *izaar* that is made of wool and embroidered with colored yarn threads. Pillow bags are also made of wool which, after being embellished with geometric designs, are filled with wool to make pillows for sleeping or cushions to lean on while sitting in a *mudhif* (*takya*). Carpet types are numerous and vary from one location to another – both by their names and by their embellishments.

3. House furniture

Houses of this and other villages in this region have simple wooden furniture, such as wooden chests made from the finest kind of wood and often studded with bronze nails and beautifully engraved bronze plates. Bamboo baskets can be seen in many households and are used for putting clothes in.

As for beds, the marsh inhabitants used bed-like structures made of palm-leaves, reed or other plants and which were called *irzaal*. These were used as beds to sleep on at night, although during the hot summer months, many people prefer to sleep in the open air outside their houses. In the villages adjoining the marshes, "sleeping platforms" were built to raise the bedding above the ground (Ochsenschlager, 2004: p. 108). Figure 3.8 shows a terracotta model of a bed from the Isin-Larsa/Old Babylonian period in which woven rush appears to have been used.

Most early furniture pieces were probably crude affairs of a basket-like construction of woven reed, which was found in abundance in the marshes of southern Mesopotamia. Moreover, this type of construction resembles types used in many of the village coffeeshops found in southern Iraq today, which are called *kursi jireed* (Figure.3.9). These are made of the spiny part of the fronds of date palm trees, which is strong and versatile, and lends itself to a kind of cage construction, as well as for more decorative types. The smaller end sections of the spine are typically used for the vertical members and are inserted through holes in the heavier horizontal pieces. The latter come from the thicker part of the palm frond, and are only partially dried so that they tighten up on the vertical pieces as they dry out, and form a fairly rigid and durable construction. Crates to hold vegetables and fruit are made in the same manner and it seems likely that we have here an example of a craft that has continued with little change for more than 4,000 years. The seats of the chairs are made of woven rush – a craft known from prehistoric times. In Figure 3.10 are examples of cane chairs depicted on ancient cylinder seals (tentative reconstructions).

4. Baskets

Several kinds of baskets are made in Khdhaboh, these depending on their proposed use; one such type is the *khassaf* basket which is a large basket used for pressing dates and is made of low-quality green fronds with

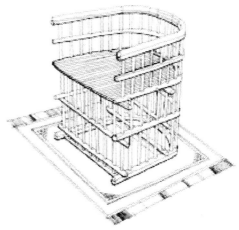

Figure 3.9 Drawing showing a traditional chair called *Kursi Jireed* in which no nails whatsoever are used. This chair can still be found in many Iraqi coffee shops today. Crates to hold vegetables and fruit are made in the same manner to this day.

Figure 3.8 Terracotta model of bed from Isin-Larsa/Old Babylonian period showing use of reed weaving.

a 10 cm *safifa* width. Women usually make *khassaf safifas* that are very long. After finishing the weaving of *safifas* men gather on a summer night in a *mudhif* or a *mudhif* courtyard and collectively plait the *khassaf* by using strands of palm-leaf stems. The lower end of the *khassaf* is first knitted and then the whole thing is sewn to a cylindrical shape to a height of about 70 cm and a diameter of approximately 40 cm, with the upper side left open. *Khassafs* are stored until the arrival of the date-pressing season, when they are drenched in water to tenderize them (Salim, 1970: p. 313).

Another type of basket is the *zibeil,* which is a small basket that is called *gosher* in some villages. It is made by weaving a thin, white-frond 3–5 cm width *safifa* and then plaiting it with thin strings from fronds, or palm-leaf stems or *nissil*. The basket's diameter normally ranges between 20–30 cm and has a height of 15–25 cm. Handles are not normally sewn to the frails (*zibeil*) which can be made of colored *safifas*. Frails have many

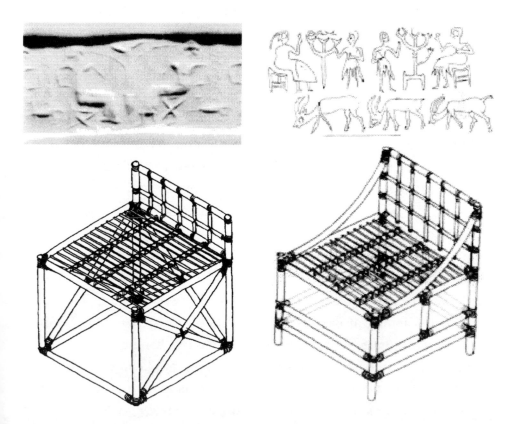

Figure 3.10 Tentative reconstructions of cane chairs based on cylinder seal impressions from the Early Dynastic period (Source: Dr Sam Kubba, 2006).

uses, from gathering dates and crops like okra and peas, to presenting food. Likewise they are sometimes used to store small domestic items. Larger baskets are available and are called *allaga*. These are typically made of green fronds, although some are made of smooth white fronds, depending on their proposed use. If the *allaga* is made for seasonal activities like gathering dates it would be made of low-quality green fronds. But if it was made for domestic use then its *safifa* would be knitted out of smooth white fronds. A handle of fiber is normally knitted for *allagas* in a rope-shape which is why the shape of an *allaga* is flattened and pressed from both sides to facilitate linking to the handles.

As for *wazna,* it is a basket of white fronds of standard dimensions. The reason it is called *wazna* is supposedly because its measurement represents a woman's daily wage and is filled with dates for that purpose. A *wazna* normally has a diameter of 50 cm and a depth of 50 cm. *Waznas* typically have two handles sewn on both of their sides by deploying a rope of fiber. In addition to the *wazna,* there are baskets called *jilla* which have the same form as the *wazna* but are of a lower standard. A *hindaal* is another small basket made of low-quality green fronds, which are sometimes interlaced and which are used daily. The *haychal* basket is smaller than the *hindaal* and is typically used by children who may sometimes put a small nightingale in it. It has a frond handle, in addition to being interlaced in a manner that would allow air circulation so as not to suffocate any small nightingale that may be in it. Most of these baskets are sold in local markets (Figure 3.11). Another popular form of basket is the *tubag* which is made of 1 cm rope-shape needle-like leaf bands after drying them and soaking them in water, or from palm-stems, after which they are all sewn together in a spiral manner by utilizing fresh fronds. A long needle (*mikhraz*) some 5 cm long that has a hole at its end is used to sew the basket. The *tubag* belongs to a family of baskets that consists of a dish roughly 50 cm in diameter, with upraised edges, and normally has two handles from the same material. Its main function is for presenting food or placing bread.

The *guffa* is a circular-shaped basket that is made in the same way as the *tubag*. The *guffa* basket comes in different sizes and serves various functions. Some *guffa* are small – not more than 30 cm in diameter and 20 cm in depth, while others are very large. Large *guffas*

Figure 3.11 Photo showing different types of mats and baskets that are currently being sold in the marketplace.

are usually coated with bitumen which renders them black in color and resistant to humidity and other climatic effects. The bitumen also increases its toughness and useful life. Tarred *guffas* are often used for moving around items like dates, wheat and barley, as well as for storage purposes. Sometimes the *guffa* has a concave base to facilitate a woman carrying it on her head. Women typically place a piece of cloth between their heads and the *guffa* to protect themselves from the harshness of it.

When baskets are weaved with colored yarn instead of palm-fronds they are called *suffat* which is basically a small container that is sewn, which often has beautifully drawn patterns on it. *Suffats* are generally provided with a lid from the same material that is fastened to it with yarn. *Suffats* are used for storing gold and silver jewelry and precious stones; they are also used for keeping women's cosmetics like perfumes, *mahlab* and *dirim,* as well as traditional medicines and money.

5. Pottery vessels

The *hib* is a common terracotta vessel found in most homes in the area; it is cylindrical in shape from the upper side and cone-like from the lower side. Its upper diameter is between 50–70 cm, and it has a height of approximately 70 cm which includes the thin part of it. *Hibs* are made of clay and are a pale green color directly after being baked. They rest on a wooden stand and are used mainly to store and cool water by evaporation; as the water oozes out of the *hib* it evaporates and cools it. Sometimes the *hib* is used to filter polluted water which is gathered in a small terracotta container called a *bouaga*. As this is a long and tedious process and can rarely satisfy a family's water needs, *bouga* water has come to be used largely for infants, the elderly and the sick.

A *habana* is smaller than the *hib* and is sometimes called *madana*; it is used primarily for storing and transporting water but also for making butter. The diameter of the *madana* ranges from 30 to 40 cm as does its height (including the pointed thin part).

Another pottery vessel type is the *sharba,* which consists of a long pottery container that looks like a kettle and is known as *tinga* in many parts of Iraq. The *sharba* is also used for storing and drinking water. *Kouz,* on the other hand, had its name derived from the word *cass* (cup) and consists of a small cup. The *kouz* has now virtually vanished along with other vessels, including the *jadah* or *kashkool.*

6. Copper containers

The village people of Khdhaboh, as in most of southern Iraq, use a variety of copper tools. Copper was particularly popular during the period prior to the appearance of aluminum (*fafun*) as the latter is cheap and light, unlike the more expensive, thick and heavy but long-lasting copper tools.

Using copper pots was linked to the *saffar* profession (copper craftsman), and many of the larger cities and towns have a market for *saffarien* or *saffafier*. Every two or three years a group of *saffarien* come to villages like Khdhaboh and take up a central position in it so that they may install their stoves and bellow (*keir*) and also find a good location for polishing customers' pots, preferably near a date palm. Traditionally, the *saffar* craftsman stands on the required pot to be polished after filling it with sand, and then grabs the trunk of the palm tree with both hands and starts twirling left and right while the *saffar* uses his feet to polish the pot.

A *saffar* would wander around the village to notify the residents of his arrival, and the local womenfolk bring him their copper utensils and tools that need repairing or polishing. *Saffars* use coal for heating the objects and tools like hammers for repair; they also use *qalay* and red paint to polish the pots. There are different kinds of copper products such as the *siphriah,* which is a pot that is made in various sizes depending on its function. While some are very large and others quite small, they all essentially have the same shape. *Sinyahs* (trays) also come in different sizes; they have a drawn-up edge, and are used mainly for offering food and refreshments. Copper dishes are also used to present food as well as to cover copper pots that are used to boil water or cook food.

A *breej* is used for washing hands and comes in two basic shapes; short and long. Normally a child would carry it in his right hand to pour water for the *mudhif* guests so that they can wash their hands before and after eating, while the water used for washing gathers in a *lagan* that has two parts – a container and a cover. As for the *maskhna,* this is a copper bowl that is used for bringing water. Its name was originally derived from the word *taskheen,* which means heating, as it was used for heating water. However, it is no longer used for that purpose. Women can be seen putting the *maskhna* on their shoulder while gripping its handle and scooping water from the river. A piece of cloth is normally put under the *maskhna* which acts as a cushion to soften the pressure on the shoulder. A bride's *maskhna* is generally a new, polished one (white) and ornamented with red drawings. The term *gidir* refers to the standard cooking pot, and is used for cooking food; it is usually provided with a lid. Traditionally, the bride would bring to the house of her groom simple furniture that is called *jihaz.* This consists mostly of a *maskhna,* a basin, a kettle, a wooden chest (Figure 3.12) to keep clothes, a wooden wardrobe and a silver anklet (Salim, 1970: pp. 108;191).

7. Wooden tools/articles

Yawan or *jawan* is a tree trunk that is hollowed out – usually with an adze or chisel; the hollowed form takes a cylindrical shape with a peaked ending. The *jawan* (pestle – a tool used for pounding and grinding a substance) is used primarily to separate grains from their husks, and is generally 60 cm high and 30 cm in diameter. The crushing tool in *jawan* is called *mejana* and it is a one-and-a-half-meter-long wooden stick that is grabbed by two opposite women who mostly take turns in crushing it and grinding it down in the *jawan* in a routine manner. During the *jawan* grinding process, the

Figure 3.12 Wooden Chest (Photo: Haydar Auda, 2008).

women may sing songs of love, sorrow or the separation of lovers and dear ones. A horizontally tied piece of wood is often fixed to the *mejana* to give it added weight and increase its crushing capability.

Ochsenschlager states that the inhabitants of the region used many kinds of mortars and pestles, which were usually made of metal, reed, clay, bitumen or wood. He states, however, that the grain pounders and pestles used by the Ma'dan were often made of palm-tree sections, and that wooden pestles were covered with bitumen to protect them (Ochsenschlager, 2004: pp.165;174).

8. Miscellaneous tools

The *hawan* is one of the most important tools used by the Marsh Arabs and is made of iron. It has a cylindrical shape and is used for crushing grains and coffee with the use of another rod called a *hawan's* hand. Most houses have two *hawans,* one used by the menfolk to crush coffee and the other used by the womenfolk to grind other things that they may need. A *hawan's* hand is a metal rod that is 20–30 cm long and its diameter varies according to the size and diameter of the *hawan*. The bottom end of the *hawan's* hand is mostly flat, while the upper end is pressed from both sides.

The *rahha* is one of the few stone tools to have survived and consists of two disks of sea stone put on each. An iron (or wooden) pole is installed at the lower disk's center, and an iron ring is fastened at the upper disk's center to be penetrated by the iron pole. A wooden handle is then installed at the upper disk's edge, and two women usually sit facing each other and pull the wooden handle each to her side in a somewhat monotonous motion so that the grindstone can twirl and crush the grain that is fed from the central gap. The resulting flour is gathered on a sheet that is put under it. In some villages grinders were made of mud (clay) and covered with bitumen.

9. Coffee preparation tools

A complete set of coffee tools is called *idda*. *Mihmas* is a one-handled pan with a meter-long handle; the reason for the long handle is so that man can maintain a safe distance from the fire. This handle is topped with a dished disk where the coffee beans are put and toasted on embers. A *khashooga* (spoon) consists of a metal piece about a half-meter long that has a flat side used to flip coffee beans while roasting to avoid burning their side. The *mihmas* is held with one hand and the *khashooga* with the other. The toasting process takes place in a stove (*awjagh*) where the coffee pots are put.

Coffee pots vary in sizes and types, but normally consist of a *mussab* which is a small pot that is carried in the left hand to pour coffee for guests into a small cup or *finjan* which is carried in the right hand. Fresh coffee, brewed in the small pots, is typically prepared upon the arrival of important guests and is served in small porcelain cups. The larger pots normally become blackened by soot.

10. Clay/mud storage and ancillary structures

Traditionally, the village womenfolk make the food storage structures called *sidana*. These are cylindrically shaped and constructed of a mixture of clay and hay and in some ways resemble the traditional kiln. However, unlike the traditional kiln, they enclose bins which are used to store grains like rice and wheat, as well as unpressed dates. They are also used to store dung and straw for fodder and fuel. The largest structures are called *haltha* and a wooden ladder is sometimes needed to reach their opening. The *jin* is a mud/clay structure which has the function of a chicken or turkey coop and is used for laying eggs or raising their chicks.

11. Boats (*balam*)

The generic term for canoes is *mashuf*. However, boats have different names depending on their size and type. For example, the larger canoe (*mashuf*) is referred to as a *tarada* whereas the smallest *mashuf* is called a *mataur* or a *houri*, and are used for hunting marsh ducks. The *tarada* is often more than 10 meters long and one meter at its widest part. Normally about ten persons can fit into it. The big plates that are used inside them are often ornamented with big-headed nails (*kirsa*).

Canoes are the primary means of transport in the marshes and are used for transportation, fishing, carrying fodder for the buffalo and reed gathering. The *mashuf* is made from wooden planks and carved wooden ribs in the center; these are bent on the sides and are painted with bitumen brought in from the town of Hit in Anbar province (Young, 1977: p. 35). The upper section of the rails is covered with wooden planks on both sides that are as long as the *mashuf* itself. The planks are wide in the middle and become thinner towards the ends, especially as they reach the neck of the *mashuf* (*al unug*). This allows it to glide through the water and make its way among the reeds. The front of the *mashuf* (*al booz*) and its ending (*al kheer*) is usually encased with wooden plates to make two benches that measure about half a meter in length and are used for various purposes. Each boat has two wooden beams to strengthen it, known as *jist*.

A big *mashuf* is usually called a *burkasha* and can carry a larger amount of reed. Bigger boats are called *giood*; these are used for crossing long distances. Sails can be installed on a *giood*, which is directed with oars. As for *balam* (regular boats) they differ from canoes by size. They can also be distinguished by having two crooked ends, one of which is used to fasten the rope (*sharoofa*) and the other is set for the boat's wheel. Still bigger boats are known as *anya*.

Boats are typically made by professional craftsmen who specialize in this industry. The main centers in the marsh area for boat-building are located in Chibayish and Hwair which are located on the Euphrates, west of Qurna; boat workshops are numerous along the banks of Shatt al-Arab especially in Abu al-Khaseeb. There are also boat handymen called *gallaf* who roam the various villages and who specialize in the fixing and maintenance of boats. The *gallaf* would replace defective plates and paint

Figure 3.13 The *balam* and car, the two necessary means of transportation (Photo: Dr Hamed Haykal).

the boats with a special oil called *sill* oil to increase their resistance to water and bugs. They utilize cotton ropes soaked with an insect-resistant material and place it between the wood plates to prevent water from oozing into the boat. There are many *ashshary* boats with crooked ends in the village. And each family has its own boat which they use for carrying and transporting dates and other farm products. But the boat industry and the use of boats as a means of transport continues to decline as the motor vehicle gradually replaces them.

Navigation by boat requires special gear like the *mardi* which is a long, strong reed used to move small and large boats in shallow water; this oar was mentioned in old Sumerian writings. It is usually made of a specially strong and lean kind of reed. The *mardi* is usually 3–4 m long and about 5–7 cm in diameter. The *gharrafa* is another kind of oar that is made of wood and ends with a flat side. It is held by the person sitting at the back of the ferry or boat. This oar is usually used on small boats and in deep water only, while the *mardi* is used in big boats and shallow water.

Boats are usually steered by hems and steering shafts. A hem is a triangular piece that is fastened at the boat's rear and a wooden shaft is fixed on it so that the person who sits at the boat's rear can steer it to the left or right. There are usually iron parts that are installed in the boat to stabilize the hem. This tool is not used in small rivers or marshes but it is necessary when sailing in big rivers like Shatt al-Arab and the Euphrates, especially when boat-sails are used. A boat's sail is a piece of cloth fastened on a wooden post with ropes. This post is settled on the boat's mast which is another pole of strong wood and is installed in the middle of the boat by setting its lower base in a wide piece of wood that fastens the sides of the boat, and it has a hole in it with a bigger diameter than the mast's diameter.

The mast is tied with a rope to fix it vertically, while the mast is tied with several ropes to facilitate its movement in the wind's direction and according to the destination required. The mast fixing and moving needs a special skill that only professional sailors have and which allows them to sail on the main rivers.

12. Traditional Dress

Marsh Arab dress differs little from those of the Bedouin or rural people as they all wear traditional Arabic clothes. The *dishdasha* is a long garment that almost reaches the floor and has long sleeves. It represents the most essential part of an Arab man's traditional wardrobe. The fabric can be white, cream or a dark color. In poor villages, especially during the 1950s, many men had only one or two *dishdashas*. Men wear jackets in winter, and long trousers (*libas*).

Rich and well-to-do people wear a *saya* or *diglah*, which is a long sleeveless dress that is open from the front. Men wrap it around their bodies and tie it with a cord over which a belt is worn followed by a jacket. Men often wear a *bishet* on their shoulders as a final cover, its textile and value depending on the person's social and income level. Head covers consist of three pieces; the first one is the *arakcheen* or *latiea* which is a hollow half ball that is made of a thin fabric in summer and a thick one in winter. It is worn directly on the head followed by a *koufiya* then an *igal* (head rope) over the *koufiya* (Salim, 1970: p. 198). The *koufiya* comes in several colors according to a person's social status. There are also various types of *igal*, depending on the area and social class; some are thin and smooth, while others are thick or straw-like (Figure 3.3). The older men usually wear the red-checked Arab headdress. Men's footwear normally consists of sandals. There are many kinds of sandals – the best ones are made of natural leather and are reportedly made in the city of Zoubair.

The marsh women typically cover their bodies with a full black *abayah* (cloak). Under the abayah, women's clothing generally consists of the *dishdasha* and the *sheila,* which is a piece of black cloth that women wrap around their heads. Some elderly women wrap their heads with a black headband, while affluent women wrap their heads with a *bouyma* that is made of silk. Marsh women use large wrappers on their heads called *laffah.* The other costume that is used on special occasions is the dress or *hashmi,* which resembles a baggy, triangular sack with three openings for the head and the arms. The *hashmi* is made of a light, sheer, adorned material, and sometimes made of brilliant colors for the young girls. Some village women also wear a *poushi,* which is a piece of cloth that covers the face completely, but it is rare and worn only in extremely conservative families in which women do not work on the farm. Working women usually wrap their legs with a cloth to prevent thorn stings.

Figure 3.14 The normal dress of a typical marsh girl (Photo: Dr Hamed Haykal, 2005).

Figure 3.15 Little marsh girl with an empty pot on her head waiting in line to receive potable water (Photo: Dr Faris Kubba).

4

THE PHYSICAL ENVIRONMENT

Sam A.A. Kubba

GENERAL

The natural and physical environment of southern Iraq exerted an all-pervasive influence on human life and the habitation of the region. Environmental conditions such as topography, geology, soil conditions, climate and irrigation and water supply have had a detrimental impact on the evolution of the social, cultural and economic situation of the region. Therefore, in studying the inter-relationship between ancient Mesopotamian settlements and their physical environment, one must take into account all these factors to understand how they affected the natural landscape and the growth and distribution of settlements (Kubba, 1987).

Throughout history, the Tigris and Euphrates Rivers bifurcated and altered their beds, and it is believed that some of the deeper portions of the marshes were initially former paths of the two rivers that have ceased to exist as the rivers' courses shifted over time (Figure 4.1). This may have impacted the natural environment of the marshland area as at Ras el 'Amiya and many Mesopotamian settlements which are now barren or desert, and which once bordered either the Tigris River or the Euphrates River. The environment may also have been impacted by the erosion/decline of vegetation or the abuse of the land by its inhabitants (e.g., by over-planting or deforestation). Evidence of human occupation is also sometimes lost through wholesale erosion or sedimentation (Wilkinson, 1978: pp. 215–216). A considerable amount of data has in recent years emerged that throws considerable light upon man's early physical environment in southern Iraq which makes possible a more comprehensive understanding of its impact upon his daily activities.

TOPOGRAPHY AND TERRAIN

The geographical features of Mesopotamia are the consequence of the interaction of subsidence (caused by regional tectonics), eustatic sea-level fluctuation, climate and hydrological changes and man's interaction with his environment (Wilkinson, 1978: pp. 215-216). The Mesopotamian terrain is a continuation of the Eurasian and Afro-Asian Steppes; the intervening mountain system, and the intermountain valleys which constitutes the northern plain, the Kurdistan highland, and the southern plains, the territories of Arabia and the Fertile Crescent. The present political boundaries of Iraq fall within all these three areas, and apart from minor local variations, there has been little change in its topography and land forms during the past 10,000 years (Butzer, 1976: p. 35).

Basically, the country can be divided into five distinctly different topographical regions. These are: 1. the desert to the west, 2. the northern steppe, 3. the foothill region, 4. the mountains of the northeast and 5. the plain and marsh areas of the south (Guest, 1966: p. 11).

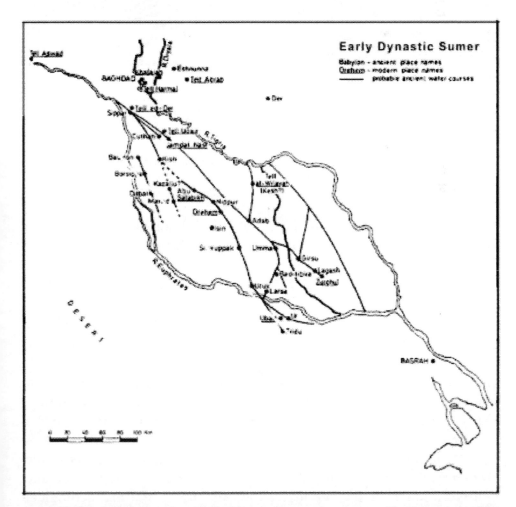

Figure 4.1 Map showing probable ancient watercourses by Postgate, 1983 (corrected from Curtis 1982: p. 49 after Adams 1981).

Figure 4.2 The current status of the Mesopotamian Marshes – North Hammar (Photo: Jasim al-Asadi).

It is the plain and marsh areas of the south that is our main focus. This area is essentially flat except for occasional mounds which are thought to be the sites of ancient towns.

The lower Mesopotamian plain is built up through a succession of alluvial sedimentation. This region can be distinguished from the upper plain by a hypothetical line passing through Hit on the Euphrates River and Samarra on the Tigris. From this line downward, the whole area is extremely flat with an altitude not exceeding 150 feet above sea level. Here the rivers flow above the surface of the plain and their overflow tends to form permanent lakes and marshes (Figure 4.2). These extensive marsh areas with their shallow waters, dense thickets of reeds, fauna and water buffaloes originally covered an area of some 15,000 sq. km. (5,800 miles) and formed one of the most fascinating regions in the world. And while these marshes may have changed in their extent and configuration over the centuries, there is substantial archaeological evidence to suggest their existence in ancient times (Roux, 1985: pp. 39–41).

Thus we find that excepting the hydrophytic (moisture-loving) vegetation of the perennial watercourses and the marshlands connected with them, most plant life in southern Iraq has had to contend, over long periods, with conditions of extreme drought, and available water is a limiting factor of major importance. By and large, precipitation increased from south to north, the desert communities of the Wadiyan and Hajara districts giving way to gradually richer plants of the "steppe". The steppe denotes an area in which the treeless vegetation is equally distributed over the ground and remains so throughout the dry summer months, unlike the desert communities which are distinguished by plant cover during the spring and which disappears during the summer. This transition from desert to steppe is gradual and depends almost solely on climatic factors, and there is no clear-cut demarcation line between the two. However, the difference between steppe and desert in Iraq does not depend solely on the degree of ground cover; it also involves the composition of the flora.

Mesopotamia is, therefore, a land of many contrasts. If the northern steppe and the southern marshes were to be considered as local variants of the great Mesopotamian trough, there is, nevertheless, a striking dissimilarity between the two regions, which had their counterpart in their cultural, political and social history.

GEOLOGY

The enormous influence of geological environment on the evolution of early settlements and architecture continues to be evident throughout the early history of the Near Eastern countries. It is responsible to a large degree for the sharp differences between the archaeological remains of cultures which, in other respects, developed on broadly similar lines.

The physiographic regions, discussed earlier, have had their basis in the geological history of Iraq, particularly in the epoch of mountain-building some 5–30 million years ago. Prior to that time the country was submerged under the sea, and in this sea was deposited the many thousands of feet of limestone (Butzer, 1965). The geological history of the country falls into three phases; the long period of marine submergence, the epoch of mountain-building and the subsequent erosion modifications.

During the periods of marine submergence, the crust beneath the sea was very depressed at a rate comparable with its rate of sedimentation, so that water remained shallow. The adjacent mass gradually rose, so that streams from the land were contributing to the sea, and shale and marl were deposited all over Iraq. When the shores retreated, the zones of mud depositions followed, and pure limestone was deposited where the water was clear and deep. This abundance of limestone in Iraq had significant cultural implications. For, apart from its use for implements and utensils, it was employed as a building material, particularly for foundations and walls, and has had considerable impact upon the growth and distribution of early settlements.

At the close of this period of marine submergence, the mountains began to rise and the seas became restricted into isolated inland seas and, because of excessive evaporations, salt as well as limestone was deposited. Beds of gypsum can thus be detected in the bluffs of the two rivers, and has varied economic cultural significance. Groundwater which moved through these beds was hard and unsuitable as drinking water, which discouraged habitation in these areas.

As the mountains rose during the mountain-building epoch, they were immediately subjected to erosion, and the outward flowing streams carried coarse gravel, sand and salt to the piedmont area. Crustal movement continued, however, and the piedmont areas themselves became folded, producing a foothill region. But as the forces of the crust deformation died out, erosional modification became dominant. Gorges were cut out and broad valleys were etched in the weaker beds.

This was later interrupted by pauses during which many of the streams were spread out to form broad basins covered with thin layers of gravel and salt, and renewed erosion left these former valley floors as terraces. The erosion stage was also punctuated by drastic climate changes reflecting the worldwide fluctuations of the Ice Age. In the highlands of Iraq, small glaciers were formed, which receded in dryer periods, leaving behind broadened valleys veneered with glacial deposits.

In the central lowland, these climatic fluctuations caused extensive flooding and inundations. Much of the salt carried was deposited in the south and was spread out in the delta region. This affected the level of sea water, the location of the coast and the changes in the river courses. During the post-glacial period, the sea level is thought to have been much higher than it is today. However, other glacial processes have interacted to produce a complex sequence of river behavior. But a more significant factor underlying the wavering character of the two rivers in the southern plain has always been the gradual subsidence of this part of the country under the weight of sediment. This was inferred by Lee and Falcon as the basis for the coastal instability, thus opposing the long-held view with regard to the Arabian Gulf that a large part of the alluvial plain was gradually reclaimed from the sea. In fact, it has been shown that the coastline's position has not changed much since historical times, and existing evidence infers that the coast is gradually advancing northward towards Basra and Baghdad (Lee & Falcon, 1952: pp. 36–38).

Nevertheless, one cannot fully accept Lee and Falcon's hypothesis until it can be significantly reconciled with ancient texts and established historical facts, such as the location of ancient Eridu "standing upon the shores of the sea", or of Merodach-Baladan, King of Babylon, who escaped to the marshes to avoid capture by the Assyrians as portrayed by Sennacherib, King of Assyria (703 BC) who says, "He fled like a bird to the swampland" and "I sent my warriors into the midst of the swamps … and they searched for five days", but the King of Babylon could not be found.

SOIL CONDITIONS

The soil's natural qualities are the result of both the prehistoric climatic circumstances as well as the underlying sediment of bedrock and topography. Deforestation and the destruction of vegetation also had a profound effect upon the nature and characteristics of the soil. Today, nearly the whole of the Mesopotamian plain is covered with a layer of new sediment, some 36 ft. deep. The Tigris and Euphrates Rivers bring down vast quantities of alluvial materials, which are deposited in the marsh areas. This alluvial deposit had in prehistoric times formed a large part of the southern fertile delta and made possible the emergence of the early agricultural settlements in Sumer, and today traces of lime, shale, marl and flint can be found well distributed throughout (Jacobsen & Adams, 1960: pp. 1252–58).

The alluvial soils of lower Iraq are chiefly calcareous loams, with occasional sandy patches. Their richness in lime is caused by the light calcareous silt brought down from the northern highlands. With certain exceptions, the soils of the whole alluvial plain of lower Iraq are comparatively uniform, differing slightly in texture and fertility, but always conforming to the same general type – a silty calcareous loam. When watered, they are usually remarkably fertile because they are rich in mineral salts, although the nitrogen content is sometimes dangerously low.

Many factors have contributed to the gradual soil deterioration witnessed in different parts of the country. The extensive and frequent Tigris River flooding of the plain, the gradual salinization of soil through the rapid evaporation during the summer months, poor soil drainage, in addition to continuous erosion of the alluvial top soil by fierce sand storms, are only some of the more important ones. This is in addition to the total desiccation of the region by the Saddam regime, particularly in the early 1990s.

The early farmers were able to control the floods by constructing canals, dykes and dams which sub-divided the countryside into walled enclosures to be watered at will. However, as the river level rose, so did the level of saline groundwater, which, together with the gradual evaporation of continually exposed poorly drained stretches of the flood areas, caused its gradual soil salinization. This turned once fertile fields into barren deserts and forced agricultural settlements northwards to the less saline regions.

In the Mesopotamian plain, soil salinization did not assume such catastrophic proportions. The water table there is very low, and greater rainfall helped to wash down saline soil. The variation in the quality of soil between the two halves of the country must have had a direct effect upon their agricultural output, population, movement and the density and distribution of settlements, and has obviously contributed to the difference in their rate of urbanization and cultural development. The north, however, encountered entirely different problems with respect to soil deterioration. Here, the moist and temperate climate has throughout time facilitated the formation of the hilly sides of the eastern flanks of the Fertile Crescent consisting of a rich and fine mantle of highly fertile red loam (Terra Rossa) which was washed down by rain, leaving behind a highly eroded plateau covered with a thin layer of winter vegetation. This, together with the systematic destruction of vegetation by a population lacking in fuel, did much to promote the deterioration of the soil (Wilkinson, 1978: p. 216). Maps A and B in Figure 4.3 gives a clearer portrayal of the total desiccation by the Saddam regime in the early 1990s.

IRRIGATION AND HYDROGRAPHIC CONDITIONS

Scholars often say that Mesopotamia is the gift of the twin rivers, the Tigris River and the Euphrates River. Throughout history, the Tigris and the Euphrates have deposited their rich alluvium on a bed of sedimentary rocks between the Arabian platform and the Iranian highland, forming in the midst of desert a massive fertile plain which in size and potential fertility had no equal (Roux, 1985: p. 22). But unlike Egypt, the vast and unpredictable inundations of the two rivers could on account of topography and the nature of the soil prove disastrous unless kept under strict control.

The Marshlands and Lower Mesopotamian Plain
Sanlaville states that downstream from the city of Kut and al-Hindiyya
to Amarah, the slope of the plane is very weak and decreases to about
0.034 per cent. In this part of southern Iraq, the Tigris and the Euphrates
split into many branches inducing the formation of an interior delta such
as the al-Hindiyya and Hillah branches on the Euphrates and the Gharraf
on the Tigris (Sanlaville, 2002). But Sanlaville points out that due to
the changed conditions caused by the building of dams and canals, etc.,
the upper fan-deltas of the two rivers have ceased to be active. The
levees here are smaller and lower than in the upper Mesopotamian Plain,
and the groundwater is closer to the surface. The formed depressions
between the channels tend to become marshy. The Interior Delta Plain
is the main sedimentation area of the rivers, especially as the silting had
increased due to irrigation practices. The Euphrates forms a fan-delta
around the Suq Ash Shuyukh area, which has numerous distributaries
bordered by levees and floodplains. Prior to 1990, the Euphrates actually
disappeared at this point, reforming northeast of the delta. The Tigris
delta is located to the south of Amarah, where it trends to the east, while
the deltaic distributaries trend to the south.

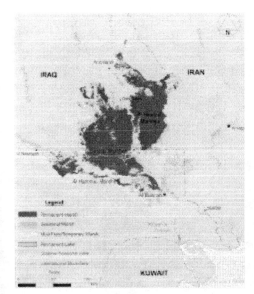 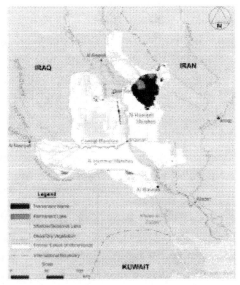

A.   **B.**

Figure 4.3 Map giving a comparative analysis of Landsat imagery from
1973–76 (A) and 2000 (B) showing the significant changes to the marshland
habitat extent and marshland land cover prior and after the desiccation of
the wetland (Source: UNEP-2001, Partow, H.).

These deltaic environments have in the past been areas of intensive rice cultivation. This inactive delta that is associated with the Gharraf River is a distributary of the Tigris, and flows southward from Kut. Once we advance past the delta environment, the waters flow into the marsh and lake areas, where the land is basically flat. Here, the remaining suspended sediments are trapped within marshes and lakes where the presence of a dense vegetation of reeds tends to support their deposition, and active evaporation of salt-loaded waters increases the lake and marsh salinity: so as we go south of the Hammar Marsh we find ephemeral saline lakes, *sebkhas* and desert (Sanlaville, 2002).

The core of the marshes is focused in the area that surrounds the convergence of the Tigris and Euphrates Rivers. Scholars normally divide this area into the three primary sectors: Hammar Marsh, which lies south of the Euphrates; Central (Qurnah) Marshes, which lie between the Tigris and Euphrates Rivers; and Huweizah Marshes, which lie east of the Tigris River.

Historically, the marshlands constituted a chain of almost interconnected marsh and lake complexes that flowed into one another. Some areas of the marshes were temporary, created during periods of high floods in which large tracts of desert were submerged under water. Usually, the separate permanent marsh areas would merge together, forming larger wetland complexes. The wetlands themselves consisted of a mosaic of permanent and seasonal marshes.

The Arabian Gulf is relatively shallow, having an average depth of about 50 meters and the water depths close to the Iraqi coast are normally not more than a few meters deep. Within Shatt al-Arab River, the tidal range averages three meters near its mouth to 0.5 meters (1.64 feet) at Basrah (Rzoska, 1980). Sanlaville states, "Due to the natural dam formed by the Widian plateau promontory and the Karun alluvial fan, the Mesopotamian plain disappears as well and the Shatt al-Arab corresponds to an estuary, influenced by the strong twice daily tidal action of the Gulf. Salt sea water does not penetrate farther than Abadan (the sea salinity tide) due to the important fresh-water discharge of the Karun river, but the river water rises and falls as far as Qurna: it is the *dynamic tide*, used for the irrigation of the date palms and gardens in empoldered areas of the lower levees, beyond which stretch extensive sebkhas, and on the northern border of the Haur al-Hammar, farmers made use of the few centimeters of the tidal water to irrigate their rice-fields" (Sanlaville, 2002).

In antiquity, both the Tigris and the Euphrates Rivers entered the Arabian Gulf separately. Today, however, they are joined in a single mouth to form the Shatt al-Arab River, a shallow well-mixed estuary which flows into the Gulf and is therefore influenced by tidal action. The Karun River, flowing from the Zagros Mountains of Iran, joins Shatt al-Arab River south of Basrah. Shatt al-Arab runs through a narrow passageway created by the formation of a large alluvial fan associated with the Karun River flowing in from the northeast, and another large alluvial fan associated with the Wadi Batin flowing in from the southwest.

The general pattern of the river courses can be divided into two segments above and below a hypothetical line passing Hit on the Euphrates and Samarra on the Tigris, above this line, the river valleys are distinct. The two streams cutting their way through a platform of hard rock, bordered on either side by high cliffs (Lloyd, 1985: pp. 14–16). Here the river courses have moved very little, and settlement which once relied largely on irrigation, are still on or close by the riverbanks. To the south of this line, the two river valleys merge to form the wide alluvial delta where the rivers flow at such a speed and gradient that they meander considerably above the plain, changing their course and creating permanent lakes and marshes.

The annual high waters of the Tigris and the Euphrates occur in the spring, when the snow in the highlands melts over and coincides with the maximum rainfall in Turkey. Thus, depending on the synchronization and character of the winter snowfall, and temperature conditions, a huge volume of water may sweep down, causing appreciable flooding of the plain. To make matters worse, the tidal effect of the Arabian Gulf, activated by the fierce southeasterly winds, contributes further to the flooding. However, more dangerous than the extent of these floods is their unpredictability. For while low waters over a period of a few years could mean drought or famine, one excessive flood could spell disaster. Every year therefore, the country hovers between desert and swamp. Thus in order for agriculture in the Mesopotamian valley to advance, the fields had to be adequately defended with dykes against flooding.

The Tigris rises earlier than the Euphrates and carries about 2.5 times as much water, but its bed cuts deeper into the plains. Thus even though the Euphrates is carrying only 40 per cent the amount of water, it remains the main source for irrigation of the land between the two rivers, as its bed is above the plains (Forbes, 1965: p. 18).

Previously, the establishment of the early agricultural settlements in the plain was no easy step, considering these harsh environments. Their expansion and growth was impossible without effective water control. This difficulty perhaps explains the subsequent settlement migration northwards to the less flood-threatened areas of the delta.

Owing to the presence of natural ridges, abandoned levees, embankments, channels and the like, the alluvial plain is thus divided into irregular basins which drain successively as the river floodwater recedes. But if the water were held back by dams, dry season reservoirs could be created.

However, this type of irrigation depends on the floods which, as illustrated above, are highly unpredictable. But as Butzer points out, "Archaeological evidence supports the suggestion that irrigation farming involved only the breaching of the natural embankments of streams and made use of uncontrolled local flooding" (Butzer, 1976: p. 60). Large-scale networks are later than the Ubaid Period. To maintain a regular basin irrigation, small gaps were dug in the riverbanks, at strategic positions, and canals, channels and streams were constructed to divert the water into the fields.

Lift irrigation was not introduced till later, and numerous canals were dug to provide more effective irrigation. These canals were usually dug parallel or at an angle to the main river course, and each time a canal was silted up, another was cut parallel to it, so that the whole countryside was covered with a network of canals which not only served for irrigation, but also provided a cheap and effective transport system.

The very nature of the southern Mesopotamian plain and of the river forced the settlers to pool their resources within an area whose size and prosperity was decided by the limits of an interdependent canalization system, the planning and upkeep of which required the direction of a central autocratic authority. Their construction, therefore, involved considerable social energy, and unlike natural irrigation, required the resources of a large and well organized community – tribes and families sharing the same inherent interest in the land. The well- known British archaeologist Leonard Woolley believes that the development of the city state was not due to the peculiar mentality of the Sumerian people but rather to the physical character of the environment.

The destruction caused by war, and social and economic change, has all resulted in their neglect. Perhaps most importantly, the frequent shifting in the river courses has caused many to lie dry and useless. This resulted in the gradual decline and eventual death of many settlements and the migration of many others to the north. Another significant factor leading to population movement has been the salinization and deterioration of agricultural soil. The irrigation of the plain by means of canals, streams and levees has led to the creation of small and completely enclosed basins, which were difficult to drain.

As a result the soil gradually hardened and became too saline for cultivation. It is thus ironic that canal irrigation which gave birth to the Sumerian civilization was to become the main cause for its demise and eventual death (Beek, 1962: pp. 12–13).

Irrigation and water supply have obviously played a prominent role in the economic, social and cultural development of Mesopotamia. From the dawn of history, the nature and extent of water supply has had a detrimental effect upon the location, growth and distribution of settlements and indirectly influenced their form and structure.

CLIMATIC CONDITIONS

The transition from food gathering to food production on the eastern flanks of the Fertile Crescent is associated by a number of authorities with significant changes in the physical environments of the area brought about by sudden worldwide climatic oscillations during the closing years of the pleistocene period. Woolley suggests that there is a cause-and-effect relationship between climatic change and the origin of agriculture. He points out that the close of the glacial periods and the advent of a more temperate climate provided the essential prerequisites for civilization, as we understand it, to begin and flourish. The most important of these prerequisites in his view are: 1. the soil, and 2. the climate. These two essential ingredients must together be so favorable as to allow man to produce sufficient quantities of food easily so that survival no longer devours all his time and energy (Wooley and Hawkes, 1963: p. 414). Some scholars, however, refute this view and reassert the significance of the role of culture in the achievement of the transition to food production.

At this time the higher middle latitudes were subjected to alternating series of glaciations and warmer periods covering at least one million years. Worldwide climatic conditions in fact approached a level comparable with those of today some thousand years ago. At present the climatic snow-line, i.e., the altitude below which as much snow melts as falls per annum, lies between 10,000–15,000 feet. During the last glaciation, the existing glaciers increased in size and advanced southward. The climatic snow-line responsible for these was estimated to have been 2,000–2,700 feet lower than that of the present day. This implies that the temperature level in those days was correspondingly lower throughout. Such a depression, if interpreted in terms of the modern average upper air lapse rate (i.e., one degree Fahreinheit for every 300 feet), suggests that the entire area was some 7–8 degrees Fahreinheit cooler on average than it is today (Butzer, 1965).

Southern Iraq's climate is generally hot and dry with limited winter precipitation. In the marsh areas, the winter temperatures range between a maximum average of 15 °C (59 °F) and a minimum average of 5 °C (41 °F). During the summer months the temperature range averages between a maximum average of 40 °C (104 °F) and a minimum average of 25 °C (77 °F). At Basrah, the mean temperature measured 25 °C (77 °F), with January having the coldest monthly average of 12 °C (53.6 °F) and July having the hottest monthly average of 36 °C (96.8 °F). The lowest mean minimum temperature is in January, at 8 °C (46.4 °F), with the lowest temperatures at –2 °C (28.4 °F), which means that frost and night frost can occur on the surface. The highest mean maximum is 42 °C (107.6 °F) in August, peaking at temperatures of up to 50 °C (122 °F). The seasons of spring and autumn are typically short.

When all other factors remain constant, the lowering of the mean temperature would cause a considerable reduction in evaporation from open stretches of water. This would allow greater percolation of moisture into the soil, thereby increasing the density of vegetation. The available evidence suggests that modern moisture conditions have remained basically unchanged over the last 15,000–20,000 years and that contemporary temperature levels have likewise maintained their current levels since about 8000 BC.

Relative air humidity is low throughout most of Iraq but is normally considerably higher near the marshes, having an annual average of about 59 per cent, going from about 47 per cent in August to 90 per cent in January. The average humidity in the marsh area currently ranges from 40–45 per cent. It is typically lower in the summer days and higher in the winter; it is also higher in the early morning than later in the day. This is a natural consequence of the great ranges of temperature. However, due to low precipitation levels and high temperatures, high evaporation rates dominate the marshes and in Basrah it averages 2,653 mm. Recent studies show that evaporative loss generally increases from east to west across the Mesopotamian plain.

Strong climate winds are common and are an important factor. Desiccating winds form two distinct patterns. The predominant wind, which occurs throughout the year, is the famous *shamal* wind that come from the north and northwest. This is a dry steady wind, and normally prevails from June through September. The breeze has some cooling effect and brings considerable relief to the inhabitants of central

Mesopotamia. The ancients usually took advantage of this phenomenon by building their temples and palaces facing it (Figure 4.4).

The gusty *sharqi* winds come into play mainly in spring and autumn. These winds originate from the south and southeast of Iraq and are frequently accompanied by violent dust storms with which they have become associated. The velocity of these winds generally varies from 7 to 18 knots (Saad and Antoine, 1978: pp. 15–45). Relief from the heat is normally brought about by the increasing rate of evaporation from the skin and not by lowering the air temperature. The wind's direction and force usually depends on the season.

However, it should be noted that the rapid desiccation of the wetlands is expected to have significant ramifications on the micro-climate of the region, including a sharp decrease in humidity levels and an increase in temperatures, particularly during the summer months. Marshland desiccation will also impact rainfall and wind patterns. For example, previously the strong, dry winds that reached temperatures of over 40 °C were broken by the reed beds; these will blow unhindered (Maltby, May 1994). Hassan Partow says that "With salt crusts and dry marshland soils exposed, windblown dust laced with various impurities will

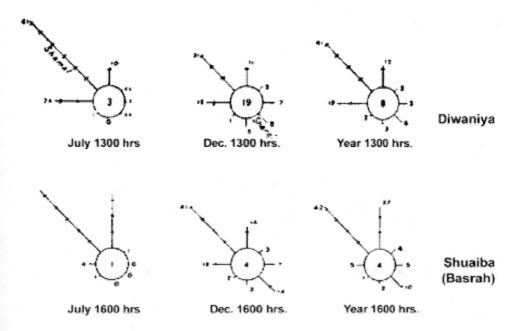

Figure 4.4 Wind diagram illustrating the percentage frequency of wind direction and calms (central figures for cities of Diwaniya and Basrah).

considerably increase, affecting thousands of square kilometers well beyond Iraq's borders. Ecosystem degradation at such a grand scale may have serious drawbacks on human health, ranging from the effects of water scarcity and pollution to increased exposure to thermal extremes and potentially toxic dust storms blowing off saltpans and dried marsh bed. Furthermore, the fragile arable lands surrounding the former marshlands are likely to suffer from land degradation and desertification, caused by wind erosion and sand encroachment from the dried marsh bed and surrounding deserts." (UNEP, Partow, 2001).

Moreover, owing to its extensive area and the diversity of its topography and physical regions, climatic conditions throughout the Near Eastern general and Mesopotamia in particular were subjected to considerable local

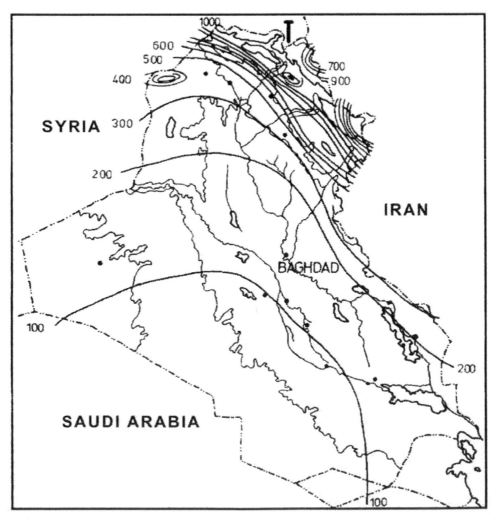

Figure 4.5 Diagram showing mean annual rainfall in Iraq.

or regional micro-climates similar to those existing at present. The mountainous region in the north and northeast presented a temperate climate when the winters were raw and cold and the summers dry and hot. The central and southern Mesopotamian plain is practically flat, with a dry sub-tropical climate where temperatures fluctuate between up to 120 °F in the summer to slightly below freezing point in winter. The mean annual rainfall at Basrah is only 15 cm, and monthly inputs range from virtually zero for the period from June through October, to 22–34 mm per month in the period November through April, with peak rainfall in January (Figure 4.5). Yearly averages vary considerably and can range from 70 to 302 mm indicating that local agriculture has to depend mainly on artificial irrigation. Low precipitation, along with high temperature, constitutes the defining climatic condition in the Iraqi marshes.

CONCLUSION

The lower Mesopotamian plain according to Sanlaville "presents a complex, coherent and harmonious but fragile organization of very different but interdependent areas that undergo a complex evolution depending on numerous factors (tectonics or subsidence, regional climatic and hydrological changes, small oscillations of the Gulf level, human factors, etc.) tending towards a slow and progressive filling up of lakes and marshes and ultimately to their long-term disappearance." (Sanlaville, 2002). Plans had been developed for various engineering works since the early twentieth century, but particularly during the 1950s and 1970s (over 30 large dams have been constructed during the past four decades). During the 1970s the expansion of irrigation projects had started to disrupt the flow of water to the marshes. By the mid 1980s, a low-level insurgency developed against Saddam's drainage and resettlement projects in the area which was led by Sheikh Abdul Karim Mahud al-Muhammadawi.

However, the wholesale destruction of the marshlands did not proceed in earnest until the Marsh Arabs revolted against the Saddam regime after the first Gulf War. In 1991 the Iraqi government retaliated by aggressively reviving a program to divert the flow of the Tigris and Euphrates Rivers away from the marshes through the building of an extensive network of dykes and channels. This also served the purpose of eliminating the primary food source and preventing any remaining militiamen from taking refuge in the marshes and using it as a cover. To facilitate this, it has been reported that reed beds were burned and the water intentionally poisoned. Once these massive drainage works were implemented in southern Iraq, the once extensive marshlands dried up and regressed into desert, with large stretches being salt-encrusted. All that basically remained was a small northern fringe of the Huwaiza Marsh, which straddles the Iran–Iraq border.

Immediately after the fall of the Saddam regime, many of the local marsh inhabitants started to breach the dykes which had taken water away from the marshes and bring back the water into the drained areas. In recent years there has been revived interest in restoring the marshlands and today the marshes are rapidly recovering with the help of international organizations such as the United Nations Environment Program (UNEP), The Center for Restoration of the Iraqi Marshlands (CRIM) and the AMAR International Charitable Foundation. However, continuous drought and damming continue to impede this recovery.

5

AGRICULTURE: PAST AND PRESENT

Sam A.A. Kubba

GENERAL OVERVIEW

The area of the Iraqi wetlands which is located in the southern part of the lower Mesopotamian plain was until recently a unique environmental phenomenon. Its people have for generations lived a life of peace and harmony with their surroundings which has few parallels in the world, yet for nearly two decades their natural habitat and the people themselves were subjected to relentless lethal attack by the former Iraqi regime.

The wetland ecosystem consists of permanent marshes dominated by giant reeds (*Phragmites communis*), seasonal marshes with bulrushes (*Typha augustata*) that normally dry up in autumn and winter, and temporary marshes with sedges (*Scirpus brachyceras*) that are inundated during the yearly floods. The wetlands are rich in biodiversity and are important breeding grounds for fish and shrimps (*Metapenaeus affinis*), wintering grounds for wildfowl and staging grounds for migratory waterfowl (pelicans, herons, flamingos).

As for the size of the wetlands, there are several different estimates given for its total area. For example, Buringh (1960) estimates the total area of the marshes to be about 35,000 km² while Fitzpatrick (2004) estimates the total area to be 20,000 km². The total marsh area today is considerably smaller. The discrepancy in the reported areas can be attributed to the variability in the freshwater flows to the marshes that depend on the discharge of the Tigris and Euphrates Rivers. As upstream developments in the upper parts of the Tiger and Euphrates basins continue, the water supply to the marshes will continue to dwindle. And many experts are warning that Iraq is now entering its third successive year of drought, and this is raising grave concerns about the economic and political fall-out.

Experts at a recent conference held in the southern Iraqi port city of Basrah warned that below-average precipitation and insufficient water in the Euphrates and Tigris Rivers have left the country basically dry for the third successive year. Drought has wrecked swathes of farmland, increased desertification and threatened drinking-water supplies. This has resulted in increasing sandstorms that in recent years have covered much of the country in brown dust.

Indeed, what is urgently needed is relevant information to all on the utilization of modern agricultural research tools to develop an Iraqi agriculture response to market forces, and begin the job of rehabilitating its land and water resources. While linking up with international agricultural research organizations and the private sector is very helpful, it is also necessary to organize the nation's agricultural institutions into a credible centralized body that can provide realistic planning and budgeting.

After the overthrow of the brutal Saddam regime, researchers from Canada, the United States, Japan, Italy and elsewhere, launched a number of international efforts to examine the marshland's devastation and the feasibility of restoring it to its previous grandeur.

The effect of upstream dam-building and continuous drought has been to suffocate the Iraqi wetlands, which throughout its history has benefited from bountiful water supplies, even during periods of drought. Today the country's lack of adequate water resources has become critical, and, with minimal apparent government planning, insignificant financial support to farmers, inadequate international aid and a lack of cooperation from its neighbors (Turkey, Syria and Iran), Iraq's prospects of regenerating the marshlands look bleak.

Many plans have been designed for draining the Iraqi marshlands; in fact a detailed plan was put in place prior to the First World War. The first major engineering work in the marshes region was the construction of the Kut Barrage which was completed in 1939, followed by the Samarra Dam in 1956. In both cases the pretext given for the construction works was to extend irrigation to the local farmers and improve agricultural opportunities.

But successive Iraqi governments have always been uneasy about the marshlands. During the Late Assyrian Period, the Babylonian king Merodach-Baladan fled to the marshes to escape death at the hands of the Assyrian king Sennacherib. During the Abbasid Period many dissidents, smugglers and bandits took refuge in the wetlands. The labyrinth of waterways gave individuals who knew the routes every advantage to hide and disappear in the flexible narrow waterways of the marshlands.

Currently, the wetland's agricultural sector represents a small but increasingly significant component of its economy. But recent population growth, coupled with limited arable land and a general stagnation in agricultural productivity, has steadily increased dependence on foreign imports to meet domestic food needs and has made Iraq a major importer of agricultural products. By the 1980s Iraq was importing half of its food requirements, and by 2002, over 90 per cent of many basic staples – wheat, rice, sugar, vegetable oil and protein meals – were imported.

After the toppling of the Iraqi regime in 2003, the country's agricultural sector remained beset by the legacy of past mismanagement and the effects of the severe drought of 1999 to 2001 and 2007 to 2009. Iraq must now rely on imports to meet the domestic food demand for many years to come.

ANCIENT AGRICULTURE IN THE MARSHLAND AREA

Before switching to farming, humans got all their food from wild plants and animals in their environment until they gradually became farmers and cultivators. The geography of Mesopotamia is such that successful agriculture cannot be attained in the absence of irrigation and good drainage, a fact which has had a profound effect on the evolution of Mesopotamian civilization. Moreover, the undeniable need for irrigation led the Sumerians and later the Akkadians to build their cities along the Tigris and Euphrates and the tributaries of these rivers. Some major cities, such as Ur (the birthplace of the patriarch Abraham) and Uruk, took root on these Euphratres tributaries, while others, notably Lagash, were built on branches of the Tigris. The rivers provided the further benefits of fish, reeds and clay.

The achievements of the Mesopotamian civilization were numerous, such as the introduction of the plow (Figure 5.1). Agriculture, thanks to the construction of irrigation ditches, became the primary method of subsistence. Farming was considered to be a complicated and methodical occupation requiring foresight, diligence and skill.

A cuneiform tablet dating to *c*. 1500 BC was discovered at the ancient Sumerian site of Nippur and may contain the oldest genuine farmer's almanac in existence. It consists of a series of instructions and directions by a farmer to his son explaining the ins and outs of the yearly agricultural activities, from the watering of the fields in May to June to the cleaning and winnowing of the harvested crops during the months of April and May (Kramer, 1981, Chapter 4).

The farmers of ancient Sumer grew numerous crops, the most important of which were wheat and barley, in a land with little seasonal rainfall and a limited water supply. However, they were able to overcome these challenges in several ways, particularly through the development of canals and irrigation systems to control the flow and direction of water from the two rivers.

Shade trees were grown to protect trees from harsh winds and from the sun. Some of the types of fruits that were planted included dates, grapes, melons, apples and figs. Probably their favorite vegetable was the eggplant, which is still very popular today. They also planted vegetables such as onions, beans, radishes and lettuces.

The ancient Sumerians worked in harmony as a community, building thick city walls and magnificent temples and digging canals that are considered the world's first engineering works. It may not be surprising, therefore, that these people from the beginning of recorded history also fought over water rights. Irrigation was extremely vital to the Mesopotamian farmer, and annual floods of the Tigris and Euphrates created serious problems for them, partly because of the significant amounts of silt these waters carried. In many respects, the marsh areas during these early periods represented the "suburbs" of great cities like Ur, Uruk, Eridu, Lagash, etc., in addition to the various mounds currently located in the marshes themselves.

The Mesopotamian irrigation system was of a simple basin type, which could be opened by merely digging a gap or hole in the lower sections of the embankment and closed by replacing the mud and filling the gap. Ancient Mesopotamian laws were considered quite sophisticated for their time; they not only required farmers to keep their basins and feeder canals in good repair but also expected everyone to assist with hoes and shovels in emergencies, such as when it flooded or when new canals were to be constructed or old canals to be repaired.

These canals sometimes lasted for centuries before they were abandoned or replaced by new ones. Even today, we can see evidence in the form of embankments of abandoned canals that were built thousands of years ago. Records show that these canal systems once supported a denser population than that which exists there today. But as time passed, Mesopotamian agriculture began a steady downward decline, mainly because of the salt that accumulated in the alluvial soil. The final blow came in 1258, when the Mongols conquered Mesopotamia and destroyed the irrigation systems.

The Laws of Hammurabi

The Code of Hammurabi (*c.* 1792–1750 BC), "King of Sumer and Akkad", contains many laws relating to agricultural crop practices such as irrigation and pollination of the date palm. Martha Roth, Professor of Assyriology, highlights a sampling of some of these laws that relate to agriculture. These laws are highlighted below:

> 53 - If a man neglects to reinforce the embankment of (the irrigation canal of) his field and does not reinforce its embankment, and then a breach opens in its embankment and allows the water to carry away the common irrigated area, the man in whose embankment the breach opened shall replace the grain whose loss he caused.

Figure 5.1. Babylonian scratch plow with seed drill (Source: Singer et al – 1954).

54 - If he cannot replace the grain, they shall sell him and his property, and the residents of the common irrigated area whose grain crops the water carried away 'shall divide (the proceeds).

55 - If a man opens his branch of the canal for irrigation and negligently allows the water to carry away his neighbor's field, he shall measure and deliver grain in accordance with his neighbor's yield.

56 - If a man opens (an irrigation gate and released) waters and thereby he allows the water to carry away whatever work has been done in his neighbor's field, he shall measure and deliver 3,000 SILA of grain per 18 iku (of field).

57 - If a shepherd does not make an agreement with the owner of the field to graze sheep and goats, and without the permission of the owner of the field grazes sheep and goats on the field, the owner of the field shall harvest his field and the shepherd who grazed sheep and goats on the field without the permission of the owner of the field shall give in addition 6,000 SILA of grain per 18 iku (of field) to the owner of the field.

58 - If, after the sheep and goats come up from the common irrigated area when the pennants announcing the termination of pasturing are wound around the m a i n city-gate, the shepherd releases the sheep and goats into a field and allows the sheep and goats to graze in the field–the shepherd shall guard the field in which he allowed them to graze and at the harvest he shall measure and deliver to the owner of the field 18,000 SILA of grain per 18 iku (of field).

59 - If a man cuts down a tree in another man's date orchard without the permission of the owner of the orchard, he shall weigh and deliver 30 shekels of silver.

60 - If a man gives a field to a gardener to plant as a date orchard and the gardener plants the orchard, he shall cultivate the orchard for four years; in the fifth year, the owner of the orchard and the gardener shall divide the yield in equal shares; the owner of the orchard shall select and take his share first.

61 - If the gardener does not complete the planting of (the date orchard in) the field, but leaves an uncultivated area, they shall include the uncultivated area in his share.

62 - If he does not plant as a date orchard the field which was given to him–if it is arable land, the gardener shall measure and deliver to the owner of the field the estimated yield of the field for the years it is left fallow in accordance with his neighbor's yield; furthermore he shall perform the required work on the field and return it to the owner of the field.

63 - If it is uncultivated land, he shall perform the required work on the field and return it to the owner of the field, and in addition he shall measure and deliver 3,000 SILA of grain per 18 iku (of field) per year.

64 - If a man gives his orchard to a gardener to pollinate (the date palms), as long as the gardener is in possession of the orchard, he shall give to the owner of the orchard two thirds of the yield of the orchard, and he himself shall take one third.

65 - If the gardener does not pollinate the (date palms in the) orchard and thus diminishes the yield, the gardener [shall measure and deliver] a yield for the orchard to the owner of the orchard in accordance with his neighbor's yield.

The Mesopotamians took full advantage of the resources that were available to them. The growth and trade of the food in the area contributed significantly to this productiveness and helped Mesopotamia to become a very powerful leader in the region. Canals and ditches were built to deliver water to the land for farming, and for redirecting the water to the fields used for farming. Farmers then applied regulators to raise and lower the water levels in the canals and ditches so that it could be used by the farmers. A major challenge the ancients faced was transportation of water from the rivers to the fields which was no simple task for early farmers. Not wanting to carry it all by hand, the early farmers were able to devise simple machines and apply basic methods or devices to move the water.

The Akkadians and Babylonians inherited many of the technical achievements of the Sumerians in irrigation and agriculture. They maintained the system of canals, dykes, dams, and reservoirs that were constructed by their predecessors and which demanded considerable engineering knowledge and skill. Mesopotamia's civilization with its many cities had achieved extraordinary cultural and literary achievements, and yet crumbled during 2300 BC mainly because of the rapid decline in agricultural productivity due to highly toxic land which was unsuitable for agriculture. It is a well-known fact that when the soil becomes too saline, crop productivity falls. And although history has recorded several important occurrences of salinity and its impact on society, the earliest and perhaps most serious occurrance was in Mesopotamia during 2400–1700 BC (Jacobsen and Adams, 1958).

Initially, only a small number of fields were affected, but these numbers grew as the saline levels increased. This deprived the marsh dwellers of the ability to use the reed wetlands for traditional sustainable agriculture and livelihood. The growing decline in crop yields led to a fundamental shift in farming strategy towards the cultivation of more salt-tolerant crops. However, this did not address the core issue and many towns and cities were devastated by the low production and inability to meet local food needs, forcing many once great Sumerian and Babylonian cities to collapse and dwindle into villages or be abandoned. Figure 5.2 is a translation of a cuneiform tablet dated to about 1300 BC, showing the layout of fields and irrigation canals near the town of Nippur.

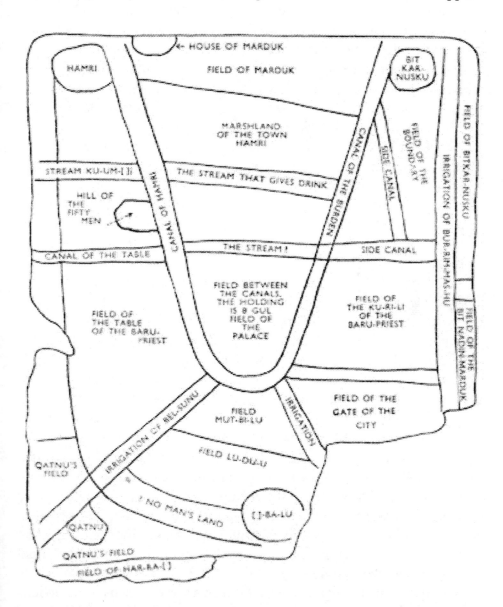

Figure 5.2 Irrigation technology – translation of a cuneiform tablet from about 1300 BC which shows a map of fields and irrigation canals near Nippur, Mesopotamia (Source: Singer et al, 1954).

WETLANDS AGRICULTURE FROM THE MIDDLE AGES TO THE FALL OF THE MONARCHY

There is little recorded information relating to marshland agricultural activity during the Middle Ages. However, we do know that from earlier times, increased production needs led to the development of controlled irrigation, involving the installation of simple dams, sluices, water wheels and an extensive network of dug canals (Schilstra, 1962). Also, as the Tigris has a higher hydraulic elevation, water from the Tigris gets redirected in a southerly direction towards the Euphrates. These canals were designed in a more geometric pattern compared to the primitive wild irrigation type previously used. The geometric pattern of the canals allowed for increased agricultural development and production above the deltaic areas. The river valley was almost completely divided into various small artificial basins bounded by the banks of the canals.

It is interesting to note that wheat and barley fields utilized more rectangular patterns, whereas for rice production a more fish-bone type pattern was used. The rectangular pattern was more prone to choking by silt, and the necessary cleaning out of the canals led to the creation of large ridges that were formed on either side of the canals, or alternatively, a new canal was dug adjacent to the former canal.

Ploughing in the wetlands was generally minimal due to its expense, but when employed the native plough was drawn by oxen, cows or men; alternatively, the land was dug with long-handled spades.

During the Abbasid Caliphate, the marshes became a stronghold of the Zanji, whose rebellion (led by Ali bin Mohammad) threatened the Caliphate's very existence. Slaves, mostly of African descent, were used to drain the marshes around Basrah. But because of their brutal treatment they revolted under the leadership of "Ali the Abominable" and became a troublesome force to be reckoned with. This was followed in 1258 AD by the sacking of Baghdad by the Mongolian ruler, Genghis Khan's grandson, Hulagu Khan. After several hundred years of Mongol rule, the Mongols were forced from power by the Turkish sultans of the Ottoman Empire. The Turkish sultans saw their southern neighbor as a buffer against the spread of Iran's Shiites. As for the collapse of the Abbasid government, it marked the end of effective central administration throughout most of southern Iraq until the British Mandate period in Iraq following the First World War.

During the centuries that followed, the marsh dwellers remained oblivious to the outside world, and for nearly seven centuries the southern Mesopotamian countryside was home to largely self-governing tribal groups which fought over the land and exploited it without substantial help or hindrance from a central and administrative authority. Salim says, "Until the end of the nineteenth century, the various tribal groups and confederations in this part of Iraq held no fixed areas of land; and it was in an effort to increase political stability and central control that, about 1880, the Ottoman government declared the whole region State Domain, thereby forcing its inhabitants either to buy titles (*tapu*) to fixed tracts of land, or to rent plots direct from the State." (Salim, 1962).

Traditional irrigation saw a meltdown under Turkish rule which was further exacerbated by the British. The colonial administration increased the power of the local sheikhs and in effect transformed them into their own "agents" within the various tribal areas. In addition, their relationship with the other members of their tribe changed fundamentally with the sheikhs now becoming landlords and their fellow tribesmen reduced to simple tenants. The British continued to increase the power of the landlords, and the numbers of peasants multiplied and were drawn into the market economy. They were then required to pay rents and taxes which they were often unable to meet.

The first major marsh-draining scheme was proposed in the 1951 Haigh Report, *Control of the Rivers of Iraq*, drafted by British engineers working for the Iraqi government. The original proposal was for a single large canal through the main Amarah Marsh from Mahmudiyya to Qurna. Construction of the large canal, called the Third River, began in 1953. Its main function was to drain off water that was excessively salty or polluted and to create more land that could be cultivated. In addition, upstream storage basins and dams were built to store the water throughout the dry season.

During the 1950s, many towns and villages suffered continuous decline in their population and prosperity. Examples of this are the town of Daghara and Chibayish. In Chibayish, for example, many families had given up altogether on cultivation and moved on to reed-gathering for their livelihood. In his study of Chibayish, Salim observed that:

> During the 1952 agricultural season, in a sample of 120 families, 50 families (41.7%) did not cultivate at all; while only 70 families (58.3%) depended on cultivation alone, 40 (33.3%) supplemented cultivation with mat-weaving, and 21 (17.5%) supplemented cultivation with other occupations. The nine families who depend on cultivation alone were able to do so because they cultivated early crops outside ech-Chibayish.
>
> In the agricultural season of 1952, only 113 habil were cultivated by the 70 families, the average cultivated per family being only 1.6 habil (1 acre). To give an idea of the amount of uncultivable land compared with cultivable land, I calculate that the *sirkal* of Ahl ish-Shaikh clan held 13 plots, totaling over 12,000 *habil* in area. Of this, 11,000 *habil* were uncultivable (88%), and 1,400 cultivable.

Crop Division

The normal procedure appears to be that the landlord or his representative is present when the crop is ready for division. Salim says that "The division is carried out either by a shallow basket, which usually holds two *wijia* (7.5 kg), or by a balance."

As far as vegetable cultivation is concerned, this is considered to be a despised occupation by many Marsh Arabs. Vegetables eaten by the villagers are therefore either brought in from Basrah or are grown by strangers called *hasawiya*, within the town (which in this case is Chibayish) itself or its outskirts. Immediately after the floods have decreased, a number of *hasawiya* families come in and lease any uninhabited islands or patches of land for the season, from September to November, to cultivate the desired vegetable crops (Salim, 1962).

Livestock

The Mi'dan tribesmen still herd water buffalo (*Bubalus bubalis*) and will likely continue to do so for the foreseeable future, both for survival and as a labor of love. Water buffalo provide milk for cheese and dung for fires, and a family might sell animals to outsiders for slaughter, for instance, only if absolutely necessary.

Significant changes in the types of livestock reared in the marshland villages were observed compared to the pre-drying period. The total number of buffaloes, cattle and sheep were estimated at just over 600,000, with nearly equal numbers among the three livestock types. In some parts of the marshes, buffaloes were the only livestock reared. Sheep were previously rarely found in the wetlands; they were generally found in drier areas. The large number of sheep documented in recent surveys may signal the consequences of the ecosystem's demise in the communities. Furthermore, buffalo require a great deal of attention; being strong and fierce, they normally need to be kept on separate floating platforms and not on the same island as the hut is located. They usually exist almost entirely on grasses, young reeds and sedges (Salim, 1962).

According to Ochsenschlager, there have been many changes over the years in Hiba. For example, "In 1970 the Beni Hasan had looked down with contempt on the Mi'dan for keeping water buffalo. They considered the water buffalo as at least partially unclean, for many would not knowingly eat its flesh, and as somewhat useless when compared with the productivity of domesticated cattle." Yet when he returned in 1990, the Mi'dan had left and yet "the number of water buffalo in the area has only decreased by about 20% to 25%." Moreover, the Beni Hassan were now keeping water buffalo (Ochsenschlager, 2004).

As far as cattle are concerned, their possession does not confer prestige on a family, and no value is attached to them other than their market price. The greatest value of cattle is in their dairy produce such as fresh and sour milk, butter and curds. Cattle live on the rushes and the young green reeds. Calves are also often used as a sacrifice, for major celebrations such as when a guest house is completed. They are also sacrificed as a pledge in the fulfillment of a prayer wish. The main value of cattle is for their food and manure as well as a reservoir of wealth when needed.

The keeping of sheep in the marshlands was fairly limited in most areas, although their numbers are increasing with the continuous draining of the wetlands. Sheep generally live on the grasses and sedges available at pasture. The primary reason for keeping sheep is their wool.

The end of colonial rule failed to stop the gradual decline of Mesopotamia's irrigation agriculture. Over the last three decades an increasing number of smallholders have sold their land to the sheikhs and have been forced to seek work outside the area, mostly in nearby urban centers.

AGRICULTURE IN THE WETLANDS AFTER THE MONARCHY TO THE FALL OF SADDAM HUSSEIN

Farming Methods
Traditionally, before the Mesopotamian farmer could work the soil, he had to flood the field with water from the irrigation ditch. Following this, the field would be ploughed to break up the large chunks of soil (Figure 5.1). The harrow is then used to smooth and level it in preparation for dropping seeds into the ground using the seeder-plough. Once it has been sown, the field has to be watered three times. When it is time to harvest and the crops are ripe, they would be picked or in the case of say wheat or barley, it is cut and gathered together and then taken to the threshing house.

With most of today's crops except for fruit and vegetables, farming operations are typically mechanized, including soil preparation, sowing, spreading of fertilizer and harvesting (except for straw and hay). In the case of planting and harvesting fruit, these operations are still done manually. Likewise, for vegetables, only soil preparation is mechanized, mainly because the plots are generally small and therefore do not readily lend themselves to mechanization.

The marshland area throughout its history has depended on river transport, but transport of goods and people started to switch to the roads, most of which do not pass near the marshes. This deprived the people of the marshlands of an important source of revenue.

Dam and irrigation projects constructed in the 1970s reduced the annual flow of water in the Euphrates by more than one third. This marked the beginning of the marshes' general demise, reducing the permanent wetlands and spring floods that had carried nutrient-laden sediments.

Construction of the Third River (also previously called the Saddam River) resumed in the 1960s, but it was not until the 1980s during the Iran–Iraq War that construction was resumed in earnest and it wasn't until December 1992 that the 565-kilometer river was finally completed. The canal was said to be needed to drain off polluted water but its main purpose was to divert most of the Euphrates away from the marshes, and this has led to extensive salination. Two other major canals were constructed on the Euphrates; one was called the Fourth River Canal, which was 120 kilometers long, and the other was called the Qadisiyya Canal.

Let us quantify the impact. All indices of agricultural production have shown an overall downturn. Whereas in the past the marsh dwellers were almost self-sufficient, they are now reliant on aid from outside, capricious state support and remittances from family members who have migrated. Dates were the basic fruit of the region. There has been a drop of 50 per cent in production, and about the same drop in livestock products. The stock of water buffalo in the marshlands, for example, has dropped to about 35 per cent of its historic levels following the drainage and desiccation operations that were instigated in the 1990s. This large drop in numbers is to be expected as a natural result of the destruction of the animal's normal habitat. Furthermore, Iraq's marsh dwellers have not been able to raise the number of water buffaloes to earlier levels, partly because of the high price being demanded for female water buffaloes.

The final blow came after the 1991 Gulf War, when the Shiites in the south rebelled against the regime. After their defeat, Saddam burned and bombed the marsh villages and then built massive canals and dykes to divert the entire flow of the Euphrates away from the marshes.

THE RUSSIAN MASTER PLAN

During the 1970s, Iraq relied largely on Russian expertise for their agricultural planning. Consequently, the Soviet-sponsored "Russian Master Plan" was developed. This plan was basically based on the theory that nature and the environment are the result of human activity. A final revision to the plan was made in 1982. Unfortunately, however, due to continuous wars, embargoes, etc., the master plan's goals were never fully met. After the toppling of the Saddam regime, the opportunity arose to revisit the Russian Master Plan and to determine whether it met the new challenges and changed conditions that now existed.

Some agricultural planners seem to think that the solution is to update and modernize Iraq's agriculture, failing to appreciate the many technical and cultural challenges that will be faced. The point to emphasize is that one cannot modernize without education. That should be the first priority if modernization is to succeed.

Based on the Russian plan many irrigation projects were developed in southern Iraq, the main consequential projects being the East Gharraf, Amarah and Shatt al-Arab irrigation projects (for a detailed description of these projects, refer to Volume 1, Book 3 – Agriculture of the *New Eden Master Plan* prepared by the Iraqi ministries of Environment, Public Works, Municipalities and Water Resources in cooperation with the Italian Ministry for the Environment and Territory and Free Iraq Foundation). These three projects are briefly discussed below.

East Gharraf Irrigation Project

The East Gharraf Area consists essentially of a very flat alluvial plain, sloping slightly from its head at Kut on the Tigris down towards the south. The area has been inhabited since Sumerian times and contains the remains of several important mounds (tells) that were former towns and remains of ancient irrigation canals.

According to a study, the *New Eden Master Plan* (Volume 1, Book 3 – Agriculture), "Since the annual rainfall in the area never exceeds 150 mm, agriculture relies entirely on irrigation. The irrigation network is supplied from the Gharraf or from its branch canals (Shatt Badaa and Shatt Ibrahim). The discharge of the Gharraf is such that regular irrigation is possible mainly during the winter and the spring."

The report goes on to say, "Since the soil is of recent or modern alluvial origin it consists of fine materials (i.e. clay, silt, fine sand) and displays distinctly hydromorphic features resulting from prolonged or periodic flooding in the vast depression and, above all, salination in the irrigated areas. Extensive farming is traditionally practiced by alternating winter cereals and fallow. More barley is grown than wheat and the high degree of salination has led certain areas to be almost completely abandoned from farming. The fact that salinity is on the increase is due to the salt content of the irrigation water (even though it is comparatively low at 0.4 g/l) and the intense evaporation observed in the area."

The Russian Master Plan divides the East Gharraf area, which consists of about 118,750 hectares, into eight hydraulic zones. Of this area, winter crops are estimated to take up 96,000 hectares, rice to take up 20,000 hectares and orchards 2,750 hectares. Below is a brief description of the eight hydraulic zones:

1. Qalat Sukkar Rafai zone: This zone contains approximately 9,275 hectares and targets three primary crops planned for the development of the area, which translates to 6,800 hectares of winter crops, 2,280 hectares of rice and 195 hectares of orchard. Based on the soil's properties, this general layout is appropriate for mixed cropping pattern.

2. Kut al-Hai zone: This zone consists of about 11,485 hectares; it is located in the northernmost part of the East Gharraf Irrigation Project upstream of the current town of al-Hai. Because the soil is of medium texture, it is generally suitable for cereals and mixed crops. The orchards consist of about 435 hectares and have been grouped near the main villages and railway station.

3. Al-Hai North zone: The zone is supplied by a new canal, known as the HNMI. Its intake is close to the al-Hai regulator. The *New Eden Master Plan* study says that "The water level upstream of the regulator makes it possible to supply the whole zone in question by gravity with the exception of the outer areas on the Shatt Al Akhdar where the ground rises and requires a lift station on the canal." Orchards take up about 555 hectares and the remaining area is allocated for cereals and mixed crops because of the medium soil texture as in the Kut al-Hai zone. Furthermore, ditches are required for all the watercourses in this zone.

4. Al-Hai South zone: The zone consists of a total area of 25,157 hectares, of which 1,752 hectares are allocated to rice and 555 hectares to orchard; this land is made up of the land supplied by gravity by canal HSM1. Rice is grown in the southeast part of the zone while the remaining part is allocated for cereals and mixed crops because of soil suitability. The main water source is the Jannabi Canal.

5. Fajir zone: The total area of the Fajir zone is 12,269 hectares, which includes 1,224 hectares for rice and 345 hectares for orchard; the remaining is for rice, cereals and mixed crops. The Fajir zone equipment consists of a combination of gravity canals and distributaries supplied by pumping stations. The area lacks a main ditch.

6. Al-Nasr zone: The land in this zone has been allocated to three crop types; they are winter crops, 7,900 hectares; rice, 1,680 hectares; and orchard, 270 hectares. The zone is irrigated by two canals which operate by gravity. The only areas that are equipped are those that are located east of road MR7. The main water source is the Gharraf.

7. Shattrah zone: The area for this zone consists of 8,562 hectares of which 1,992 hectares is allocated for rice and the remainder is for the growing of cereals and mixed crops. The zone is supplied by pumping, and the main water source is the Shatt Shattrah. Pumping stations use monocanal-type pumps.

8. Dawanish zone: The total area for this zone is 17,158 hectares of which rice (main crop) covers 11,088 hectares. The zone is located in the southernmost zone of the East Gharraf Drainage Project. The land is flat and the soil consists of a heavy texture that reduces water loss when the rice fields are submerged under water. Installation of pumping stations is required for successful irrigation. The main water source is the Shatt Abu Dawanish.

Watercourses and distributaries are intended to deliver water from a source to targeted locations such as farms. However, a watercourse generally operates on the concept of a "hit-or-miss" so that when crop demands are low for a particular month, the watercourse may deliver water continuously for a week and then stop for a week, and so on. The water flow is neither divided nor temporarily stored. Moreover, watercourses operate by upstream control; on the other hand, distributaries can operate either by control from upstream or from downstream.

The main canals of the irrigation network in the area are known by their zone names and are shown below:

- Qalaat Sukkar Canals
- Kut Hai Canal
- Al-Hai North Canals
- Al-Hai South Canals
- Fajir Canals
- Al-Nasr Canals
- Dawanish Canal

Systematic drainage of the proposed areas to be cultivated is required to suppress soil salinity. The main exception to this is the rice-crop areas which lack an underground drainage system but which require releasing the water that is drained off from the rice fields upon being dewatered prior to harvesting.

The main and secondary canals carry the water between the Gharraf River, which is the primary water source, and the distributary canals. The main canals typically operate under gravity flow from the Gharraf, except for sections B1 and B2 of the Dawanish zone. Moreover, from 1962, the number of pumping installations has dramatically decreased and currently only remain in areas where the Gharraf does not rise above ground level, such as downstream from Kut and the Shatt Shattrah Lake Zone. This is mainly due to the construction of the cross-regulators and increase in the number of gravity offtakes.

Amarah Irrigation and Drainage Project

The Amarah Irrigation and Drainage Project covers a gross area of about 285,000 hectares, and lies on both sides of the Tigris River on the southern part of the Tigris delta plain. The area is bordered by the Huwaiza Marsh to the east, the

Qurnah Marsh to the south and the Sinaf Marsh to the north and is built from alluvial deposits with very slight land slopes. The city of Amarah is the commercial and industrial center of the area.

The *New Eden Master Plan* states that "One of the most important problems concerning the area is the disruption to industrial and farming activities caused by flood flows from the Tigris River spreading over the various distributaries within the area. In the northern part of the project, the land level is higher than the level of the water in the canals and hence irrigation depends on pumping. Other problems come from the lack of gravity irrigation, soil salinity, and high groundwater level during the flood period."

Water levels in the adjacent marshlands vary and depend on the season and flood amount. The climate of this region is basically similar to that of East Gharraf and Shatt al-Arab areas – dry and hot in the summer and cool in the winter. The average annual rainfall (which takes place in the winter), also never exceeds 150 mm. Air humidity in most of the southern regions near the wetlands is fairly high.

Because of the climate conditions of the area, agricultural production relies almost entirely on irrigation for the supply of water, and the water flowing from the Tigris is typically adequate to irrigate the total project area. However, a major problem arises because of the low water level in the canals and the absence of appropriate regulators. During the flood period the high water levels in the canal make irrigation by gravity possible. This, however, applies only to the downstream areas of the project adjoining the marshes (*hawrs*). Furthermore, the high groundwater table in the Amarah area is characteristic of the surrounding marshes and is due mainly to its low topography, which, combined with its substantial network of canals, created depressions that lacked suitable outlets, thereby increasing the need for artificial drainage.

Soil: An analysis of the soils in the Tigris Delta shows that they primarily consist of deep alluvium soils and this appears to be characteristic of the region in general. The texture of the tested soils varies however between medium and heavy, with almost a complete absence of course-textured soils.

Summary of the hydrologic network
The Tigris: The Amarah Project boundary starts near the Saad Canal offtake which is roughly 34 km west of Amarah City, and ends approximately 10 km downstream of where the Tigris meets the Kassarah River. The length of the Tigris River within the project area is 128 km and this is divided in seven reaches within the area as follows:

1. Reach from the Upstream boundary to the Buteira
2. Reach from the Buteira offtake to the Chahala offtake
3. Reach from the Chahala offtake to the Mujar al-Kabir offtake
4. Reach from Mujar al-Kabir offtake to the Micheriyah Head Regulator
5. Reach from the Micheriyah Head Regulator to Qalat Saleh Barrage
6. Reach from Qalat Saleh Barrage to Kassarah Barrage
7. Reach from the Kassarah Barrage to the downstream boundary of the project area.

Some of the Tigris tributaries in the area include:
*   The Buteira
*   The Areedh
*   The Babal Hawa
*   The Musharrah
*   The Chahala
*   The Mujar al-Kabir
*   The Micheriyah

One of the unique features of the Amarah Project is that, except to the northeast, it is surrounded on all sides by wetlands. Furthermore, the entire Amarah River system, with the exception of the Tigris itself, discharges into the surrounding marshes.

Drainage Network: According to the *New Eden Master Plan* study, the project's area consists of a fairly dense network of natural canals that make up the Tigris River Delta, and which provide water to the agricultural areas of the project through a network of main, secondary and distributary canals. Another drainage network collects the excess drainage water at the lowest points of the areas, and these waters are then diverted to the adjoining marshes.

The main and secondary canals are aligned to the high contours of the land so that minimum excavation is required. Lined canals were proposed by the Russian Master Plan to reduce seepage losses, as the Amarah area is very flat.

The Amarah Irrigation and Drainage Project generally employs gravity-fed irrigation systems, except for the drainage region DR11 which is fed through the use of pumping stations from the Tigris River.

Shatt al-Arab Irrigation Project
According to the Russian Master Plan, the Shatt al-Arab project (Polservice up and Hydroproject, 1981) covers the entire Shatt al-Arab River, the Tigris River

to the 237th km, upstream of the Kassarah Barrage and the Euphrates River to Nasiriyah and their tributaries. The study states that the only source of fresh water to fully meet all future water demands of the Shatt al -Arab Project area is surface water in rivers and marshes, because the very high salinity of the groundwater makes it unsuitable for irrigation.

A soil reconnaissance survey for the entire project area consisting of about 160, 000 hectares was conducted, after which it was determined that of this area, only 89,729 hectares was suitable for future irrigation and drainage improvements. Of this, the existing date orchards within the area take up approximately 34,297 hectares. This determination was based on several factors such as the area's soil conditions, existing dykes, presence of marshes and industry.

The total project area containing the irrigation and drainage systems network with the location of main canals, dykes, pumping stations and other structures, is divided into the seven individual complexes. This is to facilitate the execution of the designed irrigation systems in line with the agricultural development plans for the area. It is intended that the drainage network will remove the saline groundwater from the upper part of the soil while keeping the groundwater table below the plant root zone. The water for this purpose was to be drawn from the Tigris, Euphrates or Shatt al-Arab Rivers using pumping stations to discharge it through a network of main and secondary canals to the areas planned for irrigation.

Of the three main irrigation and drainage projects (East Gharraf Irrigation Project, Amarah Irrigation and Drainage Project, and the Shatt al-Arab Irrigation and Drainage Project) of the Russian Master Plan of the 1980s for the agricultural development of southern Iraq, only a very limited percentage of its goals were able to achieve realization. Unfortunately, however, reliable information on what was achieved with respect to these projects is hard to come by. This is due to many factors including the Iran–Iraq War, allocated economic resources, lack of funding, etc.

Agricultural Production – Crops
The main crops produced in the wetland region are:

Wheat: This is a basic foodstuff that farmers grow as long as long as soil conditions, salinity in particular, offer acceptable yields to meet their needs. The attraction of growing wheat is that it is not a very demanding crop, thus allowing it to be grown in most of the project zone, yet current levels of wheat production are only 50 per cent of that planned.

Barley: Because of its very high resistance to salt, barley is a widespread crop in the region. Its value is mainly as animal foodstuff which together with straw is the only complement to grazing. Because of this, barley has replaced wheat in some parts of the south, bearing in mind that the cultivation periods for barley are almost the same as those for wheat. Yet the barley production yield is less than a third of that planned.

Rice: Although this crop has dwindled in recent years due to the diminution of the area of the lakes, it continues to be a basic foodstuff. Rice-growing has the disadvantage of requiring high-water and labor needs.

Maize: Although cultivated on a small scale, it continues to be important by providing complementary animal feed.

Fruit trees: Orchards are cultivated in areas along the main canals which have the best drained land and generally have a good, light texture. Having an efficient irrigation network can provide an opportunity to extend these areas and to plant new orchards where suitable soil conditions exist.

Vegetables: Vegetables are generally grown for home consumption and in small plots where the soil is the least saline. Demand is greater for summer vegetables such as tomatoes, eggplant, okra and cucumber, than for winter vegetables such as cabbages, lettuces, carrots, onions, beans, etc.

Other Crops: There are numerous other crops such as corn, legumes and sorghum, which while they may be uneconomical to cultivate, should nevertheless be cultivated because of their short growing times. These times can be modified to suit winter crop rotation. Additionally, these crops can be used for fodder consumption and their by-products for silage.

One of the more common crops that was grown annually in ancient Iraq was flax. This is because it had many uses; it was used in the production of things like nets, cloth, linseed oil and various pharmaceuticals.

Date Palm Cultivation

Date palms (*Phoenix dactylifera*) have been cultivated in southern Iraq for over 5,000 years, and Iraq is one of the largest world producers and exporters of dates. Except for oil, dates are Iraq's single largest export. Also, prior to the desiccation and draining of the marsh areas, Iraq had the largest date orchards in the world, but the wars and Saddam's draining of the marshlands depleted the number of palm trees from 30 million in the early 1960s to about 22 million in the mid-1970s and an estimated 13 million by 1985. Furthermore, Iraq is said to currently produce over 600 varieties of dates. Date production in 1987 dropped to 220,000 tons from 578,000 tons in the mid-1970s. In 1987 about 150,000 tons, or 68 per cent of the harvest, was exported to Europe, Japan and Arab countries. In fact, Iraq once produced three quarters of the world's total date crop annually; now Saudi Arabia, Egypt and Iran export more than Iraq.

Date palms were also a very important food source to the marsh dwellers' local diet – both in Mesopotamian as well as modern times. These palms grew in southern Iraq by the river marshes and supplied fibers, fodder, wood and rich food. Products from these palms are very important in mat-making, furniture and building construction.

In this regard, the Iraqi Ministry of Agriculture has already commenced with the rehabilitation of the date palm industry to increase date yields. It is also an important source of rural jobs, and will therefore be an important contributor to Iraq's economic revival. Developing nurseries to grow date palms would further increase Iraq's date production and allow agricultural specialists to increase yields of the various varieties.

The Russian master plan based its cropping intensity of irrigated lands with various irrigation systems on the need to meet Iraq's general requirements for food products. It should be noted that many factors come into play that can impact the production yield; these include things like fertilizer distribution, farming techniques and mechanization, seed quality and water availability.

Soil Salinity

Perhaps one of the more pronounced adverse ramifications associated with the draining of the Iraqi Marshlands was its reckless soil salinization. Marshland draining caused deep cracking and subsidence of the soil, and saline groundwater from the aquifers was able by capillary action to rise to the surface. Likewise, during the water evaporation process, the dissolved salts, which consisted chiefly of sulfates and chlorides, were deposited on the soil's surface, forming saltpans, which represented a very harsh and intolerant soil environment that only the most salt-tolerant plant species were able to endure.

It is anticipated that marshlands restoration will reverse soil salinization in three crucial ways. These are:

1. Flooding will solubilize the saltpans. This will initially cause a temporary increase in water salinity as the salt is flushed into the Gulf. However, once the existing saltpans no longer exist, the salinity will return to normal levels, and the areas of the original saltpans will once again become productive.
2. Saturation of the upper soil horizons will reverse the water flow, allowing percolating surface water of limited salinity to recharge the shallow groundwater, which tends to be of higher salinity. This will not only reduce local soil salinization, but will also improve the quality of the shallow groundwater, potentially to a point where it may again be used for agricultural irrigation.

3.   Rehydration of the bentonite-based soils will result in the swelling of the clay layers, thereby inhibiting the migration of shallow groundwater to the surface in regions that are flooded only seasonally. This will potentially allow the expansion of agriculture to the seasonal upland areas of the marshlands.

USAID is equipping the Ministry of Water Resources with a soil and water laboratory. In addition to the soil testing and water quality equipment being installed, staff will receive training on operating the equipment.

Capital Leaching (Soil Desalinization)

Leaching is often necessary to control soil salinity, and consists of the minimum amount of irrigation water supplied that must be drained through the root zone. However, the leaching process does not resolve the salinity problem, it only defers it to the following year. Normal values for general leaching requirements for deep and shallow drainage systems differ significantly; in the case of shallow drainage, the leaching requirements are 41 to 49 per cent higher than it is for deep drainage.

Before normal agricultural production can commence, heavy leaching may be required to wash out the excess amount of salts in the root zone of the soil profile to a level that is acceptable for agricultural production. It is also the first irrigation operation that is carried out prior to normal crop rotation and irrigation practices.

The *New Eden Master Plan* for the marshlands areas essentially extends in a triangle between the cities of Kut, Nasiriyah and Basrah. A study of the plan shows that intensive agriculture is envisioned for the area, which consists of perennial crops and rotation of winter and summer crops. Wheat and barley are the dominant winter crops, whereas orchards are the principal perennial crops (especially date palms). The irrigation and drainage projects are estimated to extend over 613,350 hectares. Generally, the agriculture of southern Iraq today is very different from what was planned and designed in the 1980s.

It goes without saying that Iraq's agricultural production is not considered to be very efficient. In practice, its efficiency can be significantly improved by simply introducing an irrigation schedule based on a simple crop water balance and improving the irrigation efficiency. There are many benefits to water use efficiency; the primary benefits are:

- increased agricultural productivity
- cost savings in the long term
- improved water quality
- reduced stream diversion

Impact of Technology on Agriculture

While traditional irrigation methods may cost less, they are pronouncedly less efficient than the more technologically modern methods that are available today. Additionally, significant water saving can be achieved by upgrading the irrigation technologies used, although, as previously stated, most farmers are unlikely to respond favorably to the application of such a process. This is especially true since farmers have for centuries used flooding irrigation water directly in the field and thus the utilization of sophisticated drip irrigation systems may be hard to swallow without first educating the farmers to the advantages of contemporary high-efficiency systems. Moreover, if the new technologies fail in their objectives due to mismanagement by people that lack the required skills, this will encourage farmers to reject other proposed innovations.

The *New Eden Master Plan* suggests the creation of some pilot farms which it is believed would help introduce the many new technologies that are currently being used, in addition to introducing new crops and a new water culture. With this in mind, USAID has established 72 demonstration farms in the wetlands, and introduced new crops and improved management practices for sorghum, wheat, barley and broad beans. It also established eight date palm nurseries with 4,500 trees that have displayed a reported 90 per cent survival rate.

Impact of Microclimate

Among the benefits that are often overlooked is the favorable impact that the wetlands impart on the microclimate of the areas adjoining them. These include higher humidity and more moderate temperatures in areas adjoining the wetlands compared with areas of dry land that are some distance from large bodies of open water.

In the marshlands, studies show that summer temperatures within these regions were typically 5 °C cooler than the dry regions. The ramifications of this are improved environmental quality and reduced cooling costs, and increased agricultural productivity by reducing heat stress on crops. It has also been shown that fields downwind from a marshland, especially in a desert climate setting with high diurnal temperature ranges, experience significant transfer of moisture from the wetlands to the fields in the form of dewfall.

THE IRAQI MARSHLANDS: A POST-SADDAM PERSPECTIVE

Kadhum Lahmoud, Director-General of the Marshlands Revival Center at the Water Resources Ministry, listed four major challenges facing the marshlands. These are:

1. major drought
2. absence of water-sharing agreements with neighboring countries
3. poor quality of water from the two rivers due to industrial pollutants
4. salt water intrusion from the Arabian Gulf

The government of Iraq has made restoration of the Iraqi marshlands one of its top priorities, and is providing the necessary financial, scientific and engineering resources. Recent studies confirm that it is feasible to remove the drainage system and restore sheet flow within the wetlands of the marshes region. However, the most important factor that will determine whether successful restoration of the marshlands and resettlement of its inhabitants is possible relies on one pivotal challenge, which is the availability of water resources.

The Iraq Marshlands Restoration Program will focus on six closely related activities:
- agricultural production and agribusiness
- integrated marsh management
- constructed wetlands
- livestock and dairy production
- primary health care
- fishing and fish farming

Agricultural and Agribusiness Initiatives
As Iraq's agricultural sector grows, it will represent an important source of revenue for rural communities. Unfortunately, agriculture in the marshlands currently provides poor returns, preventing marsh dwellers from participating fully in the growing agricultural economy. Access to agricultural inputs, extension services and improved production techniques is limited and transportation presents a significant barrier to farmers.

Working with the Iraq Ministry of Agriculture, the Iraq Marshland Restoration Program will work to jumpstart agricultural production and business around the marshes and identify job opportunities for former marsh dwellers. Two primary activities will further this goal:
- The IMRP has established eight date palm nurseries to resuscitate the south's most prosperous industry, which was destroyed by the Hussein regime. The program planted 4,500 palms, which will provide between 30,000 and 45,000 offshoots for replanting and distribution.
- Large-scale crop demonstrations in the drained areas for field crops and horticulture, combined with farmers' field days will give hands-on experience with new techniques. The IMRP program has already planted sorghum in 31 demonstration sites in three provinces to expand crop production, and which have already been harvested.

Livestock and Dairy Production

The draining of the marshes and continuous drought has disrupted traditional livestock production which has resulted in shifting the emphasis from water buffalo to sheep and cattle. Livestock herding in the marshes is crucial as a source of basic nutrition and income for families, although serious constraints do exist. The Marshland Restoration Program is moving to address these constraints by: "Extending Veterinary Services to Marsh Communities: Poor animal health is a serious constraint for local herders. This activity will bring together service providers and users under the Ministry of Agriculture and establish a small number of veterinary centers. Veterinary staff will make regular visits, and monitoring will determine if services boost production and income." The Marsh Restoration Program also proposes to assist people in the region to replenish their livestock, which consists largely of sheep and water buffalo.

Below is a list of points taken from Iraq's National Development Strategy (NDS) Report (2007–2010) that needs to be considered to successfully plan Iraq's future agricultural policy. The majority of points below also apply to the marshland areas:

1. Support production and stop agricultural inputs subsidies in different period according to their kinds and impact over the development process.
2. Encourage private sector investment in agriculture and agro-industry fields by creating a secure investment environment.
3. Reactivating credit systems through an Agriculture Development Fund by paying for the list of requirements instead of paying the credit amount which was the mechanism used in the past.
4. Encourage establishing specialized agricultural associations.
5. Trying hard to reach a fair division of water shares in quality and quantity with concerned countries.
6. Completing irrigation and drainage systems for irrigated projects using comprehensive reclamation system and rehabilitate existing ones as well as implementing main outfalls.
7. Adding new lands especially those that could be cultivated by establishing irrigation projects in rain fed zones such as al-Jazeera, KRG and Kirkuk projects.
8. Using supplementary irrigation in semi rain zones.
9. Using modern irrigation technologies specially closed irrigation systems to reduce water wastes which could result in creating new lands.
10. Reusing heavy and salinity water after treatment and planting crops that resist salts.
11. Using renewable underground water in all agricultural and livestock breeding fields without being consumed through digging wells in promising areas.
12. Completing large and small dam's projects systems achieving (water security); increasing water resources to add electrical power to the network.

13. Maintaining existing irrigation projects, pump stations, irrigation and drainage network, main rivers cleaning.
14. Increase vegetal production (including vegetal and orchards) through vertical expansion (production increase) and horizontal expansion (adding new lands) according to the irrigation project plan and water shares.
15. Derive and input high productivity species resisting dryness and salinity.
16. Reviewing seeds legislations and regulations.
17. Revitalizing and developing Iraqi Marshes according to development comprehensive programs within provided water resources.
18. Develop appropriate agricultural courses for farmers in each region and using bean fodder.
19. Looking after livestock breeding and artificial fertilization transferring genes according to development breeding programs.
20. Treating severe lack in fodder supply by planting them and developing green spots and forests, natural protectorate and reconstruct the damages.
21. Investing water sites for fishing breeding, activate sea fishing and develop poultry sector.
22. Develop guidance and veterinary services as well as supporting agricultural research in this field.
23. Develop infrastructure and building capacity upon world practices.
24. Providing guidance and educating the new generation and rural woman training her to participate in developing this sector.
25. Expanding the use of comprehensive control (IPM), expanding natural fertilizers and move to bio-agriculture production.
26. Developing environment in all agricultural projects and staying away from negative practices on it.
27. Utilizing renewable natural power such as wind and sun energy and other in developing remote areas and agricultural lands.
28. Completing the program of agro-environment dividing maps for guiding farmers.
29. Enhancing agricultural trade by increasing production and quality improvement as well as creating competition to face consequence effects on current international economic changes.
30. Review agriculture and environment legislations related to lands ownership and rent.
31. Follow up Iraq accession to international and regional agreements related to agriculture, environment and water resources.

The post–2003 Iraqi governments have committed to rehabilitating the Iraqi wetlands, and Kadhum Lahmoud, Director-General of the Marshlands Revival Center at the Water Resources Ministry, said his Ministry was working on a US$120 million project to boost the flow of water into the area by building dykes on marshland inlets. Each dyke would use satellite technology to track water quality and levels every 15 minutes, with the aim of retaining inflowing water in the marshlands for longer periods.

In the final analysis the successful restoration of marshland agriculture will depend on several factors, the most important of which is the climate (drought and precipitation issues), and resolving transboundary issues with Iraq's neighbors, namely Turkey, Syria and Iran. A typical example of this is the building of new dykes by Iran with the professed purpose of selling water to Kuwait. This will threaten the Huwaiza Marsh which is a refuge for plants and animals that it is hoped will return once the areas are restored. This is discussed in other sections of the book.

6

THE WETLANDS WILDLIFE AND ECOSYSTEM

Sam A.A. Kubba
Mudhafar Salim

GENERAL

The Iraqi Marshes serve a variety of functions for human and other ecosystems including:

- Acting as a natural sponge storing water during high river flow and releasing water during low flow.
- Nursery grounds for fish, aquatic birds and refuges for terrestrial animals.
- Natural filters that purify water, trap sediments and pollutants and facilitate desalinization of salty water.
- Highly productive in vegetative cover (e.g., reeds) harvested commercially for building material, mats and cattle forage.

Environmental Importance and Uniqueness

Iraq possesses a special moderate geographic location as it lies between the Eurasian cold (Pelarctic) and African warm (Ethiopian) zones. In addition, the topographic diversity of the surface in Iraq enriched its biodiversity and this in turn helped form wide spectra of biological diversity.

This local diversity reflected in forming a unique ecosystem in the lower part of Mesopotamia: the marshes (al-Ahwar). The Iraqi Ahwar are vast extensions of reed beds and open theaters of water that geologically formed thousands of years ago as a result of the Tigris and Euphrates sedimentations in this plain area.

The formation of such an ecosystem in such an area, considering the uniqueness of Iraq's location mentioned above, gave the wetlands such a singularity, which differs from other wetlands in the cold Eurasian zone and the warm African zone. The lower Mesopotamian wetlands, thanks to this singularity, harbors indigenous species and lie within the global birds migration routes passing over the Middle East.

As for birds' migration routes, the Iraqi wetlands lie within very important global flyways that originate from those birds' breeding grounds in west Asia, Siberia and east Europe, heading towards their wintering areas. Some of those migrating birds (mainly waterfowl) are wintering in the vast surfaces of water of the Iraqi wetlands (Ahwar), which do not look like any other in the Middle East. Others continue their journey towards the south using the Iraqi Marshes as essential stopovers and refueling rests.

There is an important morphological dimension that enhanced the "harborability" and sojourning of the resident and migratory birds. The existence of open theaters of water is ideal for grebes, pelicans, ducks, geese, otters, fish, etc., while the dense reed beds are ideal for rails, songbirds (*Passerines*), and the edges of the marshes are typical for waders, herons, storks, amphibians, snakes, etc. Such diversity in micro-habitats gave the Iraqi Marshlands (Ahwar) irreplaceable value.

Global, Regional and Local-level Wildlife Importance

The panorama mentioned above, characterized by the healthy biodiversity, made a globally, regionally (Middle Eastern) and locally important part out of this area. With the application of the global Important Bird Area (IBA) criteria, which includes intensive sub-criteria, we find that most of the IBAs in Iraq lie in southern wetlands. The criteria of the IBA's scale are based on the occurrence of the birds from the conservational standpoint (threatened, vulnerable, endangered, etc.), and the occurrence densities of some groups of birds, regardless of their conservational status. The Iraqi Marshes enjoy these characteristics because it already harbors different resident birdlife content and attracts huge numbers of migrant birds.

According to the Key Biodiversity Areas (KBA) criteria, marshes are one of the richest areas in the world as they contain this rich mosaic of birds; the diversity of floral content that ranges as submerged and emerged plants as well as the plants that inhibit the marsh margins; and other contents of fauna represented by a considerable list of insects, amphibians, reptiles, fish and mammals.

The marshes contain another important component, the Marsh Arabs, which directly effect and are affected by their ambience. Marsh Arabs inhabited this area thousands of years ago and became an integral part of the ecosystem of the wetlands. This vulnerable community is still practicing the same customs, traditions, lifestyle of their Sumerian ancestors. The same reedhouse (*mudhif*), canoe (*mashhoof*), five-headed spear (*fala*) that can be seen on the Sumerian cylinder stamps are still made and used by Marsh Arabs in the marshes. Sumerian cylinder seals, as well as mud clays and other remains, tell us much about the way they lived and interacted with the marsh ecosystem.

COMPONENTS OF THE WILDLIFE ECOSYSTEM

Micro- and Macroorganisms

Given the fact that the marshes constitute an aquatic ecosystem, it has features that distinguish it from other ecosystems. Generally, the wetlands' ecosystems are the richest in biodiversity, where considerable numbers of species complete their yearly life cycles effecting and being affected by each other.

The initial cycle that we can start talking about is the phytoplankton that is suspended in the water. Phytoplankton forms the everlasting source for the fauna under the water. The life of this huge group of microorganisms relates tightly to the physical and chemical characteristics of the waterbody, and the latter in turn relates tightly to other controls like the water level (compared to the normal water level), water flow, light conditions, etc.

There is another group of microorganisms, zooplankton, which forms an essential component of the wetlands ecosystem infrastructure. This group relates with the same controls we mentioned above, in addition to abundance of the phytoplankton. Zooplankton is essential to the food chain in the marshland ecosystem, as many insect species, animals – e.g., ducks and flamingo and birds depend on it as an essential food resource. Additionally, the Iraqi wetlands include a considerable biomass of Algae that represents another important link in the food chain.

FLORA

Ancient Flora in Iraq

Natural vegetation in as much as it consists of specific regional plant associations is the product of the sum total of local climatic factors. Indeed one of the basic principles of plant geography is that vegetation is a function of climate and is determined by it. For instance, the lack of adequate rainfall imposes restrictions on dry farming and pastoral economy. Similarly, severe

Figure 6.1 Two Sumerian cylinder seal impressions depicting plough and seeder funnel and banqueting scenes.

or repeated frost sets restrictions on the cultivation of such plant as citrus fruit, date palm, olives and grapevines. These arid limits have obviously had a decisive effect upon early domesticated plants. But local and regional plant cover can be destroyed by a number of other processes in addition to climate. These include deforestation, field clearance, fire, animal grazing, and or "overworking" the land (Butzer, 1982:124). Thus we find, "Forests have given way to fields, or have been reduced to barren scrub by fuel-gatherers and browsing goats. Extensive grasslands have been ploughed up or impoverished by overgrazing. Desolate steppe or the few isolated pines or oak trees preserved in a Muslim cemetery may be the only evidence of a once luxuriant forest" (Butzer, 1976:35).

While there is still insufficient polynological evidence available to form firm conclusions, it does appear that an improvement in the climate (ie., an increase in temperature and precipitation) occurred in the Zagros region from about 12800 – 6100 BC, which in turn facilitated the re-emergence in the foothills of the first oak and pistachio trees which were wiped out during the last glacial period (van Zeist, 1969; Wright, 1968, 1976). At Shanidar B2 (c.10000 BC), a scrub savanna was already developed and oak was becoming significant (Wahida, 1981:30). Oak, tamarisk and poplar are also attested at Palegawra in about 12000 BC (Ibid., 1981:30).

Flora in the Iraqi Marshlands

For thousands of years, most of the marshes were covered by natural wetland vegetation. In this respect, common reed or *qasab* in Arabic (*Pharagmites communis*) was the main covering component in the permanent marshes (Figure 6.2), followed by reed mace (*Typha augustata*) in the ephemeral seasonal zone. Salt-tolerant vegetation consisting of low sedges and bulrush (*Carex* and *Juncus* spp., *Scripus brachyceras*) sometimes inundates

Al-Hawizeh	Suq al-Shuyukh	East Hammar
Phragmites australis	*Phragmites australis*	*Phragmites australis*
Salvinia natans	*Ceratophyllum demersum*	*Myrophyllum verticillatum*
Ceratophyllum demersum	*Schoenoplectus litoralis*	*Schoenoplectus litoralis*
Typha domengensis	*Typha domengensis*	*Jussiaea repens*

Table 1 The cover of major species for each marsh is given in Table1. Common reeds (*P. australis*) provided the main cover in all marshes. *S. Natans,* followed by *C. demersum* and *M. Verticillatum*, were next in importance.

overgrown mud-flats whereas deeper, permanent lakes tend to support rich submerged aquatic vegetation as exemplified by species like eel grass (*Vallisneria* sp.), hornwort *(Ceratophyllum demersum)* and pondweed (*Potamogeton lucens spp.*). Likewise included is bottom vegetation like stonewart (*Chara* spp.). One can also often find in the smaller lakes and back swamps several species of floating vegetation such as waterlilies (*Nymphaea* and *Nuphar* spp.), water soldier (*Pistia stratiotes*) and duckweed (*Le mna gibba*) (Scott, 1995; Rechinger, 1964).

In fact, scholars of Iraqi Marshland flora, including Hilli, Mayah and Zubaidy, state that the marshes were characterized by high aquatic plant productivity for both emergent and submerged plants. Likewise, in the Qurnah Marshes we also see evidence of high primary productivity of phytoplankton. This high aquatic plant productivity in the marshes proved vital to the fisheries of southern Iraq (Hilli, 1977; Mayah, 1994; and Zubaidy, 1985).

The plant cover (including submerged) is the most important component in the marshlands ecosystem. It provides the shelter and the food resource for all faunal components like insects, birds and other animals. The plant component of the Iraqi Ahwar consists of nearly 60 plant species, of which 25 like *Myriophyllum* and *Lemna* are submerged or floating plant species; 6 like *Typha* and *Phragmytes* are emerged plant species, and around 25 like *Tamarex* and *Juncus* marshland margins plant species.

Figure 6.2 Marsh Arab in Chibayish transporting reed for fodder, construction or weaving of reed mats (Courtesy: Canada-Iraq Marshlands Initiative – CIMI).

With respect to the emerged plant species, it has been found that the reed beds (*Phragmytes*) and reed mace (*Typha*) are the dominant plant species that we can see everywhere in the Iraqi Marshes. The distribution of these plants differs in the areas of the marshes, for instance the typical plant cover of the area of northern Huweize may differs from that of west Hammar, and this gives additional dimension for the plant diversity in distribution that means various ecological subsequences. It is also natural to find both types in the same place; on many occasions, they might be found mixed together. In describing these reed beds, Thesiger says, "This giant grass, which looked like a bamboo, grew in the dense reedbeds to a height of more than twenty-five feet. The stems, each terminating in a tasselled head of aplest buff, were so thick that the marshmen used them as punt-poles" (Thesiger, 1964: p39).

Each of these emerged plant types constitutes a niche for different insect and fauna species. This plant cover is essential for the harboring of many of the resident bird species for nesting and raising their chicks till fledging as the plant cover is also a shelter for the insects that these birds are taking for food resources. In addition, the emerged plant group is very important for harboring a number of large migrant birds where they can hide from hunters or to be away of disturbance. Also, the reed beds and the reed mace are important for harboring and movement

Figure 6.3 An illustration of the diverse plant cover found in the Iraqi Marshlands (Courtesy: Canada-Iraq Marshlands Initiative – CIMI).

during foraging of some mammal species like otter, jungle cat, mongoose, etc. The waterbody itself includes a considerable biomass of submerged plants, which also constitute an essential niche for different aquatic species.

Most of the plant species have economical importance as food resources for a number of species of fish and water buffalo. The Reed *Phragmytes* has its own specialty in the building of the Sumerian civilization, as the marsh dwellers engaged these golden sticks deeply with their life some thousands of years since.

When the Mesopotamian farmers first descended on to the plain, some 10,000–12,000 years ago, they tried cultivating einkorn wheat, but found it unsuited to irrigation agriculture, with the consequence that emmer wheat became the exclusive species there. The earliest evidence we have to date of the cultivation of emmer wheat dates from the end of the first half of the eighth millennium BC at Tell Aswad, (Kislev, 1984:67). Similarly the northward expansion of agriculture communities was clearly hindered by cooler temperatures. Grapes, figs and olive trees could not be moved north with them; instead, more frost-resistant species were selected. On poorer soils under hard climates, wheat and particularly barley proved uneconomical. To off-set this, more modest crops such as rye and oats achieved a prominent position in cool temperature latitudes. It is therefore no coincidence that the focus of ancient civilization was located approximately in the most favorable climatic zones, for their economies were based on agriculture intrinsically associated with sub-tropical products.

This so called optional zone which falls within the southern part of the central mountain belt also coincides with the natural distribution of wild plants which archaeology has identified as the first to be domesticated. Hans Helbeck was able to show that these were emmer wheat and two-rowed barley, probably grown in association in areas overlapping only on the banks of the Fertile Crescent at an altitude of 2,000–4,300 feet above sea level.

Thus while plant cultivation progressed in the foothill region from the sixth millennium onwards as attested at Yarim Tepe I (Bakhteyev & Yanushevich, 1980: pp.167–178), there were no traces or similar agricultural settlements in the south until late in the fifth millennium BC, although Queili may prove much earlier. This southward movement of plant cultivation, from the middle latitudes to the environments have inevitably caused the disturbance of the plants' genetic constitutions and forced them to create a multitude of morphological and physiological forms which in the long run only those suited to them were able to survive (Jacobsen & Adams, 1960: pp. 1255–58). But despite its drawbacks, the alluvial plain watered by the two rivers was rich farmland, where the entire population of the country could easily be fed on its produce. The surplus produce was exchanged for imported metal, wood or stone, which the local inhabitants badly needed.

Moreover, the hot and humid climate in the south provided conditions highly favorable to the cultivation of date-palm, which grows along the rivers and canals. As early as the third millennium BC there were extensive palm groves in the shades of which citrus fruit, olives and vegetables were grown. Barry Warner, a plant ecologist from the University of Waterloo, Canada, adds that many plants have begun to thrive once again in the region, and "We're getting a formidable response in the newly reflooded areas."

Finally, in an interesting article by Mudhafar Salim (Nature Iraq), Richard Porter (BirdLife International), and Clayton Rubec (Centre for Environmental Stewardship and Conservation), the authors summarized the results of a four-year KBA (Key Biodiversity Areas) survey, concluding that, "The most encouraging finding of the 2005 to 2008 KBA bird surveys is that no bird species had become uprooted in the southern marshes of Iraq despite the drainage and water flow reductions of the previous 25 years." It goes on to say that "What may be Iraq's most important species, the globally endangered Basra Reed Warbler, was found in good numbers in several areas. It was also exciting to discover that the African Darter, Sacred Ibis and Goliath Heron still breed here."

Figure 6.4 The status of the Hammar Marsh in August 2006. The narrow waterways can still be navigated (Photo: Dr Faris Kubba).

BIRDS

The Iraqi Marshes is considered to be one of the most important wetland complexes in the Middle East, if not the world, and are essential for the conservation of many species of birds and other wildlife. Moreover, recent surveys show that the Iraqi wetlands is possibly one of the only recorded sites in the Middle East where the African Sacred Ibis *Threskiornis aethiopicus* and the African Darter *Anhinga rufa* were observed. Avibase provides a bird checklist that includes all bird species found in Iraq, and is based on the best information currently available. It puts the number of species in Iraq at 415, the number of globally threatened species as 14 and introduced species as 2 (based on Clements 6th edition – updated 2008).

Figure 6.5 Photo of flock of migrant birds in the Iraqi wetlands (Courtesy: Canada-Iraq Marshlands Initiative – CIMI).

Perhaps the earliest ornithological work in Iraq took place at the beginning of the twentieth century, largely by amateurs and researchers, many of whom were enlisted in the British army. These early pioneers covered much of Iraq and were able to record for the first time sightings of several important species, both resident and migratory.

The New Eden Master Plan (Volume 1, Book 4 – 2006) says that the late B. E. Allouse was the first Iraqi ornithologist whose first major publication was *Birds of Iraq* in 1962. Allouse also conducted several other studies during the 1950s. He was followed by Khalaf al-Rubaie who published several excellent studies in 1986, 1994, 1995 and 2000.

Rubaie also conducted a four-year field study concentrating on ducks. The results indicated that among other things, some five million birds were being hunted and sold in the local Najaf and Amarah markets.

In 1974, the Basrah Natural History Museum made a judicious decision to establish a field station at al-Shafi village which lies 90 km north of Basrah. This was a conscientious effort by the museum to study waterbirds in the marshes. To facilitate such research, the station was equipped with appropriate nets to assist in bird collection.

Richard Porter, BirdLife International's Conservation Advisor for the region and author of *Birds of the Middle East*, says that "In 1994 BirdLife International published *Important Bird Areas in the Middle East*. This identified 44 Important Bird Areas (IBAs) in Iraq, of which 28 were in the marshlands of southern Iraq." According to Porter, "The marshes hold 18 globally threatened species, as well as three endemic (or near endemic) species – birds that are found practically nowhere else in the world." Figures 6.2 A–H are several examples of birds that can currently be found in the Iraqi wetlands.

There were also a number of bird studies and surveys conducted by various international and national organizations including the International Waterfowl and Wetlands Research Bureau (IWRB), Wetlands International (WI), Avibase, the Key Biodiversity Project (KBP), BirdLife International and Nature Iraq (NI).

The list below shows the globally vulnerable, near-threatened and endemic bird species that have been seen in the Iraqi Marshes since the reflooding in 2003 (as outlined by Richard Porter). Species that breed are marked *; others are migrants/winter visitors.

Species	Latin name	Status
Sociable Lapwing	*Vanellus gregarius*	Critically Endangered
Slender-billed Curlew	*Numenius tenuirostris*	Critically Endangered (last recorded in 1979)
White-headed Duck	*Oxyura leucocephala*	Endangered
Saker Falcon	*Falco cherrug*	Endangered
Basra Reed Warbler*	*Acrocephalus griseldis*	Endangered
Dalmatian Pelican*	*Pelecanus crispus*	Vulnerable
Lesser White-fronted Goose	*Anser erythropus*	Vulnerable
Red-breasted Goose	*Branta ruficollis*	Vulnerable
Marbled Teal*	*Marmaronetta angustirostris*	Vulnerable
Greater Spotted Eagle	*Aquila clanga*	Vulnerable
Imperial Eagle	*Aquila heliaca*	Vulnerable
Lesser Kestrel	*Falco naumanni*	Vulnerable

Ferruginous Duck	*Aythya nyroca*	Near-threatened
Pallid Harrier	*Circus macrourus*	Near-threatened
Red-footed Falcon	*Falco vespertinus*	Near-threatened
Corncrake	*Crex crex*	Near-threatened
European Roller*	*Coracias garrulous*	Near-threatened
Semi-collared Flycatcher	*Ficedula semitorquata*	Near-threatened
Black-winged Platincole	*Glareola nordmanni*	Data deficient

(note: Clements 6th edition – updated 2008 – has the Black-winged Platincole as near-threatened).

Endemic or near-endemic marshland species in Iraq

Basra Reed Warbler*	*Acrocephalus griseldis*
Grey Hypocolius*	*Hypocolius ampelinus*
Iraq Babbler*	*Turdoides altirostris*

Endemic or near-endemic marshland sub-species present in Iraq

Little Grebe*	*Tachypaptus ruficollis*
African Darter*	*Anhinga rufa*
Black Francolin*	*Francolinus francolinus*
White-eared Bulbul*	*Pycnonoyus leucogenys*
Hooded Crow*	*Corvus cornix capellanus*

Some other bird species for which the Iraq marshes are important:
In winter, the marshes provide a refuge for migrant waterbirds, especially when freezing conditions occur further to the north. Other species occur as breeders – these are marked *

Black-necked Grebe	*Podiceps nigricollis*
Pygmy Cormorant*	*Phalacrocorax pygmeus*
White Pelican	*Pelecanus onocrotalus*
Night Heron*	*Nycticorax nycticorax*
Goliath Heron*	*Ardea golith*
Sacred Ibis*	*Threskiornis aethiopicus*
Greater Flamingo	*Phoenicopterus ruber*
White-fronted Goose	*Anser albifrons*
Ruddy Shelduck*	*Tadorna ferruginea*
Teal	*Anas crecca*
Gadwall	*Anas strepera*
Pintail	*Anas acuta*
Shoveler	*Anas clypeata*
Tufted Duck	*Aythya fuligula*
Smew	*Mergus albellus*
Marsh Harrier*	*Circus aeruginosus*
Coot *Fulica**	*atra*
Avocet*	*Recurvirostra avocetta*
Kentish Plover*	*Charadrius alexandrinus*
Little Stint	*Calidris minutus*
Black-tailed Godwit	*Limosa limosa*
Whiskered Tern*	*Chlidonias hybridus*

Figures 6.6A–H A. Ruff (*Philomachus pugnax*) B. Iraqi Babbler (*Turdoides altirostris*) C. Rufous Bush Robin (*Cercotrichas galactotes*) D. Wood Sandpiper (*Tringa glareola*) (Courtesy: Canada-Iraq Marshlands Initiative – CIMI).

The Iraqi Marshes and wetlands provide one of the most important wintering areas for the many migrating waterbirds from Siberia and Northern Europe. They offer migrating birds such as ducks, geese and coots, and wintering birds of prey such as rapters, a resting place, warmth, available food and protection. For many of these species, the marshes are located roughly mid-way along their migration route. In addition, the marshes typically offer a large expanse of water and a safe haven from large predators. They also provide significant plant cover with relatively minor human activity. The period spent in the marshes is therefore devoted mainly to rest and feeding, thus allowing the migrants to better prepare for the breeding and wintering seasons. In fact, out of the total historically recorded species in the Iraqi wetlands, nearly half were dependent upon these marshes for their general feeding grounds and/or as a primary stop on their migration route. This is further confirmed by surveys of the International Waterfowl and Wetlands

E. RedShank (*Tringa totanus*) is one of the more common wintering sandpipers (Courtesy: Canada-Iraq Marshlands Initiative – CIMI).

F. The Marbled Teal (*Marmaronetta angustirostris*) is one of the vulnerable bird species (Photo: Mudhafar Salim).

G. Chiffchaff (*Phylloscopus collybita*) (Courtesy: Canada-Iraq Marshlands Initiative – CIMI).

H. Little Crake (*Porzana parva*) (Courtesy: Canada-Iraq Marshlands Initiative – CIMI).

Research Bureau (IWRB) which found the threatened Dalmatian Pelican (*Pelecanus crispus*) in large numbers and using the marshes as important wintering grounds.

Bird-Breeding in the Marshes
In this respect, the New Eden Master Plan (Volume 1, Book 4 – 2006) says that "Nests differ in their position, location, building methods and materials used depending on the species in question. Nests are necessary for protection and the laying of eggs, besides offering warmth and protection for chicks. Most birds camouflage their nests within growing reeds or branches. Most of the nests are cup-shaped (open from above) but others such as pigeon nests are dome shaped with the entrance from the side. Other species, such as Bee-eaters, Kingfishers, and Sand martins, dig a burrow in the river banks and sand dunes.

In most cases, the females start laying eggs after they finish building the nest, laying one egg daily or every two days. Falcons, buzzards and pigeons lay two eggs, gulls lay three eggs, water hens and ducks lay from 8 to 15 eggs and some time even 20 eggs in one nest. Average incubation time in the nest depends on the species."

It was also noted that during the nesting and breeding phase, the birds tend to conglomerate to form breeding colonies. These colonies are typically located between thick reed settings and away from human activity and movement of large animals. These breeding colonies are generally well camouflaged and their presence is only discernable by the noise and sounds they make. Moreover, it is likely that these sites will be used year after year unless confronted by human danger or predators in which case they will seek another location to breed.

Effects of Marshland Desiccation
According to a recent UNEP report (UNEP in Iraq – Post-Conflict Assessment, Clean-up and Reconstruction), the entire Marsh Arab community suffered huge social and economic upheaval resulting from the marshlands' destruction, and that "The impact on biodiversity has also been catastrophic. Prominent losses include extinction of the endemic smooth-coated otter (*Lutra perspicillata*), and the probable disappearance of two waterbirds: the African darter (*Anhinga rufa*) and the sacred ibis (*Ibis Threskiornis aethiopica*) from the Middle East. A further 66 bird species are considered to be at risk. A wide range of migratory aquatic species were affected, including penaied shrimp that migrate between the Gulf and nursery grounds in the marshlands, causing serious economic consequences for coastal fisheries."

In the same report it says, "The majority of sites important for biodiversity conservation have no protected area status, although many have been recommended for designation. For example, BirdLife International has recognized a total of 42 sites as Important Bird Areas (IBAs). These cover a total area of 35,000km², or about 8 per cent of the country's surface area. However, none benefit from any legal protection from a biodiversity perspective and many of the wetlands, in particular, are critically threatened by flood control, irrigation and drainage projects being carried out in Iraq and in neighboring countries."

By 2006 there were indications that the marshes were providing an improved habitat for the bird populations, although the drought that followed in 2008 and 2009 made it difficult to sustain this improvement. Likewise, the discovery of a large number of breeding and nesting sites was a welcome indication that bird habitat restoration continued, although the numbers of birds were still low compared to earlier natural environment bird counts. Furthermore, the return of winter visitors such as ducks, geese and coots provides another clear indication that the reflooded marshes have managed to retain their previous role as wintering grounds. But it is important to determine the location of important breeding colonies that have been re-established, and how these breeding colonies can be protected.

M. I. Evans, an ecologist, says that the Iraqi Marshlands provide a globally important center of endemism for birds, and is one of only 11 such wetland centers identified internationally. Evans also points out that "Two species, Iraq Babbler *Turdoides altirostris* and Basra Reed Warbler *Acrocephalus griseldis*, breed only in Mesopotamia, as does the majority of the world population of Grey Hypocolius *Hypocolius ampelinus399*,400). A further five species are endemic to Mesopotamia at the subspecific level – Little Grebe *Tachybaptus ruficollis iraquensis*, Darter *Anhinga rufa chantrei*, Black Francolin *Francolinus francolinus arabistanicus*, White-eared Bulbul *Pycnonotus leucotis mesopotamiae* and Hooded Crow *Corvus corone capellanus* – while two subspecies, Zitting Cisticola *Cisticola juncidis neurotica* and Graceful Prinia *Prinia gracilis irakensis*, are near-endemic to Mesopotamia, occurring elsewhere only in the Levant. Clearly, for such a degree of endemism to have developed in a continental (rather than island) setting – and the endemism is apparent in fish, reptiles and mammals too – marshland habitats in the lower Tigris/Euphrates basin (including the Persian Gulf during the lower sea-levels of previous Ice Ages) are likely to be of ancient origin (at least, millions of years old) and are likely to have persisted for a very long period of time up to the present, even during the most extreme hyper-arid climatic phases that are known to have affected the region at the height of the Ice Ages during the last two million years."

FAUNA

Ancient Fauna

The only way available to us to study faunal change and human prehistory is by analyzing the chance remains of ancient people and animals. But as we pointed out earlier, the beginning of the neolithic period witnessed in the Near East the earliest attempts towards the domestication of wild plants and animals. This fundamental change from hunter to farmer started initially in the marginal habitats in Western Asia and then moved to other parts of the world. The cause of this change is still the subject of considerable debate, with some scholars suggesting it was in response to population increase (Clutton-Brock, 1980: pp. 37–40), which in turn necessitated an increase in food requirements. Reed suggests that this may have been "more by trial and error than purposeful forethought" (1969: p. 361).

Animals supplied man with a wide range of raw materials: hides and furs for clothing, matting and shelter construction; skins, horns and organs for containers; sinews for fiber; bones, antlers, teeth and shell for tools and ornaments; fat and dung as fuel, in addition to being his main food source (Cornwall, 1968: Chapter 4). It was also evident that the optimal zone of wild herd animals coincides conveniently onto the wooded, moist and rugged flanks of the Fertile Crescent.

Data on the fauna of Iraq dates back as far as the twelfth millennium BC and includes gazelle, wild goat, sheep, wild cattle, red or roe deer, boar, onager, red fox, wolf, lynx and hedghogs. Of these, the wild goat appears to be the earliest to be recorded. By 7000 BC agriculture provided the primary subsistence of village farmers, who grew einkorn, emmer and barley, but who also kept domesticated sheep and goats. According to Stampfli, domesticated pigs also appear at the time of Jarmo in the northeastern mountain region of Iraq (Stampfli, 1983: pp. 445–47).

Bokonyi distinguishes two main phases of animal domestication, they are: 1. Animal keeping and 2. Animal breeding (1969: p. 219). Furthermore, "Domestication as a process involves three main factors: the man who carries it out, the wild animal that has been domesticated, and the domesticated animal that is the result." (Ibid, 1969: p. 220).

With the passage of time, a number of different species of cattle, became commonly known in Mesopotamia. First, there was "*Bos primigenius*" which were the ancestors of the oxen of modern Iraq. There were also the '*Bos bubalus*' which originated in India/Pakistan, reaching Mesopotamia at the time of the Akkadian dynasty, and inhabited the plateau; it was the ancestor of the buffalo, which populated the swamp areas of the south. Another variety now extinct was the bison, which probably died out at the beginning of the historic period, but featured frequently in Assyrian reliefs (Van Buren, 1949: p. 123).

With the development of larger scale agriculture in the lower Mesopotamian plain, farm help animals such as donkeys, oxen, etc., were used extensively for hauling, carrying and plowing. During the third millennium BC the wild ass was used a great deal for military purposes and herds of these were to be found roaming the countryside. These were later replaced by the horse which first appeared during the first Babylonian dynasty and was imported from Asia Minor, Anatolia and northern Iran. The camel was originally introduced into Mesopotamia from the Arabian Desert, but it was not widely used until the middle of the first millennium BC.

Mammals

Mammals are pivotal components of the overall marshland ecosystem, usually herbivores and carnivores. In ancient Mesopotamia, the marshlands contained a great diversity of mammals, including lions (*Panthera leo*), fallow deer and the Goitered gazelle (*Gazella subgutturosa*). However, by the twentieth century, few large mammals remained, especially after the introduction of the rifle during the First World War. Of the many mammals that inhabited the wetlands, only the deer and gazelle were killed for food by the marsh dwellers. Otters were generally killed for their fur as well as to reduce competition for fish (Figure 6.9).

Figure 6.7 Water Buffalo in the Iraqi wetlands (Courtesy: Canada-Iraq Marshlands Initiative – CIMI).

During the 1950s, Gavin Maxwell observed, "The water buffaloes (Figure 6.7) are by far the most important unit in the marshman's economy, and much of the family's life revolves around them." (Maxwell, 1957: p.62). Maxwell also states that there is evidence to suggest that these animals were first introduced into Mesopotamia in about 3500 BC, although they may have been wild in the marshes prior to domestication (Ibid, 1957).

"Wild boar (*Sus scrofa*) were larger than some varieties known elsewhere. They could grow as tall as 1 m at the shoulder and sported formidable, razor-sharp tusks. Quite a few local inhabitants bore sizable scars; others died of their wounds." (Ochsenschlager, 2004: pp. 9–10). For this reason and because the wild boar posed a major threat to the marsh dwellers' crops, it was considered a primary enemy. And even though wild boar meat was edible, Islamic prohibition prevented Muslims from eating pork. Although wild boar was previously the most common mammal in the marshes, their numbers have witnessed a dramatic decline in recent years.

Hassan Partow, a Senior Program Officer with UNEP, and expert on the Iraqi Marshlands, adds, "Three globally-threatened species of mammals inhabit the marshes. These are the Grey Wolf (*Canis lupus*), the Long-fingered Bat (*Myotis capaccinii*) and a subspecies of the Smooth-coated Otter (*Lutra perspeicillata - maxwelli*) which is endemic to the marshes. Other large animals, notably the Honey Badger, Striped Hyena, Jungle Cat, Goitered Gazelle and Indian Crested Porcupine have been reported in the marsh area. All had become rare by the 1980s and are now thought to be locally extinct. Other frequently-sighted mammals include the Small Indian Mongoose, the Asiatic Jackal and the Red Fox. Common reptiles in the marshes include the Caspian Terrapin, a soft-shell turtle, and a variety of snakes." (Partow, UNEP, 2001; Maltby, 1994).

A number of small mammals were also recorded in and around the marshes including the short-tailed Bandicoot (*Nesokia indica*), which represents the most common rodent found in the wetlands, and an endemic species of gerbil (*Gerbillus mesopotamicus*). Also recorded were hedgehogs, three species of shrews, several species of insectivorous bats, and jerboas.

Prior to the drainage of the marshes, it was believed that some 40 mammals were thought to inhabit them. However, little reliable data is currently available regarding the present status of mammals in the Iraqi Marshlands, although the International Union for Conservation of Nature (IUCN) wildlife species has put together a list for Iraq which also includes reptiles and amphibians, such as toads (*Bufo viridis*), tree frogs (*Hyla arborea*), the marsh frogs (*Rana ridibunda)* and the edible frogs. It has recently been noted that frogs have returned in great numbers in the reflooded marshes, but these returned species and their level have yet to be identified.

Figure 6.8 This sub-species of the endemic smooth-coated otter is now considered extinct (Photo by Gavin Maxwell in Young, 1977).

Zooplankton
There were recorded differences in the number of zooplankton individuals at the various monitoring stations. The predominant recorded orders of zooplankton populations in the Iraqi Marshlands are Rotifera, Copepoda, Cladocera and free Nematode. The highest recorded zooplankton counts were observed to be in the spring, reflecting the same trend as before marsh desiccation.

Invertebrates
There is little recorded documentation of the rich invertebrate fauna of the marshes. Recorded dragonflies include species such as *Brachythemis fuscopalliata*, which is considered to be near-endemic to the Tigris/Euphrates basin. Also recorded were species of dytiscid water beetle (*Dytiscidae*), the gyrinid beetle (*Gyrinidae*) and nearly 40 butterfly species (including *skippers Hesperidae*).

Michael Evans says that, "Invertebrate species endemic to the marshes are or were likely to exist, with distributions restricted to the marshes and physiology dependent on the marshes' continued existence, but none are well documented at present – they are or were likely to be more frequent among non-flying groups of invertebrates. With the near-complete destruction of the marshes, any such species would now be critically endangered."

Although little appears to be known about the atyid shrimps of Iraq, other than that two species of Atyidae have been found in Shatt al-Arab and Karmat Ali, Evans also observed that, "The commercial penaeid shrimp *Metapenaeus affinis* was abundant (with individuals up to 125 mm total length) at its nursery grounds in the inland waters of Iraq, mainly in the slightly brackish Haur al Hammar..." Moreover, Evans considers the discharge of the Shatt al-Arab may be an important factor in regulating recruitment, and that spawning at sea typically appears to occur immediately after emigration (Evans, 2001).

AMPHIBIANS AND REPTILES

Drainage and desiccation of the marshes by Saddam Hussein obviously had a disastrous effect on marsh amphibians and reptiles, including frogs, salamanders, the soft-shelled turtle and water snakes, as they are all dependent on these water bodies for survival. Moreover, amphibians and reptiles are a crucial components of the ecosystem and serve numerous functions. This includes the conversion of the material that tadpoles feed on (e.g., algae) into protein, fat, etc., that are consumed by other marshland fauna higher in the food chain. This is followed by the tadpoles developing into frogs which feed on various insects which helps maintain their natural equilibrium. The frogs in turn become prey for birds, reptiles and mammals.

Reptiles also serve many functions within the wetland ecosystem. Among the common reptiles listed by the IUCN recorded in the Iraqi Marshes are the Caspian terrapin (*Clemmys caspia*), a soft-shell turtle (*Trionyx euphraticus*), geckos of the genus *Hemidactylus*, two species of skinks (*Mabuya aurata* and *M. vittata*), and a variety of snakes including the spotted sand boa (*Eryx jaculus*), tessellated water snake (*Natrix tessellata*) and gray's desert racer (*Coluber ventromaculatus*).

Figure 6.9 The ubiquitous marsh frog (*Rana ridibunda*) is the most common amphibian species in the Iraqi Marshlands (Courtesy: Canada-Iraq Marshlands Initiative – CIMI).

Figure 6.10 Eels recorded in the al-Adheim Marshlands of Iraq (Courtesy: Canada-Iraq Marshlands Initiative – CIMI).

To this day, there is a scarcity of recorded information on the availablity of amphibians and reptiles in the Iraqi Marshlands (Scott, 1995). There is also a sparsity of knowledge of species' taxonomy and distribution, and what information does exist remains incomplete.

Evans says that most of the reptile species which may occur in southeastern Iraq are desert-adapted and relatively widespread in the Near or Middle East, but "a number have more restricted ranges, centered on the Tigris/Euphrates lowlands in southern Iraq: the large, spiny-tailed lizard *Uromastyx loricatus*, the as-yet unnamed local population of the lizard *Mesalina brevirostris*, the skink subspecies *Mabuya aurata septemtaeniata*, the snake subspecies *Telescopus tessellatus martini*, and the soft-shelled turtle *Rafetus euphraticus*. The last-mentioned species is clearly the most dependent on wetland habitat. It occurs widely in the Tigris/Euphrates Rivers and their major tributaries, but the bulk of its population (numerically) probably lay within the marshes, and it was considered globally threatened for this reason."

FISH

General

There is an urgent need to gather baseline data for reptile and amphibian species in the Iraqi Marshlands. Studies conducted to date have been mostly meager and sporadic and much of the information collected is based more on personal observation and random investigations than on systematic study or scientific evaluation.

The desiccation of the marshes in the 1990s fundamentally transformed the basic structure of the fish community caused mainly by the harsh environment that emanated during this period resulting from altering the largely primary production of aquatic plants and phytoplankton, prompting changes in the secondary productivity of zooplankton. "The dominant species previously were *B. sharpeyi*, *C. carpio*, and *B. luteus* while *S. triostegus* came fourth in ranking. After desiccation *C. carassius*, *L. abu*, and *Barbus lutus* dominated in number and *S. triostegus* dominated in weight. There was also an increase in small noncommercial species such as *Acanthobrama spp.* and *Alburnus spp.*" (Evans, 2001).

The Iraqi wetlands provide natural spawning grounds, nurseries and feeding places for fish. The availability of adequate food resources therefore facilitates the growth of fish in the Iraqi Marshes as compared with other Iraqi water bodies (Mohamed and Ali, 1992).

Michael Evans says that "Fish were always an important component in the diet of the Marsh Dwellers. Favored food-fish species that were known or likely to occur in the marshes were the barbells *Barbus* spp. – especially shabbout *Barbus grypus* (up to 200 cm/100 kg) and bunni *Barbus sharpeyi*, both known to be of major importance to the Marsh Dwellers – as well as *Chondrostoma regium* (up to 40 cm/1 kg), *Mystus pelusius* (up to 30 cm), *Sillago sihama* (up to 30 cm), *Acanthopagrus berda* (up to 45 cm) and *Eleutheronema tetradactylum* (up to 180 cm).

Until recently, most fish were caught by spearing – an efficient and effective method if the water is clear – but most Marsh Dwellers latterly used nets to improve their catch for export to Basra and Baghdad. Annual per capita fish consumption in Iraq between 1984 and 1986 averaged about 2.5 kg and the total annual catch from the marshes was more than 14,000 tons during this period, providing 60% of the national fish catch (including marine species)." (Evans, 2001). Indeed, in earlier times, the marshes were characterized by their substantial fish harvests which were transported (often by boat) to the local markets of southern Iraq, reaching Baghdad and beyond (Ibid, 2001).

Figure 6.11 Fish from North Hammar Marsh (Photo: Jasim al-Asadi).

Figure 6.12 Fish from Iraqi Marshlands (Courtesy: Canada-Iraq Marshlands Initiative – CIMI).

The Current Status of Fish

Following more than a decade of desiccation and the diversion of the Tigris and Euphrates waters from the marshes of southern Iraq, it is not surprising that marsh fish assemblages have been significantly altered. The disappearance of aquatic plants because of the shrinkage of the marshes led to the dominance of predator fish (*S.triostegus* & *A.vorax*) and the loss in range, cover and food for species like *Barbus spp.* that became easy prey to the fishermen and other predators.

Today's available data tends to indicate that the marsh fish assemblages are generally dominated (numerically) by *B. lateus, Carassius carassius, L. abu, A. vorax* and, by weight, *S. triostegus*, with varying percentages for each marsh. Estuarine and marine species occur in lower numbers. It has been observed that in general the fish caught are relatively small and have not reached their size potential as compared with the maximum lengths recorded previously, except perhaps for *S. triostegus*. In addition, it should be noted that several unsustainable fishing practices are now being used by some parts of the marshes including electroshocking of fish.

There remains rather limited recorded data on fish diversity in Iraqi wetlands. According to the World Resources Institute, the combined Euphrates and Tigris watershed supports some 71 native fish species, and a further 21 introduced species many of which are endemic to the basin, and of which none of these are shown to be under threat. Also according to USAID, "Native species exhibited higher abundances compared to migratory and alien species. Some alien species (introduced) with high commercial value, like carp (*C. carpio*) and grass carp (*C. idellus*), and the marine migratory fish sabour (*T. ilish*) had high abundances as well." (USAID: 2006).

"Particularly vulnerable to ecological changes in the marshes are those species apparently endemic to the marshes themselves (at least one barbel species, the bunni *Barbus sharpeyi*) or to the broader Tigris/Euphrates basin (at least six or seven of the 23 endemics are likely to occur in the lower reaches of the river), and those species that spawn mainly in the marshes or brackish/estuarial waters (the endemic giant catfish *Silurus glanis* and *S. triostegus*, and the anadromous Hilsa shad *Tenualosa ilisha* and pomphret *Pampus argenteus*). The two cave-fish species that occur in the Iraqi portion of the basin are considered globally threatened266, although this should be reviewed, given the drastic hydrological changes that have been perpetrated in recent years." (Evans, 2001).

Also according to Evans, The Tigris/Euphrates basin is a center of speciation, and contains over 50 native primary freshwater fish species (consisting of 7 families). Of the 50, nearly half (23 species) are endemic to the basin

– 12 of which are members of the carp family (Cyprinidae) and two are native secondary freshwater fish (*Aphanius* spp.). However, no definitive list has been compiled of the many species that occur in the Iraqi Marshlands (Evans, 2001).

After the fall of Saddam Hussein' government in 2003, we see a dramatic revival of fish farms in the southern Iraqi provinces. This is being implemented with assistance from the American Department of Defense, NGOs and private enterprise. These new fish farms have the potential to add thousands of direct and indirect local employment opportunities to the region. There were once thousands of fish farms operating in Iraq, but the wars reduced that figure significantly. However, today, the fish farming industry is expanding and is becoming increasingly important to Iraq's economy. Traditionally, fishing was the main economic livelihood for a number of low-status tribes, and subsistence fishing was practiced widely by these tribes, and for whom fish was a major food item.

However, Marsh Arabs are gradually moving away from fishing as the primary livelihood towards agriculture and increasing their number of cattle and sheep, and water buffalo, as sources of dairy products for home use and sale. Moreover, livestock is becoming increasingly important in the marsh economy and has already outpaced fishing as a desirable livelihood.

It is sad that the marshes have started to shrink again due to continuous drought and intensive dam construction and irrigation schemes upstream in Turkey, Syria and Iran. However, it would be prudent to collect more data before making a final judgment as to whether the restoration process is proceeding in a satisfactory manner during the coming years. Moreover, continuous monitoring and data collection of the ecological and biological situation is needed to make a meaningful assessment of the biodiversity of the Iraqi wetlands ecosystem.

TRANSBOUNDARY ISSUES

Joseph Dellapenna, an expert on international water rights and transboundary issues, says, "International law is in many respects still a relatively primitive legal system; that is, a system lacking centralized institutional structures for law-making and law-enforcing." (Dellapenna, 2001: p. 223). This situation is exacerbated by the complexity of the current transboundary issues which are highlighted by competing needs for what water is available.

There were many agreements between the various interested parties, including Britain and France during the mandate, between Turkey and France and between Iraq and its neighbors: Turkey, Syria and Iran. However, these agreements were vague and unenforceable.

Because of drought and dam building, the Iraqi wetlands find themselves decidedly caught up in the middle of regional water scarcity. Being located at the bottom of the water flow of the Euphrates and Tigris Rivers from Turkey, Syria and Iran means there would be very little water left prior to it draining into the Arabian Gulf. This transboundary issue is further aggravated by the proposed dyke to bisect the Hawaiza Marshes on the boundary line dividing Iran and Iraq, which creates a critical transboundary issue because this dyke would further reduce the flow of water into the marshlands on the Iraqi side and would have a very negative impact on the existing ecosystem. Dellapenna also says that Iraq faces a real possibility of a near exhaustion of the Euphrates as a source of water by Turkey and Syria.

Iran has displayed an interest in exploring a transboundary approach to the conservation of the al-Hawaiza/al-Azim marshes straddling the Iran–Iraq border, and in this regard has initiated a proposal to declare the remaining marshlands a wetland of international importance under the Ramsar Convention on Wetlands. Likewise, Iraq on 17 October 2007, deposited with the Director-General its instrument of accession to the Convention on Wetlands as Waterfowl

Figure 6.13 Tigris-Euphrates Major Water Projects - Not to scale (Based on: AMAR International Charitable Foundation 2001 – T. Naff & G. Hanna).

Habitat adopted at Ramsar in 1971 and as amended in 1982 and 1987. This means that the wetland named "Marais d'Hawizeh" has been designated by Iraq for inclusion in the List of Wetlands of International Importance. And in accordance with Article 10(2), the Convention entered this into force with respect to Iraq on 17 February 2008.

Most scientists agree that to fully restore the Iraqi wetlands to its past glory will require a long-term effort that will necessitate far more than just dismantling Saddam Hussein's dams to succeed. It will also require solutions to the many tough regional disputes with Turkey, Syria and Iran which have been at a stalemate and which currently limit the amount of water available in Iraq's two great rivers — the Tigris and Euphrates — for refilling its wetlands. Pekka Haavisto, chairman of the Iraq Task Force of the United Nations Environment Program (UNEP) in Geneva, says, "by the most optimistic assessments — Iraq may be able to obtain enough water only to refill about one-third of its former wetlands."

Finally, if no agreement with Iraq's neighbors is reached, the destruction of the historic Mesopotamian wetlands, which is a region of such global importance for biodiversity and home to the Marsh Arabs and Ma'dan, will go down in history as one of the twentieth century's major ecocides and a most thoughtless environmental disaster.

Figure 6.14 Photo of a typical marsh landscape consisting of huts built on artificial floating islands by enclosing a piece of swamp, and filling it in with reeds and mud (H Partow, UNEP 2001).

7

DESIGN PRINCIPLES

Sam A.A. Kubba

GENERAL OVERVIEW

Prior to attempting to reconstruct ancient buildings and spaces, one must be aware of how these structures or spaces were used and how society in general behaved in them. In ancient societies, as is the case today, the size of rooms and enclosed spaces were determined by several factors. These include the ability of the builder to roof the space, i.e., the room must not be too large to be roofed, and also on social-motivational factors. How close physically people want to be to each other depends on the closeness of their social relationship as well as their cultural background. People of different cultures inhabit different sensory worlds. For example, Arabs in general make more use of olfaction and touch than the British or Germans. Likewise, they do not interpret their sensory data in the same way that the British or Germans do nor do they combine them in the same way (Hall, 1969). It is even possible, if not probable, that certain sections of the house (known as 'territories'), as well as temples, were personalized – e.g. cooking areas, etc.

Logic has it that humans have specific spatial needs. Winston Churchill's famous statement, "We shape our buildings and afterwards our buildings shape us", certainly applied to the ancients. There are no precise calculations on the amount of information the eyes and ears gather in contrast to the other senses, nor in fact whether over the years this has varied, due to the changing complexities of society. But there is a great difference in both the type and the amount of information that the two receptor systems can process. What is not known technically is the effect of incongruity between visual and auditory space, although it is possible that early man's auditory senses were superior by the very fact that he relied on them more heavily for his very survival (this also applies to his other senses).

ANCIENT MEASUREMENT

In order to conduct foreign trade and build elaborate structures such as temples, ziggurats and palaces, the ancients required a uniform system of measurement, a more permanent standard reference. Dilke states the point quite clearly when he says, "The countries of the Tigris and Euphrates had much foreign trade with other areas, exchanging items such as spices, jewels and silks from the East for minerals or timber from the West." (Dilke, 1987).

This international trade was dependent on recognized units of weight, volume, area and length. Jens Hoyrup on the Sumerian origin of mathematics (and therefore measurement) states, "As so many other elements of our modern culture, mathematics came into being for the first time in Sumer, in southern Mesopotamia. This happened in connection with the development of writing, around 3000 BC. Outlines of pre-Sumerian temple buildings were laid out in advance by strings and thus by the use of geometry before the development of the earliest script; metrological systems for lengths and probably even for capacities, used seemingly in connection with arithmetical calculations, were employed before the rise of Sumerian civilization." (Fauvel & Gray, 1987: p. 44).

Thus the Mesopotamians invented a system of linear measurement over 6,000 years ago as a prerequisite for the construction of the many monumental buildings the new epoch demanded, and that is easily recognizable as ancestral to our own imperial system (Kubba, 1990). It was based upon parts of the body (Figure 7.1).

But just as a system of linear measurement was invented out of an urgent necessity to assist in the design and construction of temples, etc., so too it can be said that writing was invented out of a dire need to control trade and the economy. A controlling device was needed since human memory could not cope with the increasing trade figures (Nissen, 1986). It should be emphasized, however, that the ancients possibly possessed a memory ability far superior to that of the average person today, mainly because they relied on their memory much more heavily than people do today. Moreover, the ancients may have had specialist "accountants", whose job it was to memorize certain transactions, just as in many parts of the Islamic world today we find children being trained to commit the whole Koran to memory. It is also a well known fact that blind people, for example, develop their other senses to compensate for their blindness.

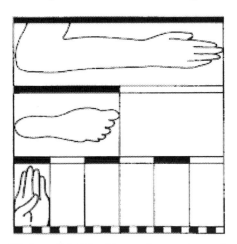

Figure 7.1 The Sumerian system of linear measurement was based on parts of the body.

And while using "tokens" as at Abada (which is in the Hamrin region northeast of Baghdad) and elsewhere may have been one method to "keep track of the economy", it seems logical to suppose, in view of the substantial evidence of the varied complex geometric principles utilized during the Ubaid period, for example (but even as early as Tell es-Sawwan), in surveying as well as in the design and construction of temples and palaces, that some form of writing was invariably in use – perhaps in pictorial form. It may have been initially applied on material that was perishable such as skins or wood, or it could have been painted on flat slabs of terracotta, which have been misinterpreted by archaeologists. Figure 7.2 is a diagram illustrating the method used by the ancient Mesopotamians to achieve 90-degree angles when laying out buildings and temples, that is based on the 3:4:5 triangle principle .

The Sumerian system of linear measurement was commonly used throughout the Near East with slight variations, and consisted of a cubit of 49.5 cm (Dilke, 1987: p. 25), measured from the elbow to the tip of the middle finger; the span from the tip of the little finger to the thumb of an outstretched hand; the palm usually measured across the knuckles; the finger width; and the foot. Moreover, the smaller units – spans, palms, finger widths and feet, were usually related as subdivisions of the cubit (Figure 7.3).

A basalt statue of Gudea, King of Lagash, dating from *c*. 2170 BC has a scale-bar inscribed on it, and in the king's lap is a plan of a building incised on stone (Figure 7.4). This, with other evidence, shows that the Sumerian cubit was usually divided into 30 digits or fingers, each finger being 1.65 cm. The foot, which may not have been used extensively as a unit of measurement, was equal to twelve finger widths. Another unit of measurement sometimes used, particularly for measuring the area of houses is the Sar, which is approximately 36 sq. m.

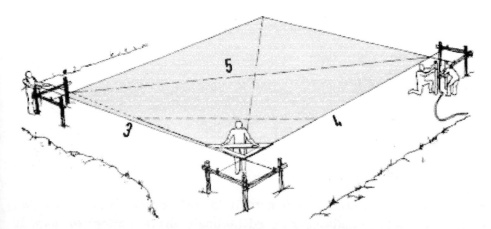

Figure 7.2 Ancient method for laying out buildings and temples.

It is abundantly clear that to construct some of the buildings of the Ubaid period, for example, the architects must have been extremely proficient in the use of mathematics and geometry and must have utilized a formal system of linear measurement.

Old Babylonian texts were found at Tell Haddad which, although from a much later period in time, are nevertheless relevant to our understanding of early measurement. They may have belonged to a library, and are quite illuminating (al-Rawi and Roaf, 1984: p. 178). The tablets show that the Old Babylonians used a sexagesimal system. Several of the mathematical problems cited are related directly and indirectly to building materials and quantities. They also show (Ibid: p. 178) that:

1 Suppam	=	5 Gar		
1 Gar	=	2 Reed	=	Approx. 6m.
1 Gar	=	12 Cubit (Kus)		
	=	12 x 30 Fingers	=	Approx. 6m.
1 Cubit	=	30 Fingers (Ubanum)	=	49.5cm.

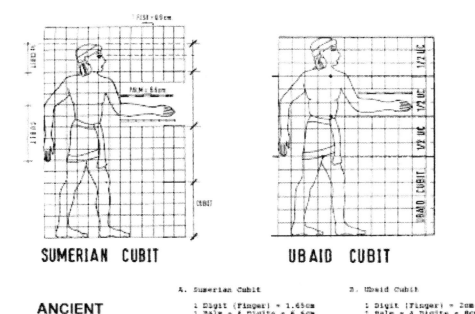

SUMERIAN CUBIT   UBAID CUBIT

ANCIENT
MEASUREMENT
(CONJECTURAL)

A. Sumerian Cubit
1 Digit (Finger) = 1.65cm
1 Palm = 4 Digits = 6.6cm
1 Fist = 1.33 Palms = 9.9cm
= 1 square
30 Digits (Fingers) = 1 Cubit
=49.5cm

B. Ubaid Cubit
1 Digit (Finger) = 2cm
1 Palm = 4 Digits = 8cm
1 Fist = 1.5 Palm = 12cm
= 1 square
36 Digits = 1 Cubit = 72cm
= 6 squares

Figure 7.3 Ancient linear measurements used in Mesopotamia. The use of the Ubaid cubit was recently discovered by analyzing a number of ancient Mesopotamian temples.

Figure 7.4 A basalt statue of Gudea, king of Lagash, dating from *c.* 2170 BC with a plan of a building in the king's lap.

Today, we have basically two major systems of measurement: the Imperial system based on feet and inches (as used in the United States) and the Metric system which was developed much later, using meters and centimeters (widely used in Europe) and which has completely displaced the cubit system. However, it is interesting to note that the cubit (*dhiraa'*) and hand span (*shibir*) measurement system is still being used in parts of southern Iraq, particularly in the marsh region to build the reed houses among other things (Ochsenschlager, 2004: pp. 152–153).

FUNCTIONAL ASPECTS (INTERNAL PLANNING)

In order to analyze the way ancient builders designed and constructed their buildings and the weight they placed on different aspects of design, we need to undertake a "post mortem" of the society or culture under analysis. To do this satisfactorily, it is necessary that we comprehend as many facets of their culture as possible, but in particular the social, religious and technological aspects. Otherwise, our findings will by necessity be flawed.

AESTHETIC ASPECTS

Proportion: Proportion is, in a sense, a composition of parts of an element or elements. It refers to the mutual relationship of these parts to the whole. Many people, however, do not differentiate between proportion and scale, and use the two interchangeably. When we think of proportion, we think of good and bad. When we think of scale, we imply large or small. Scale generally refers to the human being as a unit of measurement or to a part of an element as related to another part or to the whole. Moreover, a structure may be of beautiful proportions in itself, yet out of scale with its surroundings. An example of this is the ancient ziggurats of Babylon which were the tallest buildings of ancient Mesopotamia (Figure 7.5).

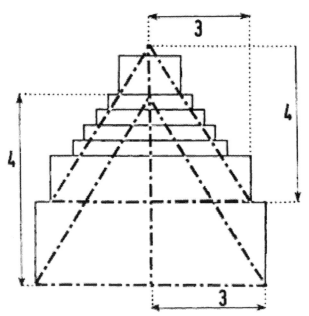

Figure 7.5 Ziggurat of Babylon as reconstructed by Stecchini. The ziggurat was the tallest buildings in ancient Mesopotamia. We also see the proportions that were considered desirable by the ancients in temple-building.

The Ubaid builders of southern Mesopotamia displayed an astonishing understanding of proportion and geometric principles in their architecture, as witnessed at Eridu and Queili. Moreover, the monumental buildings of this period appear to show an unusual grasp of harmonic proportions, the golden section and triangle, the "Pythagorean" triangle (an unfortunate misnomer, since it was in use in Mesopotamia nearly 4,000 years before Pythagoras was born, and geometric progressions. The implications of this are far reaching. This undoubtedly indicates that some form of writing, not merely numeric notation as Oates and Jasim (Jasim & Oates, 1986) are inclined to suggest, was in existence some 1,000 years earlier than hitherto supposed. As yet, this is still conjectural, but from the circumstantial evidence already existing, it seems inevitable that Mesopotamian history will be pushed back many centuries once the fourth and fifth millennium become better documented. The author (Kubba, 1990) has previously published a detailed synthesis of the use of geometric principles in Mesopotamian architecture during the Ubaid period.

Sumerians ($c.3000$ BC) found proportions in the ratio of 3:4 to be pleasing, while the early Greeks found that rectangles with dimensions in the ratio of 2:3, 3:5 and 5:8 were most pleasing (Kubba, 2003). Thus, it is difficult to define proportion in absolute terms since there are no precise guidelines, and each society has its own concept of beauty and good proportions. Value judgments that are applied to the evaluation of what is beautiful and what is not, varies considerably from person to person and from culture to culture. It is therefore probably an intuitive judgment and is inherent in the practice of perception.

Balance and equilibrium appear to be at the root of this sense of proportion. The ancient builders in Mesopotamia appear to have been aware of this, especially from the Ubaid period onwards (although at Tell es-Sawwan, an acute awareness of proportion and balance was also exhibited), and when they designed a temple or palace, they did so in relation to its surroundings.

But being intuitive in nature presents several problems, particularly when trying to evaluate ancient spaces and forms, since it is easily affected by environmental and cultural influences. For example, the proportions of a room are greatly affected by lighting, shadow placement and color. The eye is attracted to the light source and sets up an independent movement of its own. In the same space, a dark floor and light ceiling give a totally different spatial perception than a light floor and dark ceiling. Likewise, the visual perception is significantly altered by the introduction of vertical lines in a building such as the use of pilasters, recessing and buttressing (Figure 7.6) and this is discussed in greater detail in Chapter 9.

Scale: Scale is a relative quality. It is the relation of the size of an element to that of another element within the same perceived space. When dealing with furniture, interior design and architecture, the human being is the unit of measurement and scale is the relation of an element size to that of an average human being. The ancients knew that strong-colored, large-patterned and coarse-textured objects appeared larger than objects of soft, light colors, small patterns and smooth textures, and they utilized this fact to great effect, particularly in their temples as can be seen from the many seals indicating the elaborate patterns on buildings, and the strong colors – especially red, black and white – as seen from the traces found on wall fragments.

The ancient Mesopotamian lacked aesthetic subtlety; everything he did, he did for maximum effect. He lived in constant contradiction – he was humble for himself, yet he built monumental edifices for his god and his king. The gates of the temple were monumental, yet openings in dwellings were usually small. It also appears that the ancient's concept of scale differed from that of today; this is probably due chiefly to cultural differences, although security must likewise have been a pivotal factor.

Figure 7.6 A reed *mudhif* interior showing the effect of rising vertical lines (Photo: Jasim al -Asadi).

It was in monumental design (particularly from the Ubaid period onwards), that the Mesopotamian builder was most at home. By controlling the size of a space, he directly controlled the effect of that space on the statue gods, the furniture and human beings when they were present. His judicious use of pilasters and buttresses emphasized the verticality of his buildings and thereby added to the monumental effect.

Balance: When discussing balance, we are mainly concerned with visual weights (as opposed to actual weights), coordinated in such a way as to create a sense of equilibrium. The equilibrium of the temple interior changed constantly during the day due to several factors – the amount of sun entering different parts of the temple at different times of the day; the use of artificial light (probably bitumen or oil lamps); the presence of people moving or praying or the 'priest' giving a sermon. In the marshes, light also played a significant role as can be seen from the interior of a modern *mudhif* (Figure 7.7).

The ancients used three types of balance in their designs: 1. Symmetrical (sometimes referred to as formal) balance. This they often used in the placement of a prominent architectural feature such as a main gateway or door, as well as the placement of the altar. It is achieved when identical elements are arranged similarly on either side of an imaginary centre line. Symmetrical balance is used often to achieve or suggest a feeling of repose and dignity. A good example of symmetrical balance can be found in the contemporary (and ancient) Marsh Arab *mudhif,* where the door is placed in the center of the front facade (Figure 7.10). 2. Asymmetrical (Informal) balance. Here, we find visual weights are equal but not identical, such as at the Eridu Temple in Level IX. This type of optical balance or equilibrium is much more casual, subtle and interesting than its symmetrical counter-part, but also requires greater skill to achieve. To achieve asymmetrical balance, the ancients carefully juxtaposed the various elements of different weights and arranged them around a balancing point or fulcrum. But because of its informal nature, asymmetrical balance was not as widely used as symmetrical balance. 3. Occasionally, radial balance was used. As its name implies, it is based on a circular arrangement. All elements of the design radiate from or around a central point of focus. Typical examples are found on many of the pottery designs found in ancient Mesopotamia.

Emphasis: Emphasis is basically the principle of dominance and subordination. This concept (sometimes referred to as "the centre of interest") is used by the designer to focus attention on a particular area or object in a given design. When

Figure 7.7 A contemporary reed *mudhif* interior from the central marshes showing a door opening symmetrically placed with seating on either side, thereby increasing the emphasis of centrality (Photo: Mudhafar Salim).

the Mesopotamian architect/builder wanted to give the altar or god a feeling of prominence, he would place great emphasis on it. It became a dominant feature. At the same time, he would subordinate the other elements surrounding it, such as the walls, openings, ceiling and furnishings. An excellent example of this can be seen at the Eanna sanctuary at Uruk, Level V-IVb, in the Limestone Temple. A typical example of emphasizing an entrance can be found at the Innin Temple of Karaindash at Uruk which is Kassite in design. The recesses in the facade lead the eye to the entrance, thereby making it appear more important. Emphasis can also be achieved by raising a building or object as was done with the 'White Temple' at Uruk and the Eridu temples, levels VII and VI, or by the provision of a straight staircase as in the ziggurat of Ur-Nammu at Ur.

By having only one dominant element, with all the others subordinate, the worshipper got a feeling of unity and order. The ancient designer knew that emphasis was a vital element to the success of the temple, and so he arranged the entrances to the temples and palaces so that you immediately can tell where the most important feature lies, i.e., where the altar is or the throne room, etc., either by direct entry or via a "bent entry". Entrances were also emphasized by flanking them with sculpture such as lions or temple furniture. Emphasis may also have been achieved by allowing light to enter a high opening so that at certain times of the day, the sun's rays would "shine" on the god.

Unity & Harmony: Harmony is achieved when the sum total of all the other design principles are coordinated individually and collectively. Unity and discord was what the ancient Mesopotamian was all about. In nature, they found mostly unity; in man-made objects, mostly discord. Every design needed a unifying theme to hold it together, and the Mesopotamian builder/designer did this with extraordinary skill. The temples were sparsely furnished to add to the feeling of monumentality and awe. Mortal man was led carefully and slowly to the altar.

The ancient Mesopotamian builder achieved unity and harmony in his buildings in a number of ways: 1. He had a central theme and consistency of style throughout, particularly in the temples, palaces and *mudhifs* (e.g., use of buttresses, plan layout, etc.). 2. He used the element of repetition and uniformity. He used what simple materials were available to him – reed, and mud or mud brick which he plastered and painted. He also used buttresses to great effect. 3. He almost always had a strong focal point. In the temples this was usually the altar, in the palace it was the courtyard, etc. In the town it was temple or ziggurat. 4. Finally, the ancient builder often used harmonic proportions in his monumental buildings.

Rhythm: Rhythm is the repetition of an element in a regular sequence; it directs the eye and helps it to move about a space. Rhythm is essentially a disciplined movement and can be seen in the interior of a typical marsh dweller *mudhif* (Figure 7.7).

1. Rhythm created by repetition is the most common and can be seen everywhere in ancient Mesopotamia. It can be seen in the placement of buttresses (Eridu, Tell Harmal), the repetition of geometric shapes or patterns such as found in pottery and the mosaic cone patterns of Uruk Temples (Figure 7. 8) and the grooves and recesses in the facades of important structures such as temples. It can also be found in many of the ancient pottery designs. This type of rhythm is passive and had to be handled sensitively to avoid becoming boring.

2. Rhythm by alternation or rhythm by line is the regular, undulating and continuous flow of a line or space. This is seen in the design of friezes, wall murals and pottery, as well as in the use of cone mosaics.

3. Rhythm by radiation is created when an object's lines or motifs extend outward from a central axis, as for example in the circular structure discovered at Tell Razuk, and in most pottery designs.
4. A fourth type of rhythm is progressive rhythm, which was only occasionally used. It entails an ordered, gradual change in the size, direction or color of an object or space. It is more subtle, dynamic and inventive than simple repetition and rhythm is achieved by succession in size and direction. Occasionally, a building will display more than one type of rhythm.

Contrast: From the beginning of the Halaf period, contrast is used very effectively to enhance the pottery and buildings of the period. The Halaf artist learned to use color contrast (particularly red and black) and form contrast (the dome) with great virtuosity. To the Sumerians, contrast was an essential ingredient in the design of their exteriors and interiors, particularly during the Ubaid and Uruk periods. We find contrast of forms in the temples of Level XIII at the Mosaic cone temples of Uruk and Ubaid.

Contrast was achieved by the juxtaposition of two or more dissimilar or opposing elements or qualities, e.g., light-colored object set against a dark wall, or a circular object such as a dome in a square or rectangular space. The ancients used different types of contrast to achieve their goal. For example, they used horizontal lines versus vertical or diagonal lines or straight lines versus curved lines. The ancients appear to have been unconsciously fond of contrasting forms with one another, such as the use of a circular tholos with a rectangular antechamber.

MAJOR DESIGN ELEMENTS

Space: Space is to design what a foundation is to a building (Hartwigsen, 1980: p. 24). There are basically two types of space, they are: 1. Sociofugal, i.e. one that discourages social activity, such as found in Mesopotamian temples, and a sociopetal space, ie., to foster sociability and social contact such as in a living room, meeting place, etc. Small spaces, which are the norm in Mesopotamian dwellings, tend to foster greater intimacy and are therefore more of a sociopetal space. Individual spatial needs vary from culture to culture and E. T. Hall was among the first to draw attention to this cultural variability of the use and scale of space. Thus the Japanese, European and Arab concept of spatial experience differ from our own, which is much more limited. In the West, we regard anything more than the minimum requirement as a "frill".

Mosaic column from temple of Ninkhursag at al-Ubaid Ur, *c*. 3000 BC.

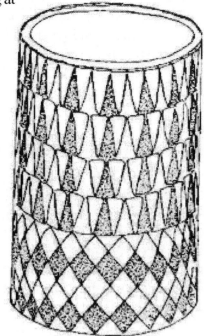

Cone of head formed with different colored stones.

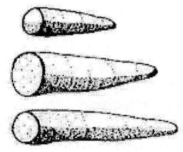

Small clay cones of different colors, red, blue, white, buff, grey, etc. about 3/4 inch in diameter and 3 to 4 inches long, driven into the surface of the mud plaster to create mosic patterns of various designs.

Figure 7.8 Mosaic cones sometimes used by the ancient Mesopotamian builder in the construction of Uruk temples.

Scholars have arrived at certain distances which are believed to be desirable distances for conversing by people in different relationships for various nations. As applied to the United States, these include: 1. intimate, less than 50 cm; 'casual' (friendly), 75–120 cm and formal, 2.10–3.60 m. However, Hall notes that these distances are culturally determined, and people from differing societies have differing preferred conversing distances (Hall, 1959). He notes that his research shows that Arabs are more intimate and prefer closer conversing distances. This is because the personal-space bubble is considered to be smaller. This proximity and combination of sensory inputs would very likely arouse a hostile reaction in the average American male, or he would give the situation an intimately sexual interpretation. Judging by the size of ancient dwellings, one may infer that this was also the case in ancient times. Also, it has been shown that the need to maintain such a distance or space is apparently deeply rooted and that spatial invasion has a disruptive effect and can produce reactions ranging from flight at one extreme to antagonistic display at the other.

In designing smaller spaces, social-motivational considerations usually dominate the design. In larger spaces, floor planning is the most important single factor. Thus the layout of a space helps us determine the use to which it was put. Activities usually correspond to organizational units. Furthermore, the Sumerians developed a sophisticated integration of line and form in the visual treatment of edges and planes that has only been equaled by the Greeks, over a thousand years later.

Form: It is impossible to separate form from space because one creates the other. Like space, form can be either two-dimensional or three-dimensional. Ancient builders were well aware of both aspects and used both successfully to improve their environment, whether in the home or in the temple.

Their two-dimensional form was depicted in their friezes and painted murals. The importance of form in ancient architecture is obvious; everything they felt, saw or touched was a manifestation of one type of form or another. But three-dimensional form consists of more than the outline shape of an object; it also contains the object's inner part as well, as well as its apparent weight. Form is the antithesis of space, i.e., if form is considered to be a positive mass, then space would be considered negative.

Texture: The term texture refers to the surface quality of an object, i.e., its roughness or smoothness, coarseness or fineness. Likewise, one should distinguish between actual or tactile textures and visual textures. Although the ancient builders used tactile textures in their buildings, such as in their frescos and architectural finishes (e.g., mosaic cones) quite often visual textures which were simulated were used mostly on pottery and small objects.

Ancient builders used texture to create contrast and variety. To this end, they made full use of the sun to get strong shadows and a sculptural effect. In addition to the various textural sensations of smoothness, roughness and softness, they were aware of other textural sensations such as that of "life" – objects such as human skin, leaves and flowers of nature.

Rough surfaces like brick and stone tend to suggest a feeling of solidity, masculinity and informality. Smooth surfaces such as plaster suggest luxury and formality. Texture was also used to create illusions, e.g., the ancients used rough surfaces to reduce the apparent height of a ceiling or reduce the apparent distance of a wall, as well as make colors appear darker and heavier. Moreover, rough textures contributed to a sense of warmth, whereas smooth textures generally felt "cold". The ancient Mesopotamians, like the people of today, preferred to live in an environment of varying textures.

Light: The sun has always been the primary source of light, and it is no wonder that in many ancient religions, it was worshipped. Darkness, on the other hand, brought fear to many, and is usually associated with evil.

Shade and shadow were used to great effect with the incorporation of buttresses, grooves, pilasters, protruding masses, etc., in the design of monumental buildings and sometimes even in domestic structures. Shade and shadow suggested substance to an object as well as volume. High windows were incorporated in temples, which allowed the sun's light rays to enter the altar chamber at a high angle, which must have had a mystical effect.

Color: The idea of using naturally occurring materials solely on account of their color first arose during the Old Stone Age. The cave drawings of Upper Paleolithic man, which antedate recorded history by several thousand years, were concerned with the representation of hunters and hunted. A very restricted palette of red and yellow ochre, ground into a powder and mixed with animal fat, was the main medium used by early man.

To the people of antiquity, particularly as we approached the advent of history, color had symbolic connotations; it was identified with the heavens, the gods and elements of science. Even clothing was worn in different hues to denote a person's caste or rank, the color purple was often considered an imperial color (probably due to the difficulty of its manufacture).

Thus, in the beginning, art arose from religion rather than from individual artistic expression. Man was more a votary interpreter of his people's aspirations than a creative genius seeking fame and fortune. And so he built magnificent monuments to his gods and his masters, brightly colored in the colors of his limited palette: red, yellow, gold, green, purple, pink, white and black. These colors he applied in flat tones with no blending or shading. Throughout the architecture of ancient times, color symbolism, emanating largely from the study of astrology, prevailed.

Unlike Egypt and Greece, Mesopotamia was a clay and reed civilization, building chiefly with only perishable materials such as mud, clay and reed. The Mesopotamian artisan, therefore, had to be more resourceful than his Egyptian and Greek counterparts. About the time that writing was invented (*c.* 3,500 BC), he conceived a highly original way of disguising the ugliness of the clay material he was forced to use.

First, he manufactured tens of thousands of Mosaic cone clay nails, about ten centimeters (four inches) long, which he sun-baked. He then dipped them in red, black and buff paint and let them dry. Once dry, the clay nails were inserted side by side in a thick, wet plaster in such a way as to create beautiful, brightly colored designs. Thus, instead of using color to emphasize the structural elements, as the Greeks did, they used it to blend in the different elements into a unified whole.

Colors can make a plane appear to advance or recede; make objects look heavier or lighter. Even sounds can be made to sound louder or softer. Color is part of a total sensory experience of our environment and as part of our perceptual system. Colors can also be related to 'moods'. For example, blue is a 'cold' color and suggests security, comfort, calm and serenity. Red, on the other hand, is a 'warm' color and suggests excitement, protection and defiance. Orange suggests distress, black suggests despondence and power, purple signifies dignity and yellow suggests cheerfulness (Bennett, 1977: p. 109). Whether the ancients were aware of the psychological effects of color, or whether indeed colors had the same psychological effect on ancient societies as they do on contemporary societies is uncertain.

In early color experiments, Guilford found that yellow was the least preferred color, red was of average pleasantness and green and blue were the most preferred colors (Ibid, 1977: p. 106). Black and white seem to be favored colors in ancient times as well as modern times.

The Babylonian taste for color is manifest in the use of distemper-painted wall paintings in many of their temples. The ancients had a strong preference for primary colors, just as young children do today; they lacked a taste for the more sophisticated and subtle pastel colors used today. Favorite colors appear to have been red, black, white and buff, although blue appears to have become a dominant color in Babylonian times.

Many of the pigments used by Mesopotamian artists were derived from minerals. "The opaque or stanniferous white as an oxide of tin; the yellow, an antimonite of lead and some tin, similar to Naples yellow; the blue, an oxide of copper. The opaque white made from tin oxide used by the early Mesopotamian artists, was afterwards handed down through the Persians and Arabs to the Italians and modern Europeans." (al-Kaissi, 1984: p.169). Cinnabar and vermilion were produced from mercury sulphide. Pink colors were made by mixing red with white pigments as is done today. Blue pigments were made from lapis lazuli, blue frit, azurite and indigo.

Pattern: Pattern as opposed to plain design is the easiest way of designating surface enrichment. It is formed by the use of line, form, light and color. The ancient Mesopotamians were well versed in the use of pattern, as is evident from the beautiful pottery that has survived.

The use of pattern in Mesopotamia was controlled and disciplined. Usually it was based on formal and geometric designs as found in Halaf and Ubaid pottery. In monumental architecture, pattern was successfully used to unify a design, in the form of a frieze or at skirting level. The ancients used pattern to create instant visual impact and mood. They also used texture to add another dimension, that of depth, as well as tactile interest.

The Mesopotamians used pattern to reinforce the impression they sought in their temples and palaces. They even used pattern to disguise the unevenness and defects of their plastered walls, either in the form of painted murals, friezes or clay mosaic cones.

Line: To the ancients, line was a very potent force. They used vertical lines with great force in the form of vertical recesses and grooves to make the temples appear higher and more monumental. This illusion is because vertical lines have a tendency to lead the eye upward. They had an uplifting quality and suggested strength, aspiration and dignity, as well as masculinity and formality. This the Marsh Arabs inherited and put to good use in their *mudhifs*.

Horizontal lines were used on the bases of podiums and terraces to make a structure appear longer. They suggest repose and tranquility. By the judicious use of line, the Mesopotamians were able to create an illusion of depth and height.

Diagonal lines suggest motion and energy, activity, dynamism and restlessness, and were used in many patterns on the facade and wall murals. Broken lines were used to give the appearance of animation and gaiety, whereas zig-zag lines and uneven broken lines indicated instability and were not used in temple architecture. Curved lines were used to suggest gracefulness and femininity. The ancients also used line to enclose space and convey form through outline and contour.

FURNITURE

Little is currently known of the early stages in the evolution of furniture and design, and much research is still required to be undertaken by scholars who are interested in this field of archaeological history. Only then can we hope to interpret the many fragments of information available – both published and otherwise – that now exists on the subject. Moreover, there are still hundreds of existing "tells" which jealously conceal the secrets of the ancient past. They breathe heavily in anticipation of the modern archaeologist's thrust into the labyrinth of history – to lift the alluvial soil and bring to life its ancient past and glory.

Modern science continues to unfold new facts which would have been impossible only decades ago. For example, in a microscopic study of twenty-nine micro-crystalline quartz cylinder seals (dating from *c.* 2500 BC to *c.* 800 BC), it was shown by the presence of "peculiar collar shapes" that a type of copper drill was probably used (Gwinnett & Gorelick, 1983: p. 45). In the same study, evidence was cited for the use of a tubular drill in early seal manufacture. New archaeological discoveries bring with them fresh glimpses of these ancient cultures and civilizations, just as the recent onslaught of computer technology and applications have created new challenges so that archaeology as a discipline will never be the same.

Looking through the annals of history of Mesopotamian furniture and design, one consciously and subconsciously compares the furniture of antiquity with that of recent years – wondering what tangible progress has been made over the millennia. It is interesting to note that most of the traditional cabinet-making techniques in Mesopotamia (and Egypt) were perfected long before the great Greek and Roman empires. Basic joinery has changed little during the past 5,000 years. Indeed, only recently, with the introduction of new materials in furniture design such as plastics, glass, laminates and stainless steel, and with the coming of modern technology, were modern furniture designers able to break away from ancient traditions and find new modes of expression and a new design vocabulary.

The Mesopotamian plain is mostly alluvial, and before systematic control of the flood waters from the mountain sources, contained large areas of marshland. Reeds and rushes were to be found in profusion, which explains why so much of the very early furniture was manufactured from this material. Although the ubiquitous palm was also used in some instances, it was usually considered unsuitable for most types of furniture construction or in buildings except by the very poor. Because the Mesopotamian carpenter was handicapped by the lack of good native timber, he had to search for it elsewhere. The best timber was imported from the Lebanon, where the famous cedars of antiquity grew.

Often the reconstruction of ancient furniture of "Clay Civilizations" such as Mesopotamia is based on fragmentary evidence which has come down to us long after the wood has decayed and disappeared, or cylinder seals in which furniture is depicted more incidentally than deliberately. But our knowledge of ancient Mesopotamian furniture is not dependent solely on these few fragments of furniture pieces. We now have a very substantial number of two-dimensional furniture representations depicted on sculpture, clay plaques and cylinder seals in addition to terracotta models which can be found in museums throughout the world (Figure 7.9).

Sometimes there is a temptation to "stretch" the information to fill the gap; to assume that what held good in Egypt, Palestine or northern Mesopotamia, for example, also held good in ancient southern Mesopotamia – e.g., the marsh areas. Although one is treading on dangerous ground, it is sometimes a reasonable assumption to make since in this case there was considerable contact between the various civilizations.

After the destruction and the rape of Babylon in 539 BC, Mesopotamia never fully recovered until the advent of Islam in the seventh century AD. The fact that some designs have lasted many centuries indicates the basic conservatism of Mesopotamian society and culture.

Some scholars suggest that historically, the chair may have been the resultant offshoot of the stool and the forerunner of a number of familiar furniture forms. "The folding-stool epitomizes how a combination of adaptability and mobility characterizes the most enduring forms of furniture. It also usefully reminds us that supreme authority, sacred and secular, has more often been represented seated rather than standing: because the throne symbolizes, at times even personifies, the power of the state or the authority of divinity." (Moorey, 1996: p. 254). Indeed, at times, it appears that the occupant of a chair with arms was instantly recognized as the most important person in the room. This may have accelerated the development of the armchair and the side chair.

The history of ancient furniture comes to us principally from the art records, artifacts and remains left to us by earlier societies. Occasionally, real pieces can be examined and described first-hand. Given that this history is incomplete and based principally upon pictorial records, generalizations are sometimes made by researchers in the field to create a cohesive picture for their readers. This chapter should be read with this in mind, yet taking note that the author is both an international architect and furniture designer/manufacturer, with extensive experience in manufacturing techniques, particularly in Iraq and Jordan.

The Mesopotamian populace in general lived at ground level on rugs or reed mats and thus the floor became their "seat" with little more than cushions for support. Even today, this tradition has survived. Sometimes they 'raised' themselves above the earth floor by building mud podiums, or mud or stone benches, where timber was scarce, or where they lacked the technical know-how to construct a bed or chair. Reed matting which was also widely used to cover the floors, was "waterproofed" by bitumen. The common people usually squatted on the floor and furniture as we know it was not in wide use (Figure 7.10). Furniture was thus restricted mainly to royalty, nobles, the privileged class and the temple.

Early furniture was probably of a basket-like construction of woven reed, which was found in abundance in the marshes of southern Mesopotamia.

Figure 7.9 A. Teracotta relief of woman and child seated on round hassock. B. Alabaster statue of Ebil-il from Early Dynastic III period. Hassocks appear to be of basket-like construction which is popular in the marshlands area. The rushes are sewn together to form a cylindrical stool. The seat and base appear to be of cane.

Moreover, this type of construction resembles types used in many of the village coffe shops found in southern Iraq today, which are called *kursi jireed*. Figure 7.11 represents a Marsh Arab ceremonial chair constructed on the same principles as the *kursi jireed* chair. These are made of the spiny part of the fronds of date palm trees, which is strong and versatile, and lends itself to a kind of cage construction as well as decorative types. "The smaller end sections of the spine are used for the vertical members and are inserted through holes in the heavier horizontal pieces. The latter come from the thicker part of the palm frond, and are only partially dried so that they tighten up on the vertical pieces as they dry out and form a fairly rigid and durable construction. Crates to hold vegetables and fruit are made in the same manner and it seems likely that we have here an example of a craft that has continued with little change for more than 4,000 years. The seats of the chairs are made of woven rush – a craft known from prehistoric times." (Baker, 1966).

One of the chief differences between ancient and contemporary furniture is the increased use of upholstery (In ancient times, chairs and stools had used cushions and limited upholstery in a small way, mainly to augment the woodworker). In addition, the introduction of new materials such as glass, plastics, laminated board and chrome has had a powerful impact on the furniture industry and the contemporary chair. Likewise, the gap between regal or "royal" furniture and that of the "common folk" in ancient times has been very significantly narrowed if not

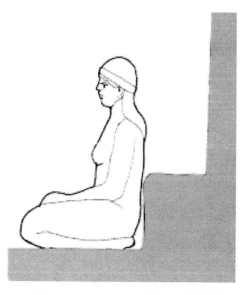

Figure 7.10 Typical sitting posture in ancient Mesopotamia (Kubba, 1990).

erased all together today. For example, much of the carved surfaces of the ivories found in Nimrud were covered with gold leaf. Little remains of this precious metal today because the conquering Medes and Babylonians, upon descending on Nimrud, stripped away the gold and then discarded the ivories.

In antiquity, the crafts of the carpenter, the metallurgist and the ivory worker were often closely related to one another. This was necessary because most of the royal furniture needed the skill of all three craftsmen. The carpenter would build the frame; the metallurgist would gild it – as well as produce the other metal sections – and the ivory worker would carve the panels that decorate the furniture, if the furniture itself was not made of ivory.

Figure 7.11 An Illustration of a contemporary Marsh Arab ceremonial armchair – central marsh (Photo: Mudhafer Salim).

These changes reflect changes in social customs and habits as well as a change in function. By the end of the Early Dynastic Period the smiths' technique developed to a pitch never excelled in later Mesopotamian history. The conquests of Sargon of Akkad put an end to the Early Dynastic Period and bronze disappears and the inferior copper takes its place.

Cabinet-making tools were perfected by the end of the Early Dynastic Period. The use of inlay was by now freely employed by the Sumerians to embellish their furniture such as the gilded and inlaid harp from the "Royal Tombs" of Ur (Figure 7.12a, b, c). The bull's head is covered with gold sheet hammered over a wooden core. The bandings on each side of the timber sound box are of lapis lazuli, red limestone and shell. A similar technique is found on a large chest belonging to Queen Pu-abi (*c*. 2700–2500 BC) which had a band of mosaic inlay, although it is not possible to say if the rest was painted or not (it probably was). The use of inlay can also be seen in her sledge chariot, and a small gaming board now in the British Museum in which the entire surface is encrusted in shell and colored stone (Woolley, 1963: p. 586). Among the objects discovered by Woolley at the 'Royal Tombs' of Ur was the "Standard of Ur" which depicted a banquet scene of the "king" with his guests seated on stools (or chairs with low backs) with animal legs, being entertained by two musicians. The animal legs appear well balanced in relation to the overall design. There are also vertical members at the side and a stretcher at the bottom. The seats were probably made of rush as the weaving of baskets was already well established, and cane and rush were often used in furniture as evidenced from the cylinder seals.

Although the Akkadian period only lasts about 150 years, it left its stamp on the development and evolution of ancient furniture. Also, during this period, a wood-turning device similar to the bow drill appears to have been introduced. From the Akkadian period to the end of the Kassite period (2370–1150 BC), we witness considerable pictorial evidence of the popularity of the cross-legged stool and box-shaped stool with lattice side panels.

The seats with the grid pattern in their sides have special interest not only because of the frequency with which they appear in the seals of the period, but also because of the resemblance to a construction popular in Iraq today. Crates to hold vegetables and fruit are made in the same manner and it seems likely that we have here an example of a craft that has continued with little change for more than 4,000 years. The seat of the chairs are made of woven rush – a craft known from prehistoric times.

Throughout this period, sitting on a stool or chair without a backrest was quite popular, at least as far as records can tell us. In the seals of the old Babylonian period the simple wooden stool with rounded legs and a single stretcher appears

Figure 7.12a Detail from the Standard of Ur, depicting the king seated on a low back chair with animal legs. Early Dynastic III (first half, third millennium BC).

Figure 7.12c Tentative reconstruction of chair in Standard of Ur (above). The seats were probably made of rush as cane and rush were often used in Mesopotamian furniture. Also, bull's legs were a popular feature of this period. Notice how the backrest is used (Kubba, 2006).

Figure 7.12b Detail drawing from the Standard of Ur (Kubba, 2006).

so frequently that one may assume that this was the seat most generally in use at this time, bearing in mind that the majority of common folk sat on the floor.

During the Old and Middle Babylonian period, chairs with curved backs appear, as in the cylinder seal impression of King Ur-Nammu seated on a curved back throne from the Ur III period. Curved backs also appear in sculptured reliefs of the late third millennium BC as in the fragment of a terracotta plaque dating from the time of Gudea showing a woman seated on a rather contemporary looking wooden chair with a sloping back. This clearly shows that the people of this period understood basic ergonomics and human anatomy and applied it to the construction of their furniture.

The Neo Babylonian periods in Mesopotamia (1350–539 BC) see the chair and table being used together in artifacts depicting eating scenes. They also become more elaborate in their design and manufacture.

Finally, in both design and construction, the techniques used in ancient Mesopotamia are still followed in much of the locally manufactured furniture today and construction of the reed huts and guest houses. In the manufacture of large pieces, particularly seating and tables, the mortise and tenon joint, familiar to the ancient Mesopotamian craftsman, is still in use although the tenon is sometimes replaced by a dowel to speed up production.

8

BUILDING MATERIALS AND THEIR AVAILABILITY

Sam A.A. Kubba

GENERAL

There are a number of factors that influence a building style, and the building material is one of these. The raw building materials that were available to the prehistoric inhabitants of Mesopotamia may be classified into several primary categories:

1. reeds, rushes, date palm, etc.
2. timber
3. pressed mud (*tauf*, *pisé*), unfired mud-brick and baked brick
4. stone
5. bitumen
6. metals
7. miscellaneous: plaster, decoration, mosaic

1. REED, RUSHES, DATE PALM, ETC.

Reed (*gramineae*) and Rushes (*juncaeae*): Unlike the cultivated palm, reed (*qasab* in Arabic), which can grow as high as 4.50 m (about 15 feet), was a natural product of the marshes and was prolific in southern Mesopotamia (Postgate, 1980: p. 102). It was used widely in building construction, especially in constructing dwellings for the ordinary folk (Figure 8.1).

For better protection the Sumerian builder covered the outside of his reed dwelling with a thick coat of mud plaster; examples of such plaster were found in the pre-flood levels at Ur.

In mud-brick buildings, a layer of reeds was sometimes placed between the old walls which formed the foundation and the new walls of the superstructure, which, with the use of bitumen, would have acted as a damp-proof membrane. Alternatively, it was used between courses of a mud wall, to improve the grip, as at Ur (Woolley & Mallowan, 1976: p. 21) and Tell Asmar (Delougaz, Hill and Lloyd, 1967: p. 151).

It appears that the earliest settlements in southern Iraq favored reed architecture and many examples are depicted on ancient cylinder seals (Figure 8.2). Traces of reed huts were also encountered by Woolley in the bottom of the Flood Pit at Ur. Similar traces were also found at other sites excavated to virgin soil, including but not limited to Eridu, Tell Ubaid, Lagash, Telloh, Uruk and Fara (Abu al-Soof, unpublished manuscript). Light doors of vertical reed paneling were found at Tell es-Sawwan and in two of the chapels in the Larsa period AH house quarter at Ur.

Reed and reed matting were used as flooring material during pre-Sumerian times and reed matting impressions were found at numerous sites including the Tell Hassuna level II floor at Choga Mami — which was of a weave that is still made, Tell Abada and Tell Hiba in the marsh area. To this day, reed matting is used for flooring and in construction (Figure 8.3).

Bulrush (*berdi* in Arabic) grows up to 3m tall and its stem is not as stiff as the reed. It is used mostly for matting. Other types of rushes are also found in Iraq which are smaller in size and are also used for mat-making.

Date Palm: The palm tree is indigenous to Iraq having been cultivated for more than 5,000 years. It thrived in antiquity and is mentioned in many pre-Sargonic texts from Lagash. Iraq is one of the largest world producers

Figure 8.1 Bundles of reed ready for market (Photo: Jasim al-Asadi).

Figure 8.2 Sumerian seal impressions show use of reed in their architecture.

and exporters of dates. After oil, dates are Iraq's largest export. Iraq once had the largest date orchards in the world but war and environmental degradation – including the intentional draining of the marshlands – depleted the number of trees from 30 million to 16 million. Iraq currently produces about 630 varieties of dates. The Iraqi Bahri date is renowned for its exquisite taste, especially in the golden amber phase – smooth and honey-flavored. The Iraq Ministry of Agriculture intends to rehabilitate the date palm industry to increase date yields. As an important source of rural jobs, the date industry will be part of Iraq's economic revival. Developing nurseries to grow date palms would increase Iraq's date production and allow agricultural specialists to increase yields of each variety.

Figure 8.3 A marsh woman making mats (Photo: Jasim al-Asadi).

The tree is usually less than 20m high, and consists mainly of a trunk and a crown of fronds. Every part of the palm tree was utilized. In southern Iraq, the wood was often used for building beams for houses, and palm fronds added strength to the mud roofs. The tree's "*karab*", which are the broad bases of the compound leaves, the *sa'af*, appear to have been used for fuel, and the leaves for mats and basketry. The palm tree also played an important part in the religious life of the early Mesopotamians.

The palm's timber is very soft with loose stringy fibers. The frond is used for making inexpensive furniture such as beds, chairs, etc., as depicted on many Sumerian seals. It can also be used to manufacture other objects like birdcages, window grills, screens and the like (Figure 8.4).

Sometimes, palm trunks were used for roof timber but this was unsatisfactory because the trunk's fibrous structure has poor load-bearing qualities. In the absence of an alternative, however, a split palm log will provide an adequate rafter, and palm charcoal has been found at Ur and Nuzi (Woolley & Mallowan, 1976: p. 21; Starr, 1939: p. 494).

Around the palm's trunk is a coarse brown fiber which is often woven into rough rope, basket handles, mesh nets, etc. In antiquity, it was probably also used to make tow-ropes as well as for tying the reeds together.

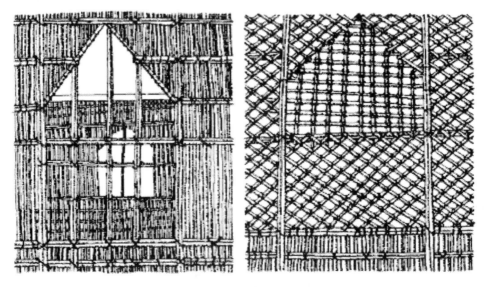

Figure 8.4 Drawing of traditional palm-frond window grills used by marsh inhabitants.

Figure 3.9 depicts a drawing of a *Kursi Jireed* – a chair made out of palm-fronds and which does not use any nails whatsoever. The chair can still be found in many coffee shops throughout Iraq today.

2. TIMBER

Wood is one of the most versatile building materials known to ancient man. Structurally, its principal use was in roofing in the form of beams or poles. It was also used as lintels over window and door openings. Likewise, it was often used to provide tensile reinforcement in mud-brick walls, as well as for the construction of complete structures, making doors, furniture, decoration, utensils, etc. And in Mesopotamia, an elaborate wood-working technology existed from early Neolithic times.

Good timber was scarce in Mesopotamia (like Egypt) and had to be imported from Lebanon, Syria and elsewhere. Evidence of this is given by Strabo who writes: "On account of the scarcity of timber their buildings are finished with beams and pillars of palm wood. They wind ropes of twisted reed around the pillars; and then they plaster them and paint them with colors, though they coat the doors with asphalt" (Strabo XVI, C.763. Loeb ed. Vol.7, 1930: p. 292). Other palm wood pillars were overlaid with mosaic in red-veined stone and mother-of-pearl set in mastic (Singer, et al, 1954: p. 256). Chappelow also wrote that the principal trees in use in ancient times were poplar, palm, tamarisk and terebinth, as well as imports of cypress and the cedar of Lebanon. Teak was also found at Ur – a possible sign of trade with India and the Persian Gulf (Chappelow, 1925).

The main tree species found in Mesopotamia and used for building purposes are poplar and date palm. At Bouqras, a Neolithic site in Syria, "The predominance of Populus and Tamarix charcoal indicates that at least part of the valley floor was covered by poplar forest with tamarisk shrub as undergrowth" (Van Zeist & Van Rooijen, 1985: p. 144). Tamarix trees were also used to protect settlements against drifting sand storms.

3. PRESSED MUD (*TAUF*), MUD-BRICK AND BAKED BRICK

With few exceptions (such as the wetlands), clay was the basic material of all Mesopotamian buildings because from the very beginning the ancients had very little to build with but mud. However, the earliest attempt to build with mud and clay must have been very disappointing due to the slow drying process and subsequent shrinkage and cracking that was experienced. Often the mud was used practically unchanged: either as it was, or with an addition of chopped straw or other vegetable matter (gravel is sometimes added) to give it better cohesion, and also it was thought to improve drainage and ventilation through the bricks and help in the evaporation of moisture from the interior. Moreover, the straw promotes uniformity of drying and tends to distribute cracking more evenly and thus reduce the risk of distortion of the finished work.

In contrast to popular opinion, results from a number of tests carried out in the United States (Neubaur, 1950) by various research workers suggest that the use of certain admixtures such as manure, for example, in fact considerably reduce the tensile strength of the bricks: apparently, it is the organic matter in the manure that is harmful. Likewise, the tests suggest that the advantage of adding straw to the mix is inconclusive. While some experienced builders still favor it, others deny its worth.

It was soon realized that it was better to work the mud or clay into lumps of suitable sizes and allow them to partially dry and shrink in the sun prior to pressing them into position on the wall. One of the main advantages of using pressed mud is that it makes it possible to erect houses which provide satisfactory conditions of habitability in areas lacking in more permanent materials such as timber, stone, pebbles, etc. Furthermore, it utilizes only such materials as may be found locally. Figure 8.5 is an example of a window and recess detail using local materials.

The advantages of using pressed mud (*tauf*) rely on the quality of the material found on the site and their ability to satisfy the conditions of composition and granulometry which are required, particularly providing adequate resistance to the weather. The other advantages of pressed mud are derived from its technical qualities, namely: good thermal insulation, fire resistance, satisfactory capillarity and impermeability. Its chief disadvantage is the large amount of labor it needs as well as the limitations imposed by certain architectural conditions deriving from the relatively low resistance of the material. This helps explain why so much of the earliest buildings were confined to simple one-storey structures. It should be noted that in prehistoric times, *tauf* house construction was most likely built with the help of the whole community or at least family and relatives, rather than a sole individual. This tradition remains to this day in the marshes. Also, because soil is heavy, its source should be close at hand, preferably directly on a building site. This may account for the many 'intrusive pits' that are found by archaeologists in their excavations, which may be nothing more than "soak pits".

Mud is vulnerable to erosion and was fragile and ephemeral; mud buildings lasted as long as their protective covering (usually plaster), and then only if the foundation of its walls was not being sapped by rainwater. Although often used for foundations, plain mud bricks are not suitable for footings because they cannot withstand water penetration. The use of emulsified bitumen or asphalt as a stabilizer was not used in antiquity. A slight crack in the terraced roof would lead to the disintegration of the wall which would return to its original state, i.e., mud.

There is still no general consensus on the life of ordinary mud buildings, but they should last a decade or so, sometimes less. Joan Oates suggests that buildings receiving regular care and maintenance, such as temples or palaces, could hope for a longer life span of, say, over forty years (Oates, 1972: p. 301). Robert Braidwood suggests 15 years as a generous average allowance for the life of a *tauf* structure but Philip Watson cites 50 years for the life expectancy of a mud structure given good maintenance (Braidwood, et al., 1960: p. 40; Watson, 1979).

In monumental buildings, the life span usually depended on prestige as well as maintenance and type of clay used, because it was largely a social matter. And even so, an amazing number of temples had to be completely rebuilt: eighteen successive states of rebuilding, without counting partial restoration, were found in one temple at Eridu.

As a result of general use or willful destruction, a building would deteriorate and the foundations of the walls become buried under the collapsed upper parts; where erosion did not remove it, the soil from disintegrated bricks protected the foundations. In rebuilding, the surface was simply smoothed over; in fact, it would have been too much work to clear the rubble, and the resulting elevation had the advantage of insulating the building from the underlying water table which was still very close.

When the surface was leveled, new foundations were dug which did not always go down to the level of the previous foundations when there was a thick layer of rubble. Raising the building improved drainage and helped make the building more imposing. Evidence of raising the building is found at Tell Madhhur (Level II house).

In other cases, where a new plan was adopted, this sometimes cut across the old foundations; but when the plan was unchanged, the walls were simply used again, such as at Tell Abada. In short, where the foundation works were not too deep, the earlier soil became, as it were, fossilized; there are cases, however, in which terracing works undertaken since ancient times have removed the first layers and the archaeologist finds to his disappointment that he cannot study the evolution of the building. However, it is generally possible to follow the successive stages.

As Braidwood points out, the tracing of a *tauf* wall in an archaeological context is usually a difficult operation requiring considerable skill, particularly trying to differentiate the various *tauf* courses. The wall stub is rarely preserved to a height of more than two or three courses. Research is needed to find out if there is some correlation between the heights of remaining walls as found by excavators and the height of the original structure. This seems possible if a site is abandoned or sacked, etc., and excessive debris may, for example, indicate a second storey. The wall is surrounded, as one finds it, by the mud disintegration product of the upper portions of the same structure (as well as earth debris from the roof construction), which collapsed upon the evacuation of its inhabitants.

The *tauf*-disintegration product is of the same general color and texture as the protruding wall stub itself. But the disintegration product does not have the vertical cleavage planes which were the original faces of the wall itself, nor does it show its horizontal bedding lines in proper position. The horizontal bedding lines appear at the top of each "course" and may be caused by a kind of capillary rise of finer mud particles to the surface of each "course" as it dried. The bedding lines show up as horizontal lines of finer and lighter (or sometimes darker) bands of mud, about half an inch thick.

The use of bricks which were manufactured to standardized units and dried beforehand increased rapidly. This allowed the walls to dry out evenly and become lighter and thereby be built higher (since mud-brick walls did not taper towards the top like pressed mud (*tauf*) walls. They also became more stable as points and lines of stress could be treated with special attention.

Mud: As a building material, clay has many inherent advantages. It is a high heat-capacity material, thus absorbing solar radiation during the day and reradiating during the evening. This mitigates the effect of the outside temperatures, thereby providing a much more comfortable interior micro-climate. But mud also has a number of serious disadvantages. These include: 1. It is easily eroded by water and wind. 2. It has a low tensile strength which sometimes hinders roof construction. 3. It is easily infested with rodents and insects which can affect its structural qualities. 4. It doesn't adhere to wood well which makes good detailing difficult, particularly around doors and windows. 5. It absorbs water very readily, which puts further pressure on beams and lintels when it rains, possibly causing them to sag. 6. It allows rising damp and salt crystallization splitting off the surface.

The ideal soil for mud wall construction should contain four basic elements: clay, silt, fine sand and coarse sand or aggregate. The aggregate tends to give the mud its strength, whereas the fine sand acts as a filler to lock the grains of aggregate (coarse sand), and the silt and clay act as a binder and adhesive for the other ingredients. If the mud mixture has too much coarse sand, it may be strong when dry, but will be less resistant to erosion when it rains. Soil structures with high clay content would be much more resistant to water and erosion, but are also weaker. An ideal clay content seems to be about 15–18 per cent (Figure 8.5).

In general, there are four principle ways of building with earth, they are: 1. Without shuttering or formwork, as in *tauf* or cob construction. 2. With shuttering or formwork, as in *pisé de terre*. 3. With mud bricks either a. with earth blocks of varying types and molded by hand as in adobe construction or b. formed in a mould and dried in the sun before use (Davey, 1961: p. 19). 4. Wattle and daub, which was popular during the Ubaid period and was used in reed structures (e.g., Eridu Hut Soundings). These are discussed in Chapter 9 (Architectural and Structural Elements).

During the fourth millennium BC, mud-bricks were usually rectangular in shape and about 48 cm long by 20 cm wide and 5 cm thick and were formed in wooden moulds. Basically, the larger the brick, the stronger the bond, ie., the wall. However, larger bricks are prone to damage during transport and are awkward to use. But the main problem the ancients encountered in brick manufacture was the soil's salinity.

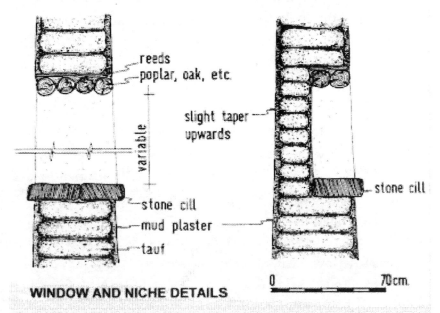

WINDOW AND NICHE DETAILS

Figure 8.5 Details of window and niche using *tauf* and other local materials..

There are a wide variety of soils that can be used for making mud-bricks. The process consists of several distinct steps:

- Finding a mud source near the site. As mentioned earlier, many of the pits archaeologists encounter in their excavations are probably the result of the brick-making process.

- A soak pit is prepared, which may be the excavation itself and which have been found in many Mesopotamian sites.

- The mud is mixed in the pit by hand or more often using the feet. At the end of the day, the pit can be "flooded" with water (with a low salt content) to allow the mud to be soaked overnight. This facilitates the mixing process the following day. The quality of mud-brick depends on its density so that a wet mixture will probably make better bricks than a dry one.

- The ground on which the moulds are placed should be level so that the bricks can be made to a uniform thickness. Sand is sometimes used to do this. The Tepe Gawra main court of Level XIII (the temple acropolis) which attests to the use of sand under the mud-brick paving may have been used initially for making bricks.

- After a mould is filled with mud, the top is scraped level with a clean straight stick. Moulds are usually made of wood, and often have handles for lifting.

- The bricks should be left flat on the ground surface after the moulds are removed, until they are dry enough to handle; this is usually 2–3 days in summer, depending on the thickness and size of the bricks. In winter it may take as long as 3–4 weeks to dry. Bricks not adequately cured will be very fragile and prone to breakage. When the bricks are sufficiently dry to handle, they should be tipped and placed on edge, thereby exposing the other side.

- If the bricks are to be stacked, they must be stacked on edge. Mud bricks have low tensile strength and are very heavy; they may break if stacked on the flat side. Bricks should be left preferably all summer to dry properly before being used.

4. STONE

In southern Mesopotamia, good building stone was not readily available for normal construction purposes. An outcrop of limestone near Samawa was used in the construction of the Limestone Temple at Uruk. It was also used for foundations at Eridu (Safar, et al., 1981: p. 36). Otherwise its use was usually confined to door sockets and grinding stones. In the north, it was available in small quantities and was mostly used for foundations as in the Ubaid sites of Tepe Gawra Level XIV as well as at the Halafian sites of Kharabeh Shattani and Arpachiya – where cobbled streets were also discovered – and for paving. At Songor B, stone was used in flooring mixed with gypsum.

At the Neolithic site of Tell Maghzaliya, a massive defensive wall, 1.5m high, enclosing the settlement was built of large limestone boulders, some weighing a few hundred kilograms (Munchaev, et al., 1984: p. 47). Stone socles were also found at Maghzaliya, as were stone pavements.

5. BITUMEN

Bitumen was used for waterproofing, as an adhesive or cement, and some of the flint implements from Kheit Qasim III showed traces of bitumen (Forest, 1983: p. 121) as well as on floors, walls, roofs, etc. At Tell Madhhur a complete bitumen handle from a wooden tool was found along with fragments of three others (Watson, 1984: p. 163). However, excessive exposure or weathering results in embrittlement, cracking and crumbling from oxidation and polymerization from the effect of sunlight (Holmes, 1951: p. 70). In Mesopotamia, it appears that bitumen was the preferred adhesive for everyday use, probably due to its availability.

It is found in abundance near Hit, but there are many other seepages. It appears to have been produced partly in the form of rock asphalt from the mountains (Singer, 1954: pp. 250–256). The bitumen produced from the seepages was free of mineral matter, and in later times the addition of suitable fillers allowed it to be used as mastic in building construction. To extract the bitumen from these seepages, one had to basically guide the floating masses to shore to dry in the sun and then break them into smaller pieces for transportation to their final destiny or to a "warehouse".

The greatest use for bituminous mixtures was in Sumerian times. The prehistoric temple mound in Uruk, which was 12 meters high and erected to form the foundation for a temple of Anu, had been built of lumps of kneaded clay interspersed with courses of dried brick and bitumen in order to strengthen the clay mound and prevent it from drying out. Bitumen was also used in the buildings of Eridu and Ur, during the Third Dynasty of Ur where many beautiful examples of corbel-vaulted chambers, etc., were bonded with bitumen mortar. Moreover, houses dating from about 3500 BC excavated near al-Ubaid consisted of a simple frame of arched bundles of reeds to which rush matting coated with bitumen had been fixed to form the walls. This is one of the earliest known uses of bitumen in building so far discovered.

Bitument is also used by the marsh dwellers to waterproof their reed and wooden *mashufs* (canoes) as well as their storage containers, etc.

6. METALS

Unlike some of its neighbors, Mesopotamia had no natural mineral resources, yet the Mesopotamian metallurgists proved to be the most proficient in the Near East. The earliest metals worked by man were probably copper and lead, followed by gold, silver and tin; then bronze and iron (Moorey, 1985: p. 1). Below is a general outline of some of the metals used in ancient Mesopotamia. It is important to stress that, generally speaking, metals played a negligible role in ancient building construction in Mesopotamia.

Copper: The beginning of copper metallurgy in Mesopotamia is normally pushed back to a mineralized oval pendant discovered at Shanidar Cave, and dating to the ninth millennium BC. Copper was the cheapest and most widely used metal in prehistoric times. Copper beads were found in the pre-Hassuna levels of Tell Sotto as well as Tell es-Sawwan, where a small copper knife was also discovered (al-A'dami, 1968: p. 59).

Although the patterns of development varies from region to region, it is generally true to say that the earliest coppers were the purest coppers, which were either native metal such as the copper awl found at Tell Maghzalia or smelted copper (Moorey, 1985: p. 5). Bromehead suggests that the impurities found in metal objects excavated in Mesopotamia indicate that the metal was probably brought from Asia Minor, where the same impurities are found, as well as Armenia and Elam (Bromehead, 1954: p. 563). However, we now know that copper was in fact imported from various sources; the main source areas for ancient smiths were Anatolia, Iran, the Gulf and Cyprus. Sumerian texts, however, cite Aratta as the main source of imported copper to Uruk during the third millennium, as well as Dilmun, Magan and Meluhha. After the Ur III period, Dilmun seems to have emerged as "the primary entrepot for all Gulf Trade" (Moorey, 1985: p. 9). Although copper is widely distributed in Anatolia, Kozlu is the only confirmed prehistoric mine, which is located some 15 km south of Horz-Tepe. Oman also appears to have been an important source of copper for Sumer from the fourth millennium BC.

In Southern Mesopotamia, copper was in use by the Sumerians as early as 3500 BC and some time before 3000 BC they found that by mixing a small quantity of tin ore with the copper ores when they smelted them, a new alloy was created which was harder and more useful than copper. This metal was bronze. Moreover, it was found that bronze was more easily worked, because by alloying a small amount of tin with the copper, you in effect reduce the melting point of the resulting metal, which meant in practice that with the same temperatures used for casting copper, you have a much more fluid metal which greatly simplified casting. It is no wonder that with the invention of bronze, the quality of casting improved dramatically (Hodges, 1970).

Metal objects discovered in the royal Sumerian tombs show conclusively that the smiths had made very significant technical advances. Complex objects were cast in molds made up of up to four pieces. They were so technically advanced for their time that they were even experimenting and implementing such tasks as joining metals with a totally different alloy, i.e., the beginning of soldering technology.

From the year 3000 BC onward we see the increasing use of bronze in Mesopotamia, particularly for the manufacture of arms and weapons, although it was also used for making tools such as the ax and the chisel. In the following centuries, these innovations which had taken place in Mesopotamia, and to a lesser degree in Egypt, were slowly being diffused into other areas of the Near East – into Syria, Anatolia, Cyprus and Crete – and a flourishing trade gradually built up between these centers.

Later, the Mesopotamian smith found that it was easier for him to add tin ore to metallic copper to produce bronze rather than by smelting the tin and copper ores together as he had done previously. As their products became more and more standardized, the percentage of tin in the bronze remained constant at about 8 per cent, which was more or less ideal to achieve a hard but not brittle bronze metal.

Lead: A lead bracelet was found at the lowest level of Yarim Tepe I, and a small conical piece was found in the 'burnt house' at Arpachiya (level TT6) belonging to the Halaf period. At Assur, we find it exploited in an architectural context, where large circular lead plates weighing some 90 kg. formed the bases of stone pivots (Moorey:1985: p. 124). However, "The role of lead in buildings where baked brick was the primary medium, and in a region where bitumen was readily available, was naturally restricted. Even in Assyria, where advanced stone construction was not uncommon, architectural uses of lead are not yet as evident as might be expected, though it was used in fixing sculptured slabs together." (Moorey, 1985: p. 125).

Silver: There is still no consensus on the origins of silver in Mesopotamia, and textual indications for the ultimate sources of the silver used in Mesopotamia are singularly rare and meager. Silver was used for plating wood and ivory objects, bricks and other metals, as well as for ornaments and currency.

Gold: The earliest appearance of gold to date is a piece of gold wire discovered at Ur, possibly of the Ubaid period (Woolley, 1956: p. 185). Gold appears to have played a significant role in the decoration and furnishing of the temples and palaces, particularly from the Uruk period onwards. Gold and gold leaf which was used in decoration was found at a number of sites in Mesopotamia.

Tin: Tin does not occur naturally in metallic form. In antiquity it was used mainly for alloying with copper to make bronze as well as a solder for copper, silver, etc. (Moorey, 1985: p. 127). The origin of tin has been a matter of much debate and little has survived from ancient Mesopotamia.

Bronze: Bronze is an alloy mainly of copper and tin (roughly one part tin to nine parts copper), possibly with lead as an additive. It appears to have been introduced into Mesopotamia some time during the first half of the third millennium BC (Moorey, 1985: p. 19).

7. MISCELLANEOUS: PLASTER, DECORATION, MOSAIC

Plaster: Plastering was an essential part of early building construction, especially in Mesopotamia. This is because without one or two coats of plaster, a mud structure would deteriorate very rapidly when it rained. The plaster, moreover, made the structure more homogeneous and gave it added rigidity.

Three types of plaster were common in ancient Mesopotamia, they are: 1. mud, 2. gypsum and 3. lime.

1.   Mud plaster has been found throughout Mesopotamia from the earliest times. It is a traditional treatment for mud-brick walls and is usually applied in two coats, both for exterior and interior surfaces. The initial coat is best reinforced with straw or some similar material, which allows the use of a greater clay content (20–25 per cent) in the plaster mix. It will also make it easier to add thicker coats for leveling the surface and for future maintenance (McHenry, 1984: p. 123). The second coat (finish coat) consists of as fine a material as attainable (with a relatively high clay content) and applied as thinly as possible. Any shrinkage 'hair cracks' that may appear can easily be rectified by dabbing a little water on the surface and working over it by hand or with a damp cloth.

Mud plaster was used in many Neolithic and Chalcolithic sites and was the normal way of treating walls and floors from the Ubaid period onwards. Fragments of mud plaster have also been found with impressions of reeds or reed bundles from southern sites like Eridu (Safar, 1950), Ur, and Tell al-Ubaid (Hall & Woolley, 1927: p. 57).

2.   Gypsum (*juss*) plaster was probably first used in the Middle East where there are extensive outcrops of rock gypsum, often as a surface sub-deposit such as at Umm Dabaghiya where the gypsum was only 30 cm below the soil (Kirkbride, 1972: pp. 3–15). To produce gypsum plaster the rock was broken into convenient lumps and then burnt with wood or charcoal. Gypsum requires a much lower firing temperature than lime and was therefore easier and cheaper to produce.

Once calcined, the fine white powder can be mixed with water to form a hard plaster which was used for walls, floors and various domestic installations and generally where   greater water-proofing than mud plaster could afford. It was used extensively during the Ubaid period at sites like Tell Abada (Building B) where it was used to cover floors and walls (Jasim, 1985: p. 18) and at Tell Songor B where gypsum mixed with pebbles was used to plaster the floors. Gypsum plaster was used at Tell Maghzaliya (*c.* 7000 BC) and Tell Sotto for floors and walls (Munchaev, et al., 1984: p. 50; Merpert, et al., 1977: p. 97) as well as at Umm Dabaghiya and other sites further south like Tell Hassan for floors and walls (Kirkbride, 1972: pp. 3–15; Fiorina, 1981: p. 279). It was later overtaken by bitumen in popularity.

3.   Lime plaster has also been used since Neolithic times. Recent research concerning the pyrotechnics for lime production show that it was well developed even before the invention of ceramics, and firing   temperatures as high as 750 °C may have been achieved in kilns of the pre-ceramic Neolithic period (Thuesen and Gwozdz, 1982: p. 99).

Fragments of wall and floor plaster, from Hama, Syria, dated to c. 6000 BC, were analyzed to test to see whether lime or gypsum was used in the Neolithic period. The plaster samples definitely show that lime was utilized during the Neolithic (Ibid, 1982: p. 101). At Madhhur, the Level II house attests to the use of "a thin layer of white gypsum of lime plaster" covering a thicker layer of mud plaster (Roaf, 1984: p. 122). It was also widely used in the Levant during the Neolithic (Wright, 1985: p. 371). Certain limes were applied to take advantage of their water-resistant qualities.

Replastering was an important part of a dwelling's regular maintenance. Furthermore, two forms of replastering would often take place: that of floors and some walls in brown mud, and that of walls in white plaster.   In the former case, earth dug from near the house is mixed with wheat straw and water to form a paste, which is then applied to the surface and smoothed over with a wet cloth. The white rock powder used to make the lime plaster is collected from outside the village, and is more carefully handled than the ordinary mud. It is mixed with sieved wheat straw and water, producing a much finer paste, and is then applied to the walls in the same way as the brown mud-plaster. Sometimes in archaeological excavations it may be assumed, perhaps wrongly, that a thick level of floor mud-plaster is due to a long occupation.

Decoration: The main form of decoration in ancient times appears to have been painting, although towards the end of the Ubaid period we find the appearance of mosaic cones being employed for decorating walls. Whether their appearance should be attributed to the Late Ubaid or Uruk periods is still uncertain.

Painted Decoration: Paint was used from the earliest times for decoration, and in some of the Neolithic village houses of Umm Dabaghiyah traces of paint were found on the floors as well as fragments of wall frescoes of onager scenes. In the "murals", red ochre appears to have been the most favored color followed by black and yellow, all painted on a white background (Kirkbride, 1975: p. 7). During the Ubaid period, we find the use of paint and murals attested to in several buildings.

At Eridu, some mud-brick houses, which are either early Uruk or "Terminal" Ubaid, bore traces of murals of red paint on their walls, and another decorated with alternate stripes of red, black and white (Mallowan, 1976: p. 330). The smaller chambers of the Eridu VI Temple were painted with white lime-wash over the mud-plaster (Safar, et al., 1981: p. 110).

At the Uruk period temple at Uqair, we find colored frescoes inside the Painted Temple, showing the continuation of painting tradition which Seton Lloyd considers the introduction of representational painting, one of the achievements of the age. Many of the pigments used by Mesopotamian artists were derived from minerals.

Mosaic Decoration: Mosaics consist of small pieces of colored materials closely set together in some cement or bitumen to create a smooth and patterned surface. Their use was first discovered in southern Iraq, from the end of the Ubaid period onwards, at sites like Tell Mismar, a small Ubaid site near Warka (Schmidt, 1978: p. 10).

The clay cones were of varying sizes, but usually 10–15 centimeters long and two or three centimeters in diameter and were pressed into the mud walls when the mud was still not dry. However, the cones were usually first dipped in red ochre, white paint or bitumen and allowed to dry. These mosaics served to protect the mud plaster of the walls as well as providing a decorative finish (Figure 7.8).

Baked clay cones have been found on a number of Mesopotamian sites, especially in the south, and Adams and Nissen, in their survey of the Uruk area, found them on eighteen sites, ranging from the Ubaid period to the Early Dynasty I period.

9

ARCHITECTURAL AND STRUCTURAL ELEMENTS

Sam A.A. Kubba

GENERAL – ANCIENT TOOLS AND METHODS

Building construction is a specialized trade, yet in traditional Iraqi construction there is no significant difference between the builder, mason and bricklayer (*banna* or *mu'mar*). They usually start as apprentices and work their way up. What is interesting is that traditional builders to this day rarely work to prepared drawings, although in ancient times temples, palaces and other important buildings may have been "sketched out" either on the ground or on a clay tablet such as the one found in the Diyala region (Akkadian), which depicted two multi-roomed houses (Delougaz, Hill & Lloyd, 1967).

The usual method was that the building was laid out on the site by "drawing" the walls with powdered lime or gypsum (*juss*). The builder or his assistant, after filling his hands with *juss*, placed them before him and let some of the lime/gypsum drop to the floor as he walked backwards in a predetermined direction. A trench was then dug for the foundations with a simple pick.

The ancient builder needed few tools other than a hatchet or adze and his hands. Edward Ochsenschlager, an anthropologist who lived in the marshes near a mound called Hiba from 1968 to 1990, found that "Blades and teeth of various kinds can be attached to their wooden or reed handles by means of daub or bitumen. In some cases they are originally constructed in this fashion. In other cases they are repaired with bitumen only when a socket or other kind of join is weakened or broken." (Ochsenschlager, 2004). For his plumbline (to check that a wall is vertical), the traditional builder would use a small pierced stone for a weight and tie a string to it. A smooth wood trowel was used to smooth the *pisé* or plaster.

MESOPOTAMIAN WOODWORKING TOOLS

Woodworking is another matter, and there is considerable circumstantial evidence to show that ancient Mesopotamian carpenters were very proficient in woodworking techniques from early Neolithic times. This can be seen from the many seals depicting furniture, etc., as well as from the much later Assyrian bas reliefs and ivory plaques that have survived. Figure 9.1a and, b show a number of simple joining details that were probably in use – based on the available technology at the time. Figure 9.2 shows simple joints used in ladder construction based on the available evidence. Notice the use of a double notch joint and the fastening detail (Kubba, 1990).

This existence of an elaborate early woodworking technology is confirmed by recent microwear analysis. Keeley, after examining a collection of tools from early Neolithic levels of Tell Abu Hureyra, indicates that some of the implements may have been used to prepare joints. These tools are variously known as "reamers", "drills", "flint rods", "*méches de forets*", etc. The bit of these tools is created by abruptly retouching both lateral edges of a blade. The drills from the early Neolithic of Abu Hureyra are very long, with unbroken specimens over 10 cm long and broken pieces longer than 6 cm, and are longer than any morphologically similar pieces from the Mesolithic levels. Microwear analysis of this sample (N=6) showed that all were used to drill or ream wood (Keeley, 1983: pp. 253–254). Moss also analyzed 109 burins and points from Abu Hureyra (*c.* 7000 BC), and concluded that the "Burins were used primarily for reed or wood working. Tanged points were used primarily as projectiles and secondarily as reed/wood working tools in the same manner as the burins." (Moss, 1983: p. 154).

Figure 9.3 shows some of the carpentry tools used in ancient Mesopotamia. Tools from the Ubaid and Uruk periods can be seen to be the prototypes of modern carpentry hand tools. These include:

1.   Scribing Instrument: This was widely used by Mesopotamian craftsmen. Knives were probably used to score lines on timber, which permitted the carpenter to work and cut it to the mark, thus replacing the need for a pencil.

2.   Try Square: The layouts of some of the Ubaid buildings, with their 90 degree angles, such as we see at Kheit Qasim III, strongly suggest the use of some form of large try square, although we have no solid evidence since they would have been made of perishable materials (wood).

3.   The Adze: The adze was one of the ancient carpenter's most valuable tools, and was used for "planing" the timber. In an Old Babylonian tablet

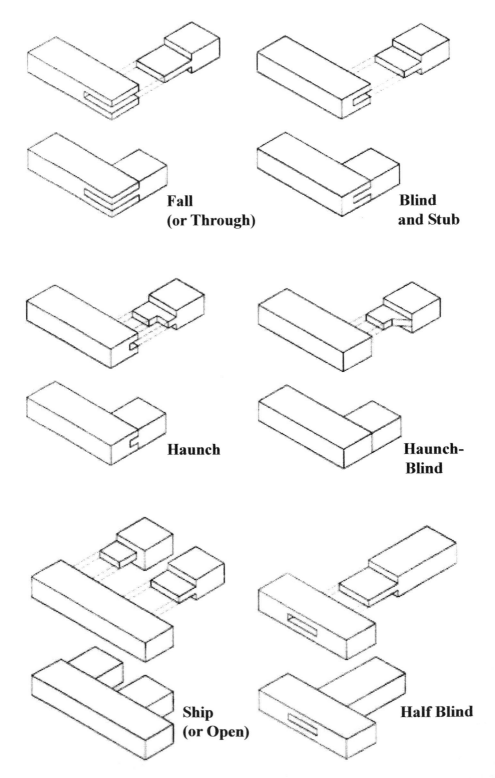

Figure 9.1a Wood joinery details used in ancient times in Mesopotamia.

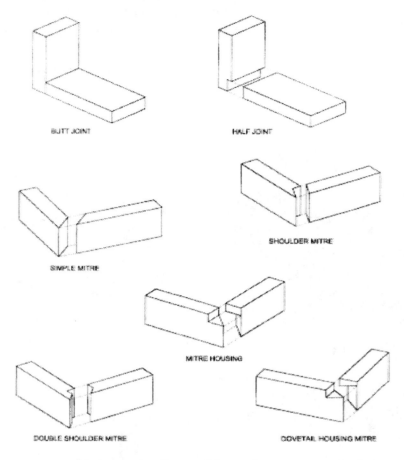

Figure 9.1b Wood joinery details used in ancient Mesopotamia.

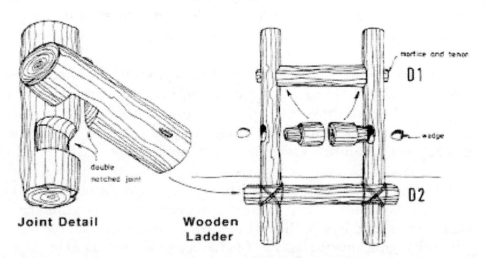

Figure 9.2 Drawing showing simple joints used in wooden ladder construction based on the available evidence.

(Figure 9.3a), we see a carpenter sitting on a stool using an adze to "clean" a piece of timber. During the Ubaid period, the adze was likely made of copper or stone. The blade was attached to a carved wooden shaft by means of a leather binding. One assumes that a small adze was used for delicate work and a larger blade for general and heavier use such as roughing and shaping the timber.

Figure 9.3a Plaque showing a carpenter using an adze. From the Old Babylonian Period.

Figure 9.3b Part of a terracotta plaque depicting a Mesopotamian craftsman with an axe.

4. The Axe: The main function of the axe (Figure 9.3b) was probably to fell trees and to cut timber to size. In Egypt, the carpenter's axe was a much heavier implement than the battle-ax. With the development of the pull saw, the carpenter's reliance on the axe must have been greatly reduced.

5. The Saw: During the Ubaid period, the saw probably consisted of flint knives with their cutting edge very roughly and irregularly serrated (Figure 9.3c). By the Late Uruk they would probably have developed to a fine serrated edge tool made of copper, probably imported from Anatolia. The ancient saw's teeth differed from those of the modern saw.

6. Chisels: Chisels were made to different sizes, some being used as 'mortise chisels' for cutting mortises. The mortise chisel would have had to have a long handle (like its modern counterpart) with the blade only partly going into the handle. The further away the tang of the blade was from the point of contact with the mallet, the less likelihood of splitting the handle.

Some chisels were small and used for engraving. These would have been made of copper. Another type of small chisel had a domed head and was used for grooves and making holes in timber and ivory. This type must have been very popular in southern Mesopotamia for making *kursi jareed* chairs, and in the north during Assyrian times.

7. Wooden Mallet: The mallet was a primitive tool, and was used in conjunction with the chisel and, being made of wood, has not survived.

8. The Bow Drill: The development of the bow drill was probably made from the bow and arrow, probably about the time the potter's wheel was invented. The bow was cut from a suitably shaped branch; at one end was a hole through which the bowstring was tied (which may have been made of plaited plant fiber, bound at each end of the bow), while at the other end the string was simply looped over a lug on the end of the bow. At the top of the timber stock was a knob which engaged a stone cup (Figure 9.d).

To operate an early bow drill, the carpenter knelt in front of the casket he was working on. In his right hand he held the bow, the cord of which was wrapped about the stock, which was held in a cup by the craftsman's left hand. Pressure was applied by his left hand through the cup and stock to the drill, which was embedded in the bottom of the stock. The bow-cord which was wrapped once around the stock was drawn backwards and forwards by the operator's right hand. This motion turned the drill which cut a hole, depending upon the sharpness of the drill.

Figure 9.3c Artist's impression of Mesopotamian carpenter using a saw to cut a piece of wood.

Figure 9.3d An artist's impression of a Mesopotamian carpenter using the bow drill.

9. Bradawl: The bradawl was probably used before the bow drill. Its main function was to bore holes through thin sections of timber (e.g., for manufacture of *kursi jareed*), or for marking timber for drilling.

REED ARCHITECTURE

Reed structures are found throughout the wetlands region. The *mudhif* or "place of hospitality" represents a well-known Bedouin tradition dating to pre-Islamic times. In the marsh region the *mudhif* is essentially used as a guest house and meeting place. Salim says that in 1953, there were about 600 guest houses in al-Chabayish – the ownership of which had become a symbol of prestige for ordinary tribesmen, whereas it was once the sole privilege of the sheikh (Salim, 1962: p. 72). The method employed is that a number of stout reeds, after being stripped of their leaves, are tied together in bundles with ropes of plaited and twisted reeds, and these fascines are planted firmly in the ground in two rows, at equal distances, facing each other, and in each row lighter fascines are lashed horizontally to the uprights so as to make a rigid framework; obviously this means that the rows must be straight and that the building will consequently be rectangular. The tops of the uprights are then bent inwards and each is tied to the head of its opposite number, forming a series of arches (Figure 9.4). Next, reed matting is attached to the inside of the framework, made fast to uprights and crossbars, and the result is a tunnel open at either end. The two end walls are constructed of strong palm trunks covered with reeds and strengthened by vertical bundles with matting and latticework. At each end wall there is a small doorless entrance in the middle and two other smaller openings at its side. At one end two specially tall and thick bundles of reeds make door-jambs which, for the sake of ornament, may be carried up like pylons above the roof line, and the space on either side and above the lintel is filled with matting.

The modern Marsh Arab guest house (*mudhif*) is a dignified and impressive building, and the prehistoric one was similar. Reed was also used for the construction of partitions and fences – as suggested by impressions of reed stems found standing vertically, and which may have been plastered on both sides. Salim states that "Such guest houses, towering over the smaller dwelling huts of the village, vary from 24 to 98 feet in length and from 10 to 15 feet in width. The number of arches ranges from 7 to 17. Traditionally they should be an odd number." (Salim, 1962: p. 72). The craft and details of building a *mudhif* has been passed on from father to son and from one generation to the next. Ochsenschlager observed that a small seven-arched *mudhif* took six days to complete from start to finish, engaging seven men for the building process and twelve women who stripped the reeds of their leaves and carried them from the marshes to the building site. Ochsenschlager observed that when the roof of a *mudhif* is new, it tends to leak during its first year and only with time as the matting is filled with dust and debris do the mats reach their "peak of efficiency". He further states that, "All measuring throughout the building process was based on forearm lengths (*dhiraa'*) and hand spans (*shibir*). Reed sticks were cut to Mersin's (the village sheikh) forearm length and hand span and used throughout in the measuring process" (Ochsenschlager, 2004: p. 152). This is a clear continuation of measurement traditions from Sumerian times.

Wilfred Thesiger in the early 1950s measured one of the *mudhifs* and found it to be, "sixty feet long, twenty feet wide and eighteen high". He goes on to say, it "gave the impression of far greater size, especially when I first entered it. Eleven great horseshoe arches supported the roof. Like the entrance pillars, these were made of the stems of giant reeds, bound closely together, and were nine feet in circumference where they emerged from the ground, and two and a half feet at the top." Thesiger states that, "The contrast between this horizontal ribbing and the shape of the vertical arches made a striking pattern seen from within. The roof itself was covered with overlapping reed mats, similar to those on the floor and sewn on to the ribs in such a way as to ensure a fourfold thickness" (Thesiger, 1967: pp. 28–29).

Thesiger also noticed that *mudhifs* on the Euphrates were larger than those on the Tigris. One *mudhif* on the Euphrates had fifteen arches and measured 84 feet long, 15 feet wide and 15 high. The *mudhifs* that Thesiger observed on the Tigris were typically 18 feet wide and 18 feet high, whereas on the Euphrates 15 feet appeared to be the normal width and height. Also, the entrance to the *mudhif* were found typically to face Mecca.

During his stay in the marshes Thesiger observed that when a *mudhif* showed signs of collapsing, the owner would reduce its height by digging a trench on the outside up to the base of an arch, "to uncover the two feet of the reed bundle in the ground, and, fastening ropes round the base, pulled it into the trench. They then cleared out the hole, cut off the bottom two feet of the bundle, allowed it to sink back into place, and filled in the trench. The process was repeated with each arch, first on one side and then on the other." (Ibid: p. 206). This practice does not appear to have been used on the Tigris because suitable reeds were more abundantly available. Also, the design of the *mudhifs* on the Euphrates was more elaborate and varied. And it is interesting that the construction of a *mudhif* is a communal effort, built by all adult males in the clan at a date to be decided by the clan head. The amount of reed required for the large arches and long transverse bundles often have to be cut and brought to the site from distant places in the marsh. Extra-large mats are specially woven for the *mudhif* and offered by each of the families of the clan.

What is most striking about early Sumerian culture, particularly during the Ubaid and Uruk periods, is the sheer magnitude of its influence, particularly on its neighbors – either through direct contact such as through trade, or through diffusion. In some areas like Degirmentepe in eastern Anatolia, we find the Ubaid culture being readily accepted, including its architecture and method of building. In other areas, like in the Arabian Gulf (Roaf, 1976: pp. 144–160), we find considerable resistance to certain aspects of Ubaid culture, particularly its architecture and construction techniques. This may be due to the materials available locally as well as to local building traditions.

In Chapter 7, we outlined basic ancient measurement standards and techniques, and we stated that in order to build elaborate structures such as temples, ziggurats and palaces as well as to conduct foreign trade, etc., the ancients required an appropriate system of measurement.

While the evidence is not definitive, it seems logical to assume that the Mesopotamians used one or more systems of linear measurement well over 6,000 years ago as a prerequisite for the construction of the many monumental buildings the new epoch demanded, and that is easily recognizable as ancestral to our own Imperial system. Mesopotamian temples and palaces, let alone houses, have left no such clues to the system of measurement used at the time.

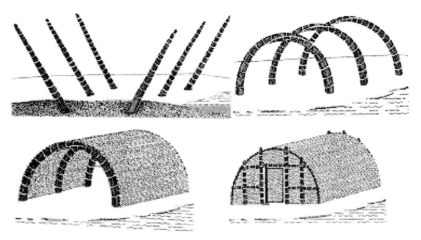

Figure 9.4 Drawing showing method of reed hut construction.

MUD BRICK CONSTRUCTION

The Mesopotamian mud-brick wall which developed from the *terre-pisé* wall construction (*murus terreus*) was, technologically speaking, unable to evolve beyond the inherited dimensional limitations of the material, i.e., the relationship between depth and height which for a wall of pressed earth is determined by the laws of gravity and the quality of the work (foundation, building technique). The thickness of the wall should preferably be one-eighth to one-tenth of the wall height. Relatively thin walls were usually undesirable both for structural reasons and because of their poorer insulating properties.

Walls were usually limited to one storey in height because a second storey created many complications and required a much greater strength for the whole structure. When a two-storey building was erected, the first- storey walls had to be about 50 per cent thicker than the upper ones. The height of a wall could be increased by adding a buttress on the outside and although this was sometimes resorted to, this type of structure had the disadvantage that it might not dry properly and evenly throughout.

1. **Building without Formwork:** Possibly the most primitive method of building an earth wall was to use turves laid with the grass facing downwards. It was acceptable for walls of structures of a primitive or temporary character, or for the revetting of minor earthworks. Another method that was used was to compact a mixture of mud and chopped straw, reed or grass in layers while still damp, without the use of formwork or timber shuttering.

For thousands of years this method has been used throughout the world. *Tauf* walls are still used in Iraq, although now confined mainly to garden or courtyard walls. The clay and straw are mixed with just sufficient water to give a suitable consistency for easy compaction so that the lowest "course" may be molded with the builder's hands, with a vertical face on either side, to a height of about 7–10 cm without slumping. Having laid the first "course" the builder simply waits a day or so for complete sun-drying before he adds the second 'course' after which he must wait again and so on.

The mud mix contains straw or grass to prevent cracking, just as does that used for preparing sun-dried mud bricks (*liben*). In times past this mixing operation was often carried out near a pond and a horse or other animal sometimes used to tread the clay and straw together, although men usually did this. In the best work, and in order to protect the lower part of the wall from rising damp and disintegration by rain splashing, a base of pebbles or stones is laid.

It is often thought that heavy torrential rains will severely erode and damage the surface of an unprotected mud wall. The clay content inherent in the brick will resist wetting, except at the surface. Natural erosion rates for vertical surfaces have recently been determined to be about 2.5 cm in twenty years.

2. **Building with Formwork:** The second method of mud construction is also very old but not used in Mesopotamia. It was to compact the mixture into wooden formwork or basketwork. In some ancient round dwellings, for example, the walls were made by compacting the mixture into the annular space, about 30 cm (approx. one foot) or so in width, between two concentric rings of basketwork.

3. **Building with mud-bricks:** The third type of wall construction is either: a. to shape the material by hand into loaf-shaped pieces of convenient sizes which after a period of air-drying are laid in mud mortar in horizontal courses or b. formed with timber moulds.

The mud often contained impurities such as pebbles, broken pieces of bone and other extraneous matter because the earth was not cleaned. The mixture is the same as that used for cob construction. The type (a) method of construction is practiced in many parts of the world and often known as "adobe", the Spanish name for mud. Sometimes the French word *pisé* is used in archaeological literature, which is inexact because it implies the pressing of rather fluid mud between built forms. This method is of great antiquity, being used prior to 6000 BC.

Mud-brick is considered one of the oldest building materials known to man, and throughout Mesopotamian history, they tended to vary in size and shape.

At Tell Uqair, a curious method of building with mud-brick was used. In Mound A, an Ubaid period building was unearthed which had large mud-brick walls nearly one meter thick. The bricks were roughly piled in succession rather than in horizontal courses as is usually the case.

The use of mud-brick was not confined to the building structure, but was also used for floor paving, as at Umm Dabaghiyah, as well as in the construction of canals, and for roof terraces, where bitumen was added to improve its weathering qualities.

Mud bricks are normally made as close as possible to where they will be used and typically near the banks of a canal or at the edge of a

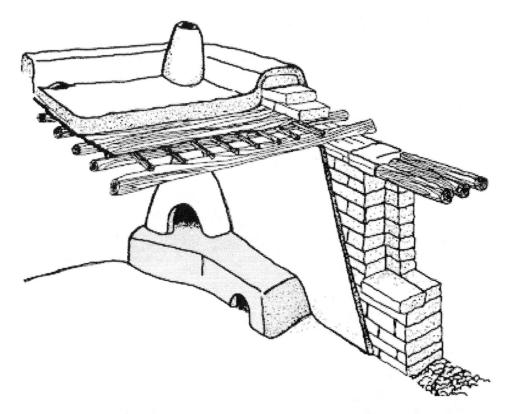

Figure 9.5 Detail of traditional mud brick construction (load-bearing wall).

marsh. It is also important to have a reasonably flat surface large enough to accommodate the quantity of bricks to be made and allow them to properly dry. In the summer, a shaded area will also be required to prevent the bricks from drying too fast (which would cause excessive cracking). Temper is sometimes added to the mud in the form of reed or straw crumbled to very short lengths. To make mud bricks, the mud mix is packed firmly into a four-sided, wooden brick mold that has been soaked in water overnight. Upon completion, the wooden mold is gently tapped on the floor (normally covered with reed mats or crumbled reed) to release the mud brick from the wooden mold. It would then be allowed to dry in the sun for 20–30 days before being used. Today, a number of mud-brick houses can be found in the villages surrounding the marsh areas. These houses normally consist of a single room where most household activities take place.

4. **Wattle and daub:** The wattle is constructed of loosely interwoven saplings and the daub is usually mud or mud-and-dung (Figure 9.6). Wattle and daub can still be seen in traditional construction in southern Iraq.

ARCHITECTURAL & STRUCTURAL ELEMENTS

Unlike Egypt and Greece, Mesopotamia was considered a civilization founded on clay, buildt chiefly with only perishable materials such as clay and reed. The Mesopotamian artisan, therefore, had to be more resourceful than his Egyptian and Greek counterpart.

A. Wall Construction: In ancient Mesopotamian building, there were basically four types of wall. These were:

1. The barrier wall, which was a defensive wall – usually to defend a city or temple enclosure. This type of wall was usually massive, but did not support any load other than its own weight. Early pre-Ubaid examples are found at Tell Maghzaliya, Tell es-Sawwan and Songor A. At Maghzaliya, the wall was more than 1.5 m (roughly five feet) high and the large limestone boulders sometimes weighed several hundred kilos.

2. The terrace or retaining wall. Its function was to neutralize the lateral thrust of the material set or piled behind it. Terrace or retaining walls were probably used at least from the Neolithic period in Iraq (as in Palestine and South Syria) for the conservation of water and for agriculture, in the building of canals and for damming. In Sumerian times, some temples were built on raised platforms enclosed by retaining walls such as Temple XI at Eridu (Safar, Mustafa & Lloyd, 1981: p. 94). In squares X28 and 29 of Oueili, a terrace wall of brownish mud-brick was also uncovered. It was used to protect the tripartite building of Level 5 (Forest, 1983: p. 20).

3. The load-bearing wall: this is the most common wall found in dwellings, palaces and temples. Its main function, as its name implies, was structural, i.e., to hold up the roof or second storey where one existed (Figure 9.5). Moreover, load-bearing walls are more effective when built on firm foundations, particularly for large structures, to avoid the likelihood of walls cracking through subsidence.

4. Non load-bearing wall. This type of wall usually consists of thin partitions, garden walls and low walls used for storage.

In Mesopotamia, unlike Palestine and Egypt, walls were almost always constructed of mud – either in the form of *tauf* or mud-brick (baked brick was later used for temples, etc.). Where *tauf* was used, its thickness was usually between 40 cm (approx. 15 3/4") to 50 cm (19 3/4") for a one-storey structure. Thicker walls of say 70 cm (approx. 2' 3 1/2") or more would suggest the possibility of the building being designed to contain two storeys. For long walls – whether *pisé* or mud-brick – some form of buttressing is required, preferably at regular intervals such as that found at Tell 'Ayyash. The wall would otherwise gradually crumble and collapse. Also, because earth walls have a low tensile strength, a bond or collar beam at certain locations would often be used to provide a horizontal reinforcement in the wall. This would also reduce cracking due to settlement.

As a rule of thumb, it is thought that a bearing wall's thickness (where *tauf* or mud brick is used) should be at least one tenth of its intended height (McHenry, 1984). Generally speaking, therefore, a 40 cm-thick mud wall can be safely built up to a height of 4 m (approx. 13 feet). It is important to note that when *tauf* construction is used, the wall usually tapers towards the top. Thus, as we see in Figure 9.5, although the wall may be 40 cm thick near the foundations, it would probably be closer to 25–30 cm near the top.

We mentioned that where a wall's width appears to be far greater than is normally required it may be indicative that the structure was designed to carry more than one storey. An example of this can be seen at Tell Uqair, where the building uncovered in Sounding IV had walls nearly one meter thick. If the Uqair building did have an additional storey, then the second storey walls would have been much thinner, thereby allowing the rooms to be larger. However, sometimes a more substantial structure is built for better thermal qualities, i.e., for stabilizing internal temperatures or for prestige purposes.

The walls were generally plastered, partially for visual reasons and partially for extra rigidity. The plaster was either mud, as at Eridu, or gypsum plaster, as at Tell Abada, Buildings A and B of Level III and Tell Madhhur.

In Tell Maghzaliya, a stone socle some 50 cm high was used to retard the rise of moisture in the wall through capillary action. At Tell Madhhur, houses of Levels 2 and 3 had heavily plastered revetments built against the base of the walls to help resist erosion through water penetration. At the Halaf settlement of Kharabeh Shattani, "The largest building apparently had stone supports added at the foot of the outer face of the *tauf* wall, and along part of the inner face also" (Watkins, 1987: p. 225). This indicates that some form of 'sandwich' construction was used. It is possible that the cavity between the two skins of stone walling which was about 25 cm, consisted of a *tauf* or "basket weave" type core with a sapling frame and plastered on both sides with mud – the stones being mainly to strengthen the structure.

B. Floor Construction: The earliest floors were of compacted mud, often covered with reed matting such as attested at various Neolithic settlements as well as in the marshlands today. However, clay floors were not restricted to Neolithic settlements; on the contrary, clay was used throughout Mesopotamia's history, as evidenced, for example, during the Ubaid period at Tell Abada in building A, level II and in the "pigeon-holes" at Oueili, Level "0" where the *pisé* floors had plaited reeds placed on them. At Uqair, a floor surface consisted of a thick layer of reed matting or rushes on virgin soil. Sometimes the reeds were laid below the mud floor to avoid humidity by acting as a damp- proof membrane (Abu al-Soof, unpublished manuscript). Gypsum plaster was also used for flooring at a number of Neolithic sites, as well as in later periods.

Usually the floor level would be raised above the outside ground level, so that any rain would not drain into the house. An excellent example of this is found at the prehistoric temples of Eridu. At Tell Madhhur, which had a heavily plastered mud-brick revetment built against the base of the outside walls, the external ground level rose faster than the internal ones so that the house floors were lower than the outside ground level. Some of the more affluent paved their houses with mud brick. The palaces and temples were usually paved with mud brick, burnt brick or stone.

The earliest bituminous floors are simply layers of mastic laid on a rammed loam foundation, such as were discovered at Tell Asmar, Khafaje and Ur, and over which matting was placed.

C. Roof Construction: There is very little direct evidence to indicate the form or material used in roof construction, except in exceptionally fortunate circumstances such as Tell Madhhur in the Hamrin region where charred timber roof beams were found.[1] However, there is substantial indirect evidence – from bas-reliefs, seal engravings, traces of wood and reed matting, etc. In many of the ancient sites, mud or plaster fragments were frequently recovered with wood and reed impressions, which help to indicate the diameter of the beams used. At Tell Maghzaliya, the roofs consisted of reed and were also gypsum-plastered and mats were used for covering the roofs of houses.

In the marsh areas today, the roofs of reed dwellings are generally made of overlapping mats. The bottom layer usually consisted of a single huge mat that covered the entire roof.

An example of a simple, low-pitched roof construction in ancient times can be seen in the Tell Madhhur house in Figure 9.10, which

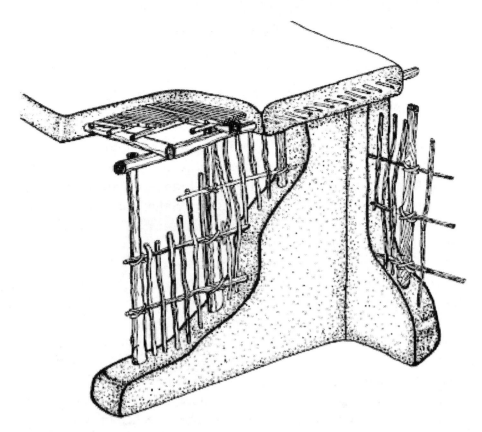

Figure 9.6 Drawing of wattle and daub construction which can still be found in traditional construction in southern Iraq.

may be typical of construction techniques in Mesopotamia during the sixth and fifth millennia. Most early Sumerian buildings probably had flat or low-pitched roofs. It should be noted that with a flat roof a structure can, in theory, expand in any direction, but buildings with a gabled or barrel roof can only be expanded in length (because of rain drainage, complication of roof construction, etc). Thus it is sometimes possible from the layout of a building or, preferably, group of buildings, to determine the shape of the roof. Timbers may have been fastened together by interlocking the notched ends and tying them together.

Typical examples of the type of designs likely to have been employed during Sumerian and Babylonian times can be seen in many of the seals and plaques discovered as well as from evidence such as mud impressions, charred beams, etc. Reconstructions are part conjecture, based on the level of technology at the time. As regards the heights of suspended ceilings or flat roofs, there are no grounds for us to assume that these buildings had very high ceilings.

Early man may have been forced to experiment, to seek solutions to many of the problems that faced him. It was through experimentation that he was able to confirm the validity of his solutions so that, over a period of time, he was able to master the flat roof, the gabled roof, the dome and the vault early on, in his attempt to control his environment.

D. Dome and Vault Construction: Dome and vault construction was practiced as early as the fifth millennium BC if not earlier. However, most of the earliest dome construction was found to be in northern Iraqi towns and villages. At Zawi Chemi, Fuad Safar apparently found a circular structure with evidence of a domed roof. If so, this would be by far the earliest dome ever found. Buildings were excavated at Arpachiyah which consisted of circular rooms made of *pisé* or clay 3.5 m or more in diameter belonging to the Halaf period. What appears to be the springing of the vaulted roof remained, but they were sufficient to suggest that they once had been roofed by a dome.

One method of forming a small domed roof can be seen at Khafaje. It covered a pit and was constructed about 2000 BC. The first course of bricks was raised up on pieces of rubble at diametrically opposite sides of the pit. As each successive course of bricks was added from each side, the dome took shape and was completed when the courses reached the crown.

Judging by the profusion of domes and vaults in traditional Iranian and Iraqi architecture, it may be that archaeologists have underestimated their use in ancient Mesopotamia, particularly since we know that throughout many periods of its history, good timber was scarce and the know-how to build domes is indigenous to the region and was known from Neolithic times. A typical example where the dome may have been used is at Umm Dabaghiya, where the uniformity of the "cells" indicate that the "storage blocks" may have been domed, particularly since no mud fragments with wood impressions seem to have been found in these structures. Likewise, at Choga Mami, the square-shaped grid-like structures suggest the use of domes, although buttresses may also mark the position of main ceiling beams, both by strengthening the wall and by shortening the span.

The use of vaults in ancient times also appears to have been miscomprehended. There is evidence that vaulted brick structures existed as early as 8000 BC in the Middle East, in which small masonry units were used to create structural roofing systems.

In the Royal Cemetery at Ur, one of the royal tomb-chambers was roofed with a dome (found intact) built of stone rubble set in mud mortar over a timber centering; it was a true dome with pendentives rounding off the angles of the square chamber. A small brick dome covered a magazine in the courtyard of Ur Nammu's ziggurat, and in several later buildings, e.g., the shrine of Dublal-makh and the temple of Nin-gal of Kuri-galzu's time, the fourteenth century BC, the ground plan shows unmistakably that the dome had been employed.

Moreover, it should be noted that the presence of structural buttresses often suggests the possible use of vaults in a building – particularly in temple structures, as they reinforce a wall's ability to resist lateral thrusts. This is also true where we have thick walls enclosing long narrow rooms.

E. Columns, Posts, Buttresses, etc.: Until recently, it had been confidently assumed that the column was unknown in early Mesopotamian architecture. The assumption was an unreasonable one, for in a land where the palm tree grows, man could hardly fail to adopt it for building purposes; it was based on the negative evidence that no columns had been found. But if the columns were of wood, their disappearance was inevitable. Having said that, columns in Mesopotamia are the exception rather than the rule, particularly prior to the Proto-Literate period, although remains of mud-brick pillars were found at Oueili Ubaid "0" which are estimated to date to the first half of the sixth millennium BC. Mesopotamia was a "clay civilization", and its architecture almost totally constructed from earth. A mud column, therefore, unless substantial, cannot take downward pointed loads as it would crumble under the weight. A mud-brick wall, on the other hand, would distribute the load, particularly if this was done via a horizontal "wooden tie beam" just below the roof.

However, when the Mesopotamian architect was determined to incorporate columns into his design, he made them massive, as was done in the Eanna sanctuary at Uruk. Also, one or more timber members would have been used at ceiling level to distribute the load of the structure.

Furthermore, because of the scarcity of timber, the ancient Mesopotamians sometimes used the inferior palm wood for columns and pillars. They would wind ropes of twisted reed round the pillars. They would then plaster them and paint them with different colors, though when the palm was used for door construction, it was usually coated with asphalt. Sometimes, the columns were sheathed in copper. Typical examples of this can be found at Tell Ubaid, Uruk and Kish, where the polychrome incrustation is applied not only for protection, but also for decorative effect. We also have the huge mud-brick columns of Uruk (Warka) whose mosaic sheathing may well have been suggested by the triangular frond-bases of the palm trunk. Likewise we have brick columns at Kish of the Early Dynastic period as well as at Ur of the Third Dynasty and an attached column of Warad-Sin (*c.* 1800 BC), which is specially molded to reproduce the frond-bases.

It is very likely that the column was simultaneously invented by different people of the ancient world independently of each other. This is because the concept of supporting one member by another is a simple and fundamental one. In fact, in theory, the load-bearing wall may be construed as connecting columns side by side and of standard width – just as a line is made up of an infinite number of points.

Wooden posts were the main source of auxiliary support in ancient Mesopotamia, propping up roofing members and porches (Figure 9.7). However, except for the existence of post holes, which are often difficult to detect, there is little archaeological evidence of their use. This is largely because the timber members were constantly reused and discarded buildings were cannibalized for their timber parts. Also, being organic, wood is not a durable material and decays very rapidly, being attacked by fungi, termites and insects, depending on its type and susceptibility.

There has been much speculation as to the origin of the buttress. Some authorities consider it derived from a form of reed-construction used in domestic buildings of the same period at Eridu, and surviving

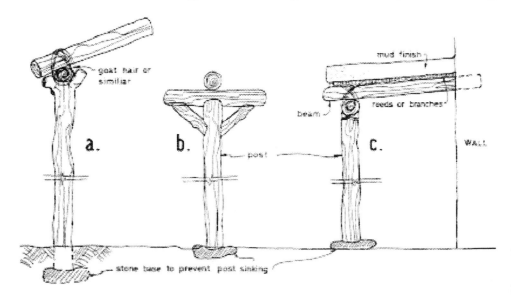

Figure 9.7 Conjectural drawing showing porch and post details that may have been utilized in ancient Mesopotamia.

today among the Marsh Arabs of the neighboring Hammar Lake in the form of the *mudhif* (guest houses). If so, this would mean the existence of settlements in southern Iraq, as yet undiscovered, which predate Tell es-Sawwan, which already exhibits a mature form of facade treatment consisting of similar buttresses and recesses.

Buttresses were a very important feature of Mesopotamian architecture during the Sumerian and Babylonian periods. From early Neolithic times, we find ancient builders using buttresses in the construction of their buildings.

At sites where pressed clay (*tauf*) was used such as at Hassuna, the use of buttressing was more necessary because *tauf* is much less stable than mud brick. Also because *tauf* construction is unbonded – i.e., it is essentially a form of "monolithic" construction, it is more liable to "crack" through subsidence, expansion, etc., with a correspondingly lower load-bearing capacity.

Some of the buttressed walls found at Choga Mami, however, "did not form part of any particular structure. Those walls constituted boundaries of large lots reminiscent of the present Arabic *bayt* in terms of a domestic complex." (Oates, 1973: p. 169). The structural utilization of internal buttresses also raises the possibility of the presence of vaults in a building – designed to withstand the outward thrust of the vault.

From the Ubaid period onwards, buttresses find their greatest expression in ancient Mesopotamian construction. They ceased to be used only in a structural context; instead, they are now exploited to articulate the facades of temples, palaces and civic buildings, using the sun to form deep shadows, creating strong vertical lines and pleasing rhythms, what would otherwise have been a monotonous blank wall. It is not often recognized that rhythm was an important factor in Mesopotamian design aesthetics. There were precise relationships of the parts to each other and to the whole (Kubba, 1987).

Typical examples are the Eridu temples of Levels XVI–VI, in which they are used initially on the inside and later largely on the exterior. At Tell Abada, "building A" of Level II had 29 buttresses and other Abada buildings also contained buttresses but in smaller numbers. We also find them at Tell Ayash and Kheit Qasim III as well as in the Acropolis temples of Level XIII at Tepe Gawra, where they find their boldest and most sophisticated expression.

F. Arch Construction: Timber beams were the main source for lintels over doors and for supporting a roof's structure in ancient times. But because of the scarcity of wood in Mesopotamia, builders had to seek ways to reduce their reliance on it, and since mud had little strength in tension, it could not be used as a beam or lintel. Through trial and error, ancient builders found that by resting two inclined slabs of mud brick against each other they could do away with the lintel. Moreover, they soon discovered that larger spans could be bridged – as long as the walls could take the outwards thrust. One method of constructing an arch is illustrated in Figure 9.8, which is still used in traditional construction.

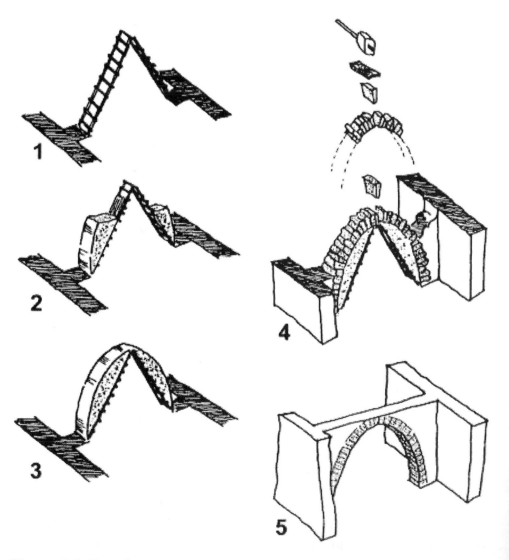

Figure 9.8 Drawing showing ancient arch construction methods.

Also, a space can be bridged over by a succession of short units held in place side by side by lateral pressures. The units of the bridge are kept from falling to the ground under the vertical force of gravity by a strong force exercised laterally. The problem with this type of construction is that the arch transmits its load at the supports not vertically downwards like the beam, but thrusts out its supports laterally. This creates an inherently unstable situation because of the constant threat to overtopple the supports. Furthermore, when the arch is being constructed, it needs a continuous support from below until it is complete; otherwise the whole system will collapse. Upon completion, this support may be removed.

It is most likely that the arch originated in Mesopotamia, and at Umm Dabaghiyah, an arched doorway was uncovered which was constructed as early as 6000 BC. It divided a room into two spaces by spanning the whole width of the room (Kirkbride, 1974).This may be the earliest arch in existence. Semicircular brick arches found at Ur were formed of kiln-burned voussoir bricks excellently made and fitted.

G. Window & Door Openings: Although we have little direct evidence of window openings, we can infer from the many seal drawings and bas reliefs that have been recovered. By being placed high up in the wall, more rapid cooling of the ceiling is achieved by the air's movement and the removal of the hot air layer below the ceiling. Small windows roofed with mud brick were found at Tell Madhhur and may have been a common feature of Ubaid buildings. High windows are also useful for natural ventilation through the indoor-outdoor temperature differential when there is no wind. Window openings would logically, therefore, have been small and high up on the wall. They were, as a rule, rectangular or arched, although sometimes they appear to have been round or triangular. Examples of rectangular windows are not difficult to come across, and can be found at such sites as Tell Madhhur, Level 2, dating to the Ubaid period, *c.* 4500 BC, and at Tell Asmar where there is an Early Dynastic period structure – the "arched house" (Frankfort, 1934: p. 11). The latter is particularly interesting in that it is excellently preserved and clearly shows how two large mud bricks were carried on five "stout sticks" which formed the lintel.

Incense burners with triangular perforations were found at Eridu. Triangular windows were formed by inclining two mud bricks diagonally against each other to form an equilateral triangle. In this way, no wood is required for use as a lintel.

We have no direct evidence of the use of window grills during the early Sumerian periods, but they appear to have been common in later times and a typical grill can be seen in the "arched house". Anchorage of windows or grills was not as critical as a door because there was little vibration. During the summer months, windows may have been covered on the outside by a thick mat of woven local bush or packed into a timber frame (called "*agool*"), which was constantly drenched with water. This was a customary feature of traditional houses in Iraq and Iran until recently. It created a form of natural air conditioning by evaporative cooling, "since the process of evaporation absorbs heat, a breeze evaporating the water can cool a room by as much as 15 degrees F" (Bourgeois, 1983: p. 68).

Door openings is a rather vague term, and in this discussion will include gates, door frames, sockets and any other components or door furniture. In domestic architecture, door openings were often quite small. At the Neolithic sites of Umm Dabaghiyah and Bouqras, for example, one had to crawl into a room. At Yarim Tepe III during the Ubaid period, doors were 60–80 cm wide (23.6 inches–31.5 inches) and 70–90 cm (27.6 inches–35.4 inches) high. This obviously served a defensive purpose, i.e., it was easier to keep intruders out. Sometimes, entrance to a room was through a small opening in the wall rather than via a "proper" door. This too was probably a defensive precaution. At Tell Sotto, a door opening was 55 cm (approx. 21.7 inches) wide, and at Tell Madhhur in the Level II house, a number of similar openings were uncovered that were raised about 1 m (39.4 inches) from the floor and measured approximately 40 cm (15.75 inches) wide x 50 cm (20 inches) high, which the excavators consider to be windows, but which may in fact have been designed mainly for children, and raised to prevent stray animals from entering the house. A similar opening, but at floor level, was found between rooms 10 and 11 in the same building (Roaf, 1987).

Generally speaking, door openings were either rectangular or arched. Rectangular door openings such as at Tell Madhhur were spanned by wooden beams in the form of wooden logs to carry the heavy load over the opening, since mud and mud brick had no strength in tension and therefore could not act as a beam. However, the early Mesopotamian builders invented the arched lintel to overcome this and to avoid having to use wood which was not as readily available as in the neighboring areas. As early as Jarmo (*c.* 6750 BC), we find evidence of door sockets, and door sockets are found at most sites during the Ubaid and Uruk periods. Openings without doors may have been covered with skin to keep the cold winds out.

In southern Mesopotamia, door leaves were probably often made of reeds, tied together with string lacing within a wooden frame. At Tell es-Sawwan (Level III), remains of a pair of doors were found which were made of reed and coated with bitumen.

The hanging or setting of door leaves was well understood in ancient times. Door leaves were made with strong lateral posts, projecting from top and bottom and incorporating pivots, placed in such a way so as to constitute a vertical rotation. The lower part pivoted in a hollowed socket set in the floor or sill, and the upper part through a ring fixed in the wall or jamb. The ancients must have used many different methods to "hang" the door leaf – an example of which is shown in Figure 9.9. In smaller buildings

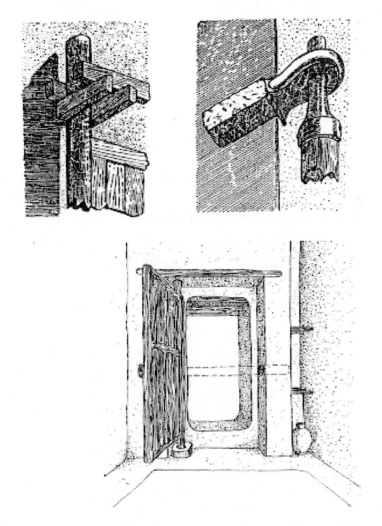

Figure 9.9 Tentative reconstruction of entry to house – Tell Madhhur (Kubba, 1990).

doors constituted a single leaf, although in monumental buildings and gates a double leaf was not unusual. We cannot be certain if locks were used, although one can presume that some form of locking mechanism was in use.

H. Stairways and Ramps: In ancient times, there were three chief ways to move vertically from level to level (e.g., for access to an upper storey or roof). These were by: 1. stairs, 2. ramp, and 3. ladder.

1. Stairs: Basically there are three types of stairs: A) Straight or single flight stairs, B) "dog-legged" stairs and C) spiral – this type is not known to have been used in Sumerian times.

A) The straight stair was probably used externally more than internally. As an exterior stair, it was used at Tell es-Sawwan, built against one of the exterior walls. This is largely because it was unsuitable for most interior spaces due to confinement of interior space, although some of the long narrow rooms in the Tell es-Sawwan houses may have housed a straight flight of stairs.

At Eridu, we find a straight flight of stairs used to connect the ground level with the raised platform leading to the temples. An example is found in Temple VII where an axial staircase led up to the main entrance in the side of the building and which may be an early prototype of the monumental ziggurat staircases of historic eras. It should be mentioned that the stairs may have been among the first elements to be constructed in a building, as it would minimize the need for scaffolding. The builder's assistants could use the stairs (or ramp) for delivering the bricks and mortar to the mason.

B) Dog-legged staircases are the most common type found in early Mesopotamian buildings because they are more economical in area and more comfortable to use. This type of stair rises in one direction and approximately half way up the stairs, a half landing is built which returns and continues to rise (Figure 9.10). What archaeologists consider to be "dog-legged" staircase enclosures comprising two parallel narrow rooms are found in many ancient buildings, particularly with the advent of monumental architecture, but definite proof of their use as a staircase is often wanting.

At Eridu, there is evidence of stairs in Temples XI (connecting ground with platform), and stair enclosures are assumed for Temples VII and VI, although no trace of the stairs themselves was found. Schmidt during excavations at Uruk in Temple I found similar stair enclosures (Schmidt, 1974).

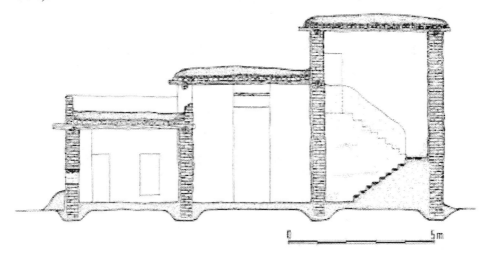

Figure 9.10 Reconstruction of Tell Madhhur house showing section through stairway (Kubba, 1990).

2.   Ramps: Ramps were often used in ancient times, but usually it is difficult to discern their presence in archaeological excavations. Temporary ramps must have been used often in building construction, particularly to build the upper parts of a building. They were easy to construct and only needed to compact the earth to the grade required. "At Eridu, the southeast face of the platform of Temple XI contained a formally constructed ramp, leading up to it from the lower level. It was supported on the outside by a parapet-wall 35 cm (approx. 14 inches) thick that rose from ground-level to the height of the platform (100 cm) in a distance of 4.50 m (14 3/4 feet). Its width was 1.20 m (nearly four feet)." (Safar, Mustafa & Lloyd, 1981). This was later replaced by a mud-brick stairway.

3.   Ladders: We have no proof of the use of ladders during the Sumerian period, although we find them depicted much later in Assyrian bas-reliefs. However, since they are constructed of wood and easily constructed, it is logical to assume that they were in common use, particularly in the absence of formal stairs (Figure 9.2).

NOTES:
1. Information regarding roof construction at the Tell Madhhur house is based on a personal communication with Professor M. Roaf.

10

RESTORATION OF THE MARSHES OF SOUTHERN IRAQ: PROSPECTS AND CHALLENGES

Barry G. Warner
Ali Douabul
Jamal Abaychi

INTRODUCTION

The marshes of southern Iraq represent a watery oasis surrounded by parched scrubland and desert in this arid region of the world. The marshes are an anomaly because there is an abundance of water and therefore there is an abundance of life, both human and non-human – or at least this was the case until recently. The source of the Tigris and Euphrates Rivers originates in the mountains in Iraq and adjacent Iran and Turkey and the two rivers join the Shatt al-Arab many hundreds of kilometres to the south before emptying into the Gulf. These vast marshlands of Mesopotamia (Greek for "between two rivers") as they are aptly and commonly called are actually a complex of many wetland types and many types of marshes. However, for ease of discussion they can simply be referred to as the marshes of southern Iraq (as they shall be referred to in this chapter). This unusual water-dominated landscape has given rise to and sustained a great many forms of life, some representing wide-ranging geographic disjunctions, others which are unique endemics found nowhere else in the world, while others yet have been assembled into habitats that are not so different from other comparable wetlands in the northern hemisphere. We do not usually think of humans, being terrestrial creatures, as important components of life in wetlands, but the marshes have also attracted humans, who have built habitats, livelihoods and sophisticated societies uniquely adapted to the marshes; an intimate relationship with the natural environment that has existed continuously for the last 9,000 years. These attributes have contributed to the marshes in southern Iraq being among the most unique and important wetland ecosystems in the world.

Environmental alarm bells were sounded in the 1980s and 1990s when most of the marshes were destroyed. For many within Iraq, there was little they could do to stop it. The marshes were declared a military zone during this period and were off limits to all Iraqis except military forces. Decades-long traditions of scientific, archaeological and anthropological research ceased. No more could local citizens, even the residents of the marshes, maintain a presence and enjoy the beauty of their historical and unique homeland. The global importance of the marshes of southern Iraq was also recognized outside the country, mostly spearheaded by Iraqis who fled and lived outside the country. The United Nations prepared environmental assessments on the state of the marshes in southern Iraq (Partow 2001). The media, mostly British and Canadian, reported on this environmental and human calamity of global proportions (e.g., Pearce 1993, Savill 1993). The AMAR International Charitable Foundation, a non-governmental organization, was formed in 1991 in the United Kingdom mostly to provide basic needs, education and public health for refugee communities in Iraq and throughout the region as a consequence of the loss of the marshes (Nicholson and Clark 2002).

The fall of the Iraqi government in April 2003 provided the long-awaited opportunity to stop the ongoing destruction of the marshes. Vast tracts of dried-out soils formerly covered by marsh were re-wetted and flooded, which immediately attracted the return of marsh plants and marsh residents to southern Iraq. The international community quickly mobilized to assist Iraq in bringing aid, development assistance and scientific expertise to help restore the marshes. By 2004, the governments of Canada, Italy, Japan and the United States committed to the marshes of southern Iraq about US$5–10 million, and by 2005–2006 there was over US$50 million allocated to assist Iraq with marsh restoration and repatriation of the local population. The Iraqi government realized the magnitude of the challenge and welcomed the assistance of the international donor community. Indeed, the new Iraqi government created the Centre for the Restoration of the Iraqi Marshes (CRIM), an inter-ministerial committee under the direction of the Minister of Water Resources to coordinate and plan restoration of the marshes.

Teams from the various donor countries all recognized some common principles necessary for longer term restoration and creation of a fully self-sustaining marsh ecosystem with a resident population in and around its borders. The thinking in 2003–2004 was: (a) in view of the extent of flooding and encouraging early signs of recovery through uncoordinated flooding efforts, restoration was shown to be feasible but likely not at a great enough scale to replace what was lost since the 1970s; (b) organized and thoughtful planning for restoration would be necessary, and (c) restoration will only succeed with sound science and an understanding of the quantitative relationships between wetland processes and environmental characteristics of the area.

The American contribution provided a general overview of some of the most obvious environmental features of the marshes in 2004 and 2005 (Richardson and Hussein 2006; Richardson et al. 2005; USAID 2006). A few selected sites, such as reflooded parts of the Central Marshes around Abu Zirig were studied in detail (USAID 2006). The Japanese funded installation of water treatment facilities for local residents and organized environmental training workshops on the marshes. The Eden Again program was supported by Italy. Hydrology and hydrological modelling was the emphasis of their contributions. They used field data supplied by the Ministry of Water Resources and applied them to HEC-RAS and HEC-Res-Sim software models developed by the Hydrologic Engineering Center of the US Army Corps of Engineers in an effort to provide decision-support tools for analyzing and predicting present-day and proposed future flows in and around the marshes. The Canadian effort, referred to as the Canada–Iraq Marshlands Initiative (CIMI), focused on the biodiversity and ecological features of the marshes. CIMI was a capacity-building and training program aimed at teaching Iraqis current wetland science and modern ecological field survey methods in accordance with international protocols and standards. A university-led collaborative network of fieldworkers and researchers were trained and remains very much the central group most capable of ongoing biodiversity monitoring of the marshes.

The marshes were probably one of the few good news stories coming out of Iraq between 2004 and 2008. Environmental conditions and human actions were just right and demonstrated what was required for successful restoration. Unfortunately, all that was gained during this period was jeopardized in 2009 when water supplies to the marshes were cut off. The marshes were reduced again to the state they had been in prior to 2003 (Figure 10.1).

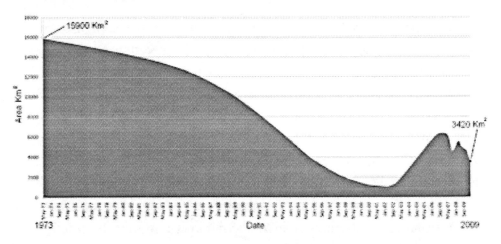

Figure 10.1 Plot of area covered by the marshes (km²) from 1973 to 2009. Data are estimates based on aerial photographs taken during this period.

It is clear Iraqis regard the marshes as an important part of their history, culture and environment that must be restored. To what degree restoration, if any, is achievable remains to be seen. The ecological work and biodiversity surveys undertaken as part of the CIMI program show that despite decades of soil desiccation and harsh arid climate, marsh ecosystems. that once supported the marshes can be reestablished within a few short years. The Iraqis have the technical expertise for making science-based choices for setting restoration goals. However, given the current state of the marshes, successful restoration will require collaboration between engineers who control water distributions within Iraq and outside its borders in neighbouring countries and scientists who can predict the ecological results of water movements in southern Iraq.

We cannot provide a detailed restoration framework in this chapter. Rather we will highlight some key considerations and summarize some key attributes acting on the marshes of southern Iraq that ought to be included in setting goals and planning for successful restoration in the future.

WHAT IS RESTORATION?

Before we can discuss restoration of the marshes in southern Iraq, we must define the term, because restoration is poorly understood and often misused in wetland science. Discussions about the marshes in Iraq are no exception.

Restoration is intended for natural wetland sites that have been disturbed or totally altered by human activity and there is a will to revert them back to some pre-existing condition, presumably something resembling a natural condition (Figure 10.2). Restoration may occur in two ways. What is referred to as active restoration is where management options are deliberate and facilitated by humans so as to allow the wetland to return to the pre-existing condition. Passive restoration is also possible where natural processes within the wetland itself may change, leading the wetland to return to something resembling pre-disturbance conditions without any human interference (Lewis 1990; Middleton 1999; Keddy 2000). In the case of the marshes in southern Iraq, it seems that both active and passive restoration will be needed for restoration.

Successful restoration requires the reversal of factors responsible for the degradation and destruction in the first place. Drainage and de-watering is the primary reason for loss of the marshes. Local inhabitants were quite right in recognizing the need to divert water back onto the land formerly covered by the marshes. However, an organized approach of assessing current conditions in the area of the marshes and defining clear goals is required for restoration success. Involvement of local residents and decision-making bodies responsible for local government is also key, without whose input it could be impossible to achieve restoration. The CIMI project has aimed to do this and has given the Iraqis many of the tools to develop a sound restoration framework for the marshes.

While restoration may be the most desirable option, not all variables responsible for degradation and destruction can be changed. Thus, full restoration may not occur. Consequently, there are other possible outcomes (Figure 10.2). Perhaps only one or some subset of variables responsible for degradation and destruction can be changed. The wetland does not approach a pre-disturbance state and remains only partly "restored". This condition is referred to wetland rehabilitation. Rehabilitated wetlands are still viewed as degraded wetlands because necessary components remain lacking to sustain a complete and viable ecosystem in the longer term. Rehabilitation is usually not preferred, but can be an acceptable compromise if full restoration is not possible. Another fact is that no matter how hard one tries, it may not be possible to remove or change the factors that are responsible for the disturbance and destruction. The extent or magnitude of disturbance will maintain and perhaps spread the extent of

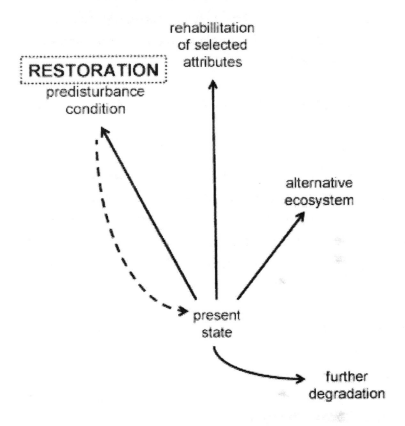

Figure 10.2. The possible different states resulting from disturbed or destroyed ecosystems (Adapted from Keddy 2000).

degradation. Finally, degradation may be so severe so as to remove the wetland altogether and convert it to another kind of ecosystem. The expansion of desert and scrubland dominated by *Tamarix* and *Suada* trees and shrubs around the marshes in southern Iraq are examples where former marsh has been replaced by a completely different ecosystem.

In planning for restoration of the marshes in Iraq, restoration is clearly the desired outcome. However, Iraqis will have to accept the reality that perhaps some parts may only be rehabilitated and others will remain degraded.

Next steps include designing and implementing the plans for restoration. Maintenance and perhaps some mid-course changes will be required. Field monitoring of the physical attributes, hydrology and success of biological re-establishment will be an ongoing process. The marshes comprise a large area. Restoration will be long, arduous and expensive. It ranks among the largest wetland restoration projects in the world, such as the Everglades of Florida and the coast of Louisiana in the United States, Lake Karla in Greece and Lake Hula in Israel.

GEOLOGICAL AND BIOPHYSICAL CONSIDERATIONS

The marshes lie on the Mesopotamian Plain in a broad flat valley (about 200 km at its widest point) of the Tigris and Euphrates Rivers at the north end of the Gulf basin. It is an extremely flat alluvial and fluvial plain, with a north-south grade of about 5 per cent (Aqrawi and Evans 1994). The Tigris, Euphrates and Karkha Rivers meander lazily across the plain crossing natural levees, active channels, meanders, flood basins and large shallow water bodies and lakes. While the Tigris and Euphrates have flowed across the Mesopotamian Plain for at least the last 9,000 years, the modern fluvial network and associated marshes were formed only in the last 1,000–2,000 years. When considering restoration of the marshes it is important to note they are part of an ever-changing geomorphology. River avulsions, the process where river flows are diverted from existing channels into new channels, are important in this part of the Tigris and Euphrates watershed (Morozova 2005). Consequently, erosion and transport of sediments both as bed and suspended loads are high. Aeolian dust storms carry sediments off the surrounding desert and add it to the sediment load of the rivers and marshes, mostly silt (around 60 per cent) with some clay and fine sand. The sediment load of the Euphrates River tends to be at least ten times greater and more saline, especially in summer, compared to the Tigris River. The large expanse of marshes adds considerable organic matter to the suspended load which is a source of nutrients to plant life and other biota (Aqrawi and Evans 1994; Aqrawi 2001).

HYDROLOGY AND HYDROGEOCHEMICAL CONSIDERATIONS

The marshes in southern Iraq represent a typical complex of riverine wetlands influenced by seasonal ebb and flow of water from the river channels onto adjacent marsh-covered floodplains and water bodies. A pulse of freshwater from the north during spring floods the marshes, significantly raising water depths and expanding the lateral extent of marshes. Water depths gradually drop and a real extent shrinks in the summer, at which time seed germination occurs at the water's edge and on the moist seasonally exposed mudflats that were under water weeks earlier during the spring. A reduction in water flow volume and velocity in summer no longer pushes out into the Gulf brackish and saline waters of the Shatt al-Arab as happens during periods of high river flow. Shatt al-Arab waters flow northwards and reach the marshes, making waters more saline in summer compared to spring and other periods of high river flows. Water levels rise slightly during the wetter autumn and winter seasons before the spring flood pulse is received again the following spring and the cycle repeats itself. There can be a change of several meters in some areas between the spring high and summer low stage. Hydrologically, the Iraqi marshes operate a "flood pulse" system typical of many riverine, coastal and deltaic wetlands (Middleton 1999).

The Tigris River supplies several orders of magnitude more water to the marshes compared to the Euphrates River. Figure 10.3 is a representative hydrograph for the marshes in the mid-1970s showing the spring flood in March, April and some of May typically. This spring pulse is all but absent currently because upstream dams and reservoirs intercept spring flows and reduce sufficient volume to raise waters enough to flood the marshes. Flows are artificially regulated by upstream dams which maintain constant flows throughout the year, which has resulted in a more static hydrological regime. The natural hydrological regime on which the marshes depend is one where there is a short-term annual flood and lateral expansion in spring and one that must be returned if the marshes are to be restored.

The geochemistry of the marshes is closely linked to the hydrology which influences periods when the marshes contain more freshwater than other periods when the marshes contain more brackish and saline waters. The Tigris River flows over quartzite and carbonate derived soils and bedrock and through forest and steppe vegetation in the foothills of mountain belts. Consequently, Tigris River water is fresh, making the marsh waters fresh during the spring during the flood period. The Euphrates River, with smaller volumes compared to the Tigris, is not as fresh and has slightly brackish water because it flows through desert and gypsum-rich salty soils. The western part with the Euphrates River is slightly lower in elevation compared to the eastern side which allows more brackish and saline waters from the Shatt al-Arab to flow north during summer. Thus, salinities in Hammar Lake are typically up to four times more saline in summer than winter (Aqrawi and Evans 1994).

The biggest flood pulse in the marshes in decades occurred after April 2003, for two main reasons. Immediately following the American-led invasion, maintenance operators abandoned all field posts on dams and reservoirs on the Tigris and Euphrates Rivers. Great volumes of water poured out leaving most upstream reservoirs and artificial lakes dry. This was coupled at the same time with the uncontrolled destruction of dams, dykes and diversion canals by local residents in and around the marshes, which further contributed to releases of great volumes of water in the marshes. Flooding was so great and immediate, with no warning, that homes and farms were drowned by the new waters. These actions were largely responsible for the great rebirth of the marshes for the next few years. By the time upstream dam operators returned to their field posts in 2005 or so and captured water to re-fill reservoirs, there were heavy snowfalls in the winters in the mountains of northern Iraq, Turkey and Iran that supplied enough water to keep all reservoirs full. Operators were able to release surplus water which benefited the downstream marshes greatly. By 2009, there was a dramatic reduction in water volumes available to the marshes. Construction of several new dams and reservoirs, within Iraq and by its neighbouring countries, held back even more water than before and winter snows were much reduced in the mountains. The marshes appeared in 2009 very much like they did before April 2003.

It has been estimated that there was nearly 16,000 km^2 of marsh in the 1970s and about 1,000 km^2 by 2002. At its greatest extent in 2007, there was close to 16,000 km^2 again but this shrunk in November 2009 to less than 3,000 km^2 (Figure 3).

There are some good lessons to be learned about what is required for successful restoration of the marshes from the flood period after April 2003. Human-controlled releases from upstream dam structures have a negative effect on the marshes because flow volumes are constant and do not include a spring flood. There is no seasonal rise in water levels and no lateral expansion in spring which is a critical factor in the natural ecosystem. Engineering structures and human manipulation of water on the Tigris and Euphrates Rivers and throughout the marshes must be minimized or at best managed to include a short-term flood in spring if the marshes are to be restored.

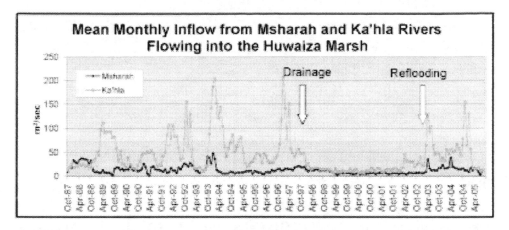

Figure 10.3 Hydrograph showing mean monthly flow (m3/sec) of two tributaries of the Tigris River flowing into Huwaiza Marsh. Note similarity in flows pre-1997 and post-2003 and similarity in flows during the period of drainage between 1997 and 2003 and the period post-2005. Data provided by Iraq Ministry of Water Resources.

BIOLOGICAL CONSIDERATIONS

Macrophytes, including algae, mosses, ferns and vascular plants, are the most obvious and perhaps the biggest biotic components of most marshes. As primary producers, they are the foundation of food webs because they capture energy from the sun and transform it into other energy sources for higher organisms. Macrophytes also influence abiotic characteristics such as light levels, water currents, sedimentation processes and biogeochemical characteristics such as pH, conductivity, nutrients, dissolved oxygen and dissolved organic concentration (van der Valk 2006). Thus, macrophytes can be useful bioindicators of hydrological regime, soils and nutrient regimes if relationships between plant species and specific ecological parameters are known.

Al-Hilli undertook in the mid-1970s an important study of the macrophytes in a representative part of the marshes in southern Iraq (al-Hilli et al. 2009). It was possible to recognize five major groups of macrophyte growth forms: submerged, floating, herbaceous tall emergent, herbaceous low emergent and woody emergent. The common reed (*Phragmites australis*) and cattail (*Typha domingensis*) were the most common. Water level proved to be a dominant variable on determining macrophyte distributions, which emphasizes the need for the high water period in the spring and low water levels in the summer. Salinity proved to be a co-dominant factor.

The macrophytes showed differences in the Central marshes between the 1970s and after flooding in 2006–2007 (Hamdan et al. 2010). Most of the macrophyte species and communities widely distributed in the 1970s were present in 2006–2007. The environmental attributes are likely hindering the macrophyte re-establishment. In addition, a much more subdued seasonal fluctuation in the quantity of water inputs and outputs where there is no flood event in spring appears to have been responsible for delay in vegetation recovery in the Central marsh (Hamden et al. 2010). Many macrophyte species and communities known to exist prior to drainage returned, but floating and submerged species such as *Myriophyllum verticillatum*, *Nymphoides indica* and *Utricularia sp.* did not return in the new marshes. Overall species diversity was lower than before drainage too. The two most dominant macrophyte communities, *Phragmites australis* and *Typha domingensis*, reappeared but were not as productive as previously. The bulrush, *Schoenoplectus litoralis*, seemed to be more widespread, likely due to low suspended sediment load and clearer water conditions.

At least 100 taxa of algae (including what used to be called the blue-green algae) have been recorded in the marshes of southern Iraq (Maulood et al. 1981; Hinton and Maulood 1983). The distinctive feature of the algae is the great abundance of attached (i.e., periphyton) forms of both diatoms and non-diatom species which is not surprising in a fluvial high energy marsh such as in southern Iraq. Similarly, diatoms dominate the phytoplankton (i.e., free-floating) in terms of biomass, though species diversity is greatest among the non-diatom groups. Encrusted mats of algae (and Cyanobacteria) are common along the margins and on exposed sediment surfaces in the marsh during the low water periods in the summer and autumn. High water pH, conductivity, salinity and turbidity appear to be important environmental variables associated with algae communities in the marshes. While still high, these parameters are much lower in areas where there are less boating and other human activities (Maulood et al. 1979, 1981).

In general, the algae do not show great differences between the periods before and after drainage. Our preliminary work in 2005–2007 shows that there is abundant periphyton and planktonic algae in the reflooded marshes today.

Salinity and total suspended solids are two important parameters associated with algae abundance. Other abiotic and biotic parameters, such as water depth, water temperature, light penetration and dissolved oxygen tend to exert significant impact on algae communities at more local scales depending on the physical setting and hydrological influences. Algae responds to high nutrients (i.e., nitrogen and phosphorous) which can be derived from both point and non-point sources from human activity.

Fish found in the marshes are comprised of those which spend their whole lives in fresh waters and those which are primarily marine but move inland into fresh waters or waters under tidal influence from the Gulf (Coad 2010). The Hammar Marsh is one part of the marshes that is influenced by tides from the Gulf. A total of 31 species were recorded in reflooded sections. There were 14 native freshwater fish, 6 exotic freshwater fish and 11 species of marine origin. Resident species (present for 9–12 months) numbered 10, seasonal species (6–8 months) numbered 5 and occasional species (1–5 months) numbered 16, indicating a low diversity. The number of species was lowest in December at only 5 species and diversity increased in March–April and in July, which was the highest at 22 species. In contrast, the Huwaiza Marsh, which is the most intact part of the marshes remaining today and is not influenced by tides from the Gulf, had 15 species, 12 being native and 3 exotics (none of marine origin) in the same study. Resident species numbered 9, seasonal species 3 and occasional species 3. The number of species was lowest in December at 5 species and diversity increased in March–April, in July and September, the latter two being highest at 13 species (Coad 2010).

OTHER CONSIDERATIONS

Sociological and political factors are important components of restoration planning. There must be opportunity and will for restoration by all stakeholders. Those who own and control the land such as the residents, farmers, fishermen and business-owners must be included. Local through national levels of governing and decision-making bodies must be involved too. There must be the technical and scientific knowledge available to know what is possible and how best restoration options might be accomplished. Wetland restoration projects of comparable size as that in southern Iraq have proven successful because a multi-stakeholder decision-making body was put in charge of developing and implementing the restoration plan. The Everglades in Florida and the Gulf Coast of the southern United States are good examples of where restoration has been successful (Keddy et al. 2007; Richardson 2008). The CIMI project has provided guidance to Iraqis for pulling together the necessary multi-stake holder group that might be required for the marshes in southern Iraq. Results from this process are to be completed in 2010.

Among the biggest challenge is to obtain consensus in setting priorities and goals for restoration. Scientists can provide advice and educated guesses on what might be achievable based on an understanding of the processes responsible for shaping the marsh ecosystem. There may be a number of options. The decision for future goals is not a scientific issue alone. However, good science should be used to guide the needs and goals of restoration.

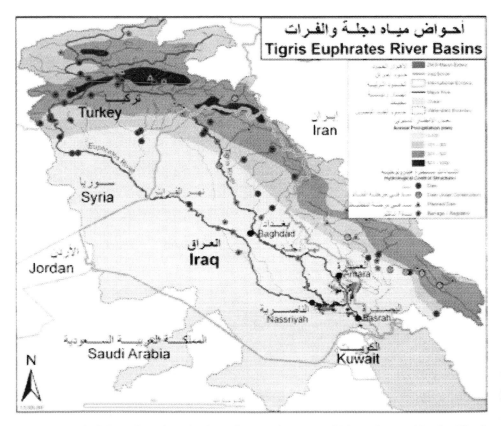

Figure 10.4 Map showing the location of dams as of 2009 situated in the Tigris and Euphrates watershed (Courtesy: K. Holmes, University of Victoria).

Figure 10.5a Photographs taken in 1973–74 of selected macrophyte communities in the Central Marshes. Courtesty of Dr M. R. al-Hilli. Submerged aquatic community *Potamogeton nodosus.*

Figure 10.5b Emergent tall aquatic community *Typha domingensis* and emergent low aquatic community *Polygonum salicifolium* in foreground.

Figure 10.5c Emergent tall aquatic community *Phragmites australis.*

Figure 10.5d Submerged aquatic community *Myriophyllum verticullatum,* floating leaved aquatic community *Nymphoides indica* in foreground and emergent tall aquatic community with *Typha domingensis* in background.

Figure 10.5e Floating leaved aquatic community *Nymphoides indica* on wet mud during low water period and emergent tall aquatic community *Typha domingensis* in background.

Figure 10.5f Gathering *Polygonum salicifolium* for cattle feed.

RESTORATION GOALS

Perhaps the most important step in any restoration program is defining goals and targeting what pre-existing condition is desirable and attainable in the context of environmental conditions and the time frame of the project. Any assessment of restoration success in the future cannot be determined unless expectations and wetland thresholds have been clearly defined at the outset of the restoration planning process. Restoration goals must include the whole ecosystem. This is especially difficult for large areas such as the marshes in southern Iraq.

Wetland of some kind or another has probably existed in southern Iraq for as long as the Tigris and Euphrates Rivers have existed. Geological and archaeological evidence and sediment age dating suggest wetlands of some kind existed for most of the last 9,000 years in southern Iraq. It was probably not until the last 1,000–3,000 years, however, that the modern-day marsh ecosystem as we know it was established with freshwater-dominated and brackish/saline water influences (Aqrawi and Evans, 1994; Aqrawi, 2001; Morizova, 2005). The emergence of agriculture and urban settlement, a milestone in the development of modern humankind, occurred in this part of the Fertile Crescent. The inhabitants today practice a way of life inextricably linked to wetlands that remains much as it did from these early times when people first migrated to the region. Despite this important history, it is unreasonable to target the marshes of several thousands of years ago as a reasonable restoration goal, even if we had accurate information on what they looked like at the time.

It is nearly impossible to find a period in the history of the marshes when humans were not present. Other chapters (ie., chapters 1 and 2) in this volume summarize the long history of humans in the marshes. Given the human presence for most if not all of their history, a true pristine state probably never existed. The marshes very much represent an altered landscape that has been modified and disturbed by humans living in and around them. Thus this history makes it difficult to use the pristine state as a suitable restoration target.

We would suggest that a more reasonable goal might be the state of the marshes as they existed in the 1970s prior to the recent period of greatest impact and destruction. There is a reasonable body of knowledge about what the marshes looked like then. We know what the primary forces are that have degraded and destroyed marshes, and hence the forces that need to be reversed to achieve restoration.

CONCLUSIONS

The marshes in southern Iraq represent a large geographic area. The natural system is highly variable and dynamic geologically, hydrologically, hydrogeochemically and biologically in both space and time (i.e., daily, seasonally and annually). There is an intimate relationship between the natural ecosystem and its human residents, a relationship that has existed and evolved for centuries. For this relationship to continue in the future, full restoration will be required. Restoration must adopt an ecological and not an engineering approach alone to be successful. Figure 10.6 is an attempt to summarize some of the most important environmental factors acting on the marshes of southern Iraq which should assist in understanding the consequence and impact of choices in setting restoration goals.

Based on our experience, field observations and scientific studies, we indicate the following is a limited list of some key factors that need to be considered if restoration is to be successful for any parts of the marshes in southern Iraq:

a. the geomorphology of the main river channels, secondary channels, and backwater is dynamic and susceptible to major erosion and deposition events, which will elicit immediate response by the biota, most macrophyte communities.

b. suspended sediment loads of both organic and inorganic materials are sources of nutrients for plants and food for animals; upstream engineering structures such as dams and reservoirs minimize suspended sediment loads and thus have a negative impact on life in the marshes and on restoration potential.

c. water flows and ebbs must maintain a seasonal cycle of high water levels for two to three months (March to May) in spring followed by a period where water levels fall to annual low levels in summer (June–September), and then minor increases in winter (December–February); the timing of releases from upstream dams and reservoirs do not follow this rhythm of change and would lead to greater restoration success if they did.

    d. macrophytes respond well and almost immediately to reflooding even after old marsh soils have been desiccated for decades because: (i) local seed banks remain viable and new seeds can be transported from long distances to establish new communities, and (ii) desiccation has oxidized nutrients from old marsh soils that are remobilized and reintroduced to the marshes; reduced suspended sediments and nutrient supplies create macrophyte communities in a way in the new marshes that did not exist previously.

    e. open connections between the upstream Tigris and Euphrates Rivers and the downstream Shatt al-Arab are required for fish populations in the marshes.

    f. control structures and artificial water regulation have a negative impact on all aspects of the marshes; greatest restoration success will result if engineering is minimized or removed completely.

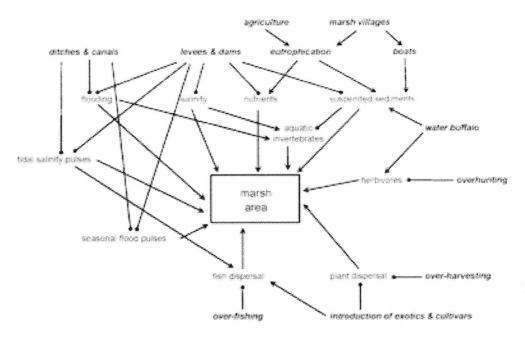

Figure 10.6 A summary of some of the most important environmental factors acting on the marshes of southern Iraq. The symbol ⟶ indicates a positive effect and the symbol ⟶• indicates a negative effect. Human factors, shown in bold italics, can augment natural factors and can contribute to marsh degradation and loss. (Adapted for the Iraqi marshes after a similar diagram for Louisiana wetlands in Keddy et al. 2007)

g. maps, geographic information systems and models of hydrology, hydrodynamics and ecology are all available and should be used; these data need to be verified by ground truthing and field work.

h. local residents are adapted to and have developed their unique lifestyles and livelihoods based on a dynamic and highly variable aquatic habitat; inability to restore these natural processes that sustain the marshes will limit the success of the local inhabitants in their natural and traditional way of life.

11

SUSTAINABLE HOUSING UTILIZING INDIGENOUS MATERIALS IN THE MARSHES

Mufid A.Samarai

INTRODUCTION

The marshes consist of 4,000 sq. km. of marshes during drought time and 15,000 sq.km. during flood time. The altitude varies between 1m below mean sea level to 4m above mean sea level. The area is strongly characterized by marshes and marshland (Maxwell, 1998). The subsoil for the whole area dates from the recent Pleistocene. It is fully covered by recent quaternary river alluviums. Marshland soil is normally characterized by continuous water presence, near or above the land surface, which creates exceptional conditions for lacustrine life. The water level in the wetlands varies from 50 cm. to 400 cm., and may increase somewhat during exceptional flood. The climate in the area is of a sub-tropical type, hot and dry in summer and cool with little rainfall in winter. Dominant winds are northwesterly. The mean air temperature ranges from about 12 °C in January to about 37 °C in July, the mean relative humidity in the same period goes from 78 to 49 per cent – i.e. an amplitude of 29 per cent.

The main types of plants are palm trees, cane/tall reed (*Phragmites karka Trin.*) and bullrush (*Typha latifolia*) which grow on the edge of marshes between 0.5 and 2.5 meters of water level. These plants have been used as building materials throughout the past and the techniques have gradually improved over the millenia. Reed houses are the most characteristic features of the wetlands. Such houses are built on small artificial islands made from layers of reed and mud. Traditional utilization of reeds and mud in houses in all its forms has reached a high level of proficiency taking into account that reeds are natural materials and do not require treatment. Moreover, they can be transformed manually with the use of simple tools (Salim, 1970). Figure 11.1 shows a large village guest house (*mudhif*) in the process of being built of reeds using traditional techniques.

These techniques highlight the richness and inventiveness of local builders and their ability to make the best possible use of the limited variety of locally available building materials. It also meets the needs of the local inhabitants in a manner that is appropriate to the regional and environmental conditions of their natural habitat. In this aquatic environment a close relationship and bond with nature has been formed over the years one which has existed since the earliest forms of civilization. The rural population has kept the local characteristics of their homeland settlement and this became the rational and emotional necessity (Samarai & Azawi, 1997).

The adoption of imported sophisticated building technology contributes to high energy consumption and expensive maintenance and contrasts with the call for the utilization of lower-cost housing technologies to raise the living standards of the low-income population in developing countries. Local authorities and standards do not typically encourage the use of indigenous materials. What is indigenous is often considered by many to be outdated and substandard. This has led many builders to turn to the use of concrete blocks which are not environmentally friendly and which require high energy in their production. Among the many challenges the marsh dwellers will face in the twenty-first century will be to safeguard and conserve the environment. This requires the use of renewable and ecological materials of low energy and low cost like vegetable plants and natural fibers.

The intellectual framework for the integrated marsh management approach recognizes that people are at the heart of the ecosystem, and that restoration must be compatible with a wide range of economic activities that contribute to human welfare and sustainable development. The approach also recognizes

Figure 11.1 Photo depicting marsh dwellers in the process of constructing a traditional *mudhif*.

the limitations imposed by available water and the importance of achieving ecological, environmental and human equilibrium. Healthy restored marsh-land ecosystems support biodiversity, improve environmental quality and generate goods and services, such as fisheries and grazing, providing many benefits to local communities (USAID, 2004).

With respect to earth materials, research was conducted to stabilize the soil with additives and compressing the blocks with compaction pressure of about 10 MN/m² initially using a manually operated press with hydraulic action so that the blocks produced are dense, more durable, strong in a green state, have better strength and better appearance (Samarai & Laquerbe, 1987).

Overall, the situation of the current infrastructures is substandard to non-existent. There is a lack of potable water supply except at a few select locations. Effluent disposal and lavatories is one of the key environmental problems facing the marsh dwellers in the marshes and water areas and perhaps the most difficult to resolve. Accessibility can also be very challenging and can pose considerable problems in addition to being more costly in the marshes than on dry land.

This chapter presents the planning and implementation of a major low-cost housing project for areas of a special alluvial nature. It is essential to take into account the very special natural, historical, social and economic characteristics of the wider study area. This will discourage the tendency of the native population to leave the marshes for urban areas or to seek a modern lifestyle similar to that of urban regions. The environmental and socio-economic factors could create a rural settlement fabric pattern that would be unique. Moreover, this project could be the first of its kind in the region.

SIGNIFICANCE OF THE PROJECT

Because of the drying of the marshes for many years and the devastating drought that the wetland region has been experiencing, in many marsh areas a massive tendency emerged among the native inhabitants to migrate to regional urban centers like Basrah, Nasiriyaah, Amarah and Baghdad, to seek permanent work and perhaps a more modern lifestyle . This is particularly evident among the younger generation who often lack the close connection with the wetlands that their elders have. There now exists an urgent need for a concerted effort to preserve these wetlands which have already started to lose their unique individuality. The population in this area was of sufficient size and density to commence the building of a complete and distinct settlement. The water surface and supplies are normally enough to maintain the local landscape and economic conditions and to maintain the local characteristics.

Moreover, there are good and viable economic opportunities to start agro-industrial projects in this area. The distinct geographical and exotic environmental conditions have created several remarkable potential sites, interesting land and water sequence and aura, which could create ideal conditions for a natural park.

There is a lack of requirements of an acceptable standard of living and lack of durability of building materials. Constructions are not protected from fire, and particularly the reed structure. If electricity is installed, this will increase the risks substantially. Reeds will deteriorate rapidly with insects and rot fungi. Till the reeds are improved and their life span is increased such a construction will need very frequent replacement, which puts a great burden on the inhabitants and reduces their standard of living, which is already under strain due to the high cost of reclaimed land.

Flooding is one of the most serious problems in the marshes and the zones located close to the water bodies. Mud houses were not suitable in these areas (Samarai, 2005). There is also the problem of insects as reed structures offer shelter for all species of insects.

The target of the Project is to improve the level of services, not only for the dwelling units, but also for all the social and public services, including technical infrastructures and utilities. The research is to consider all the possibilities of utilizing local building materials (reeds and earth), in a rationalized and industrialized way, adapted to the conditions of the region. The environmental and socio-economic factors could create a rural settlement fabric pattern that would be unique in the world. Preserving the traditional craft of making reed houses and the technology of building the *mudhif* was one of the main targets of the study.

RESEARCH METHODOLOGY

The project was related to an analysis and a diagnosis, with two basic lines of research:

1. A thorough analysis of all the topics, in order to check the past data and studies and integrate and synthesize the relevant and interesting planning and implementation experience, in the study region and abroad.
2. Synthesis and elaboration of diagnoses, aimed at comparison of various factors, proposals and techniques, as an input to the implementation of the project.

A methodological outline contained in this study recapitulates the overall context of the project and the retained methodology for the future work. Taking into account the very specific natural, historical, social and economic characteristics of the marshes, the target of the project is to improve, by having direct involvement from the local population, the existing housing stock and the level of services, not only for the dwelling units, but also for all the social and public services, including technical infrastructure and utilities, to reach an optimal output for settlements in the marshes as an alternative to traditional forms of construction.

Furthermore, the research is designed and aimed at considering all the possibilities of utilizing local building materials – reeds, papyrus and earth – and to seek methods for bettering them in order to have better utilization and a greater life span for improvement of housing conditions, through the utilization of local manpower, and of techniques introducing equipment and machinery minimizing the need for using ropes or sophisticated maintenance, so that there is a continuity in using these kinds of materials with the past traditions.

Regarding reeds, bulrush and papyrus, research was also conducted to determine if it is possible with a single-step process to make reeds insect-proof, rot-proof and fire-proof. There is also a need to examine further the possibility and practicality of using the reed fibers for making the panels and to examine if structural elements can be made with reeds after improving their useful life span.

To put all these factors in harmony, studies on planning all services and design of the future villages were undertaken. This led to the start of our first experiment in SEDIA, where a system of housing units based on traditional forms, materials and construction was devised. Through the use of modular coordination of units and components a great flexibility was achieved. The basic building materials were reed and papyrus. These materials were exposed to the outside and the interior was lined with a fire-proof interior finishes, such as plaster, fiberglass and eternite. In some cases the cane was left exposed to the inside of the building.

Foundations suffered different problems of settlement of embankments, waving of surface, and sometimes failure of embankment. To evaluate and assess these problems and avoid them in future development in the marshes, a full scale trial embankment was constructed in Medina experiment station. The fully instrumented embankment was 90m long, 6m high with side slopes 2:5:1. The width of the crest was 12m. Two sections were constructed; section A was reinforced with bundles of reeds (*berdi*), section B was without reinforcement. The bundles of *berdi* were placed on the marsh across the bottom of the embankment aligned perpendicular to the center line of the embankment. The two sections were fully instrumented to monitor settlement, pore pressure and lateral deformation of the embankment and the foundation soil underneath.

[234]

MATERIALS AND BUILDING TECHNOLOGY

Foundation System

Traditionally, dwellings in the marsh environments are erected on islands ranging from 150–200 sq. m. The surface is the size of the house and with enough storage and cattle areas. Provision is also kept for future expansion and for boat landing space.

Since the site bed is about 30 meters thick and made of fine soil, it is evident that in such an unconsolidated saturated soil and over such a depth, conventional foundations would settle excessively with large differential settlement, and it would be out of the question to apply pile foundations which would certainly have a prohibitive cost in this area.

Locally, a reed island is faced along its periphery with a protection made of planted and plaited reeds. This fence also provides protection against mechanical erosion due to water rippling. Inside this fencing, mud and cane are added to increase the ground level thereby sheltering the island's surface from flooding and decreasing its moisture content. The resulting platform is consolidated by means of rough manual compacting. This technique allows for construction of a light reed structure. However, due to poor subsoil conditions, the underlying layers are liable to deform and sink and constant maintenance of the island is necessary (Mohamadi & Samarai, 2004).

The Mudhif

The traditional craft of building reed houses follows a technique thousands of years old and is best illustrated in making a *mudhif* (guest house). The typical *mudhif* is built from a reed skeleton, which consists of long thick bundles making continuous columns and beams and thin bundles for purlins. The skeleton is covered with reed mats. The lower part of the *mudhif* is left open with reed grills to allow the air to pass through during the summer, and is closed during the winter with reeds (Figure 7.7).

To make a *mudhif*, a small group of workers dig holes opposite each other 75 cm. apart deep in the ground about 2 mm. apart in two parallel lines. The reed bundles are firmly placed into these holes. The height of each bundle is 3–5meters and is kept leaning to the outside and is tied at the top forming arches. The workers stand on the framework of a temporary column made of cane. One of the workers gathers the top of the cane bundle while the other brings the other opposite and they tie the two tops together. All structural reed bundles are tied with reed strips. However, these reed strips are liable to get broken and loosen after some time. We suggest tying all these parts with galvanized steel wire.

The cane bundles which make the purling run at close spacing throughout the building and tie all the columns horizontally. At this stage, the building is ready for covering with cane mats, which have a golden color, which afterwards with the passage of time gets discolored and looks earthen in color. Some parts like the front and the backs and the side grills are prefabricated on site and cut to size after fixing to the structure.

In the Sedia experiment station complete models of a *mudhif* was constructed using the same procedures and materials as in the marshlands (Figure 11.1). The construction was carried out by people from the same region. The aim was to check if it is possible to mechanize parts of the erection and to enhance the materials' durability by additives to protect against fungi attack, fire and rot.

Reeds and Bulrush/Papyrus

Regarding the use of reeds and bulrush/papyrus, research was carried out to find if it is possible, utilizing a single-step process, to make reeds insect-proof, rot-proof and fire-proof. There is also a need to further examine both the possibility and the practicality of using reed fibers for the manufacture of panels and to examine if structural elements can be made with reeds after improving their life span.

For the industrially prefabricated reed board a small production unit was built in the experiment station where those panels were manufactured and different binding materials and reinforcing frames were tested (Figure 11.4). The semi-industrial unit was established on the site for the production of two species of reeds growing in the marsh area (Phragmita communes and Typha latifolia) used for roofing, walls and doors of new dwelling units. Several types of glue were used, namely:

- Urea-formol glue (65 per cent dry extract)
- Melamine-urea-formol glue (65 per cent dry extracted); Isocynate glues
- Powdered asphalt, as urea-formol glues complement

All panels were hot-pressed at $90°C$ and the pressure was regulated in relation to the panel thickness and density.

In the Sedia experiment, a thin cement mortar was used to fill all irregularities in the surfaces of cane mats and then adhesive was spread evenly on the whole wall surface. Ordinary wall adhesive was used, and then the fiberglass wall finish was applied. This finish can be applied to surfaces such as gypsum panels or plastered surfaces.

EXPERIMENTAL WORK AND SUGGESTED IMPROVEMENTS

The Island

In the conventional method, an island is constructed with alternate mud and reed layers. Therefore, the reed reinforcement will help in reducing the lateral spread of the island and will also help the island's initial stabilization. However, this vegetal matter would entail some island subsidence due to rotting, but by then most of the settlement would be over.

A trial embankment was constructed in a typical marsh area at Medina and instruments such as piezometers, inclometers and settlement gauges were installed at different locations along the cross-section and at different depths to monitor excess and total settlement with the passage of time. The fully instrumented embankment was 90m long, 6m high with side slopes 2:5:1. The width of crest was 12 m. Two sections were constructed; section A was reinforced with bundles of reeds (*berdi*), section B was without reinforcement. The bundles of *berdi* were placed on the marsh across the bottom of the embankment aligned perpendicular to the centerline of the embankment. The two sections were fully instrumented to monitor settlement, pore pressure and lateral deformation of the embankment and the foundation soil underneath.

Mudhif Construction

In traditional reed construction methods, holes are dug in the ground for the foundations and main supports, and reed bundles are placed in these holes. After a short period when the reed is placed in the ground, it begins to decay. The decayed portion is cut off and the supporting reed post along with the superstructure which it carries, is correspondingly lowered. This process continues until the entire structure needs to be rebuilt. The improved foundation is aimed at extending the life span of the reed posts which are buried in the ground. The following improvements are recommended: 1. Treatment of the reeds with suitable chemicals to increase their rigidity and particularly to extend their useful life. 2. Giving them protective coating by dipping in hot asphalt, and preferably spraying with a simple hand pump the sides and bottom of the hole with cut back bitumen (asphalt + kerosene oil) to plug the capillary pores of the soil and provide extra protection against water.

Housing Units

In the experiment conducted at Medina, improvement of existing techniques was made by using a lightweight timber or steel framework instead of a reed skeleton. The structural elements and the completion elements can be removed or added without affecting the total structure of the building unit. The total structure is adapted for seasonal changes through the use of reed panels to fit into the cane grills through the winter and removing the panels during the summer. A framework of PVC tubes can also be made in a suitable form assembled as for a sanitary plumbing assembly. The principle is the same as for the metallic one, but with plastic tubes replacing the metallic framework.

For the above framework, which would be very durable, erection would be rapid indeed for non-skilled, non-trained builders directed by a craftsman, all belonging to the village and working on a self-help basis. On the completed framework, reed mats manufactured by the inhabitants would be placed.

Floor improvements consist in binding the body of the island and at the same time limiting moisture penetration. This may be achieved in either of the following manners:

1. A water barrier (polyethylene sheet), about 10 cm. subgrade of granular material with stabilized soil or other suitable topping.
2. Two layers of crossed reeds covered with a bitumen coating and earth.

The two basic constraints for the roof are water imperviousness and better durability of connections of various members. For waterproofing, a polyethylene sheet should be provided between the top mat and the reed structure. This will not pose much problem with regard to air ventilation in summer as the *mudhif* is left open with cane grilles to allow the air to pass through during the summer and closed during winter with reeds. For better durability of connections, different members can be tied together very firmly with the help of soft galvanized iron wire or cords instead of cane strips.

Modular Co-ordination of Housing Units

The Sedia experiment was comprised of fixed size units 6.4 m. long and 3.2 m. wide. Each unit consisted of reed panels fixed to either metal or timber frames at 1.6m centers. A combination of any of the following units can be adopted such as: guest and bedroom, two bedrooms, farm store closed or open, guest room, kitchen and store, service unit of kitchen, toilet and bathroom. This is a guide for a high standard of allocation of space. A lesser number of units could be adopted if desired. Pitched roof units are shown in Figure 11.3, and other combinations of flat roof units for larger settlements built on lands near the water utilizing reed conglomerate panels is shown in Figure 11.4.

In the Medina experiment the system adopted was an open system. Modular coordination was related to building elements and not to building units, as in Sedia. The shapes had flexible arrangements in many directions as shown in Figure 11.5a. Elements can be added or taken away in modules without

Figure 11.2a Production unit.

Figure 11.2b A semi-industrial unit was established on the site for the production of panels.

affecting the unit.Steel-framed elements were also used experimentally and proofed to be efficient and durable (Figure 11.5b).

To test the actual behavior and durability of the improvements suggested and implemented for the housing units, local families were moved to the experimental stations to occupy the units for over a year. The feedback from them was used to assess the functionality of the services, the flexibility of the units and the durability and behavior of the treated elements and frames.

RESULTS AND ACHIEVEMENTS

Boards and Panels

Physical mechanical tests of the reed conglomerate panels showed that it was possible to make boards from reed and with panels with a high percentage of cane. Typical examples of these panels are listed below:

Chipboard density (0.550 kg./cu.cm.) glues the urea-formol with 10 per cent asphalt for external uses; 80 per cent Typha l; 20 per cent Phragmita c. pressure bars 10 time pressed and 30 minutes collapse load bending in flexture. Traction is 0.44 dan./sq. cm. and Expansion 8. 20 per cent with thickness 40mm. Chipboard with pure Phragmita c. glue urea formol 15 per cent + 0.7 per cent wax pressure bars 18 times pressed 10 minutes. Board bending in flexure was with 132 DAN. Many types with great variety of glues and reed were used for the manufacturing of these panels. The above examples show that variation in physical tests is related to the use of different types of reed (Samarai, 1998).

The improvements and protections used for the roofs, floors and frames proved to be very efficient and effective. After one year of observation no deterioration or rotting was observed. This was not the case for the non-treated elements which showed some signs of defect after six months. For

Figure 11.3. Experimenting with pitched wood and reeds roofing and walls.

the framework, which was very durable, erection was rapid even with the non-skilled, non-trained builders directed by a craftsman, all from the occupants of the experimental village.

For the industrially prefabricated reed board it was observed that when using reed as raw material, with or without adding soft wood, board can be industrially prefabricated with glue and cement for use in partition walls. In this case there is also the possibility of using these prefabricated reed panels in superstructures outside the marsh area. A small production unit was built in the marshes where those panels were manufactured and different binding materials and reinforcing frames were tested.

The Island and Foundations

Based on the observations of the two trial embankments of the island, it was seen that reed reinforcement is very effective in reducing lateral spread and the settlement is more uniform throughout the cross-section. It was also observed that there was a large percentage of excess pore pressure in the first few months after the embankment construction. However, excess pore pressure is not completely dissipated even after a one-year period. The settlement of the unreinforced section B was almost twice the settlement of the reinforced section A, until the embankment height reached about 3.4 m., after which the settlement in section A increased at a faster rate than that of section B.

This behavior indicated that the bundles of reed reinforcement at the bottom of the embankment in section A were very effective in restricting lateral displacement at the interface of the fill and natural ground, thus reducing the maximum settlement. At the end of construction, the settlement of the reinforced section A was still smaller than that of the unreinforced section B by about 17 per cent. The difference in settlement between sections A and B was maintained throughout the process. At the end of the consolidation stage the settlement of sections A and B were 460mm and 540mm respectively. This difference is attributed to the use of reed reinforcement in section A which had reduced the settlement by about 16 per cent. The maximum measured lateral displacements at plates near the toe of the embankment were 28 mm. and 61 mm. for the reinforced section A and unreinforced section B respectively. This result clearly indicates the effectiveness of the reinforcement used in the experiment.

In the conventional method, an island is constructed with alternate mud and reed layers. Therefore, this reed reinforcement will help in reducing the lateral spread of the island and will also help the island's initial stabilization. However, this vegetal matter would entail some island subsidence due to rotting,

ELEVATION

SECTION

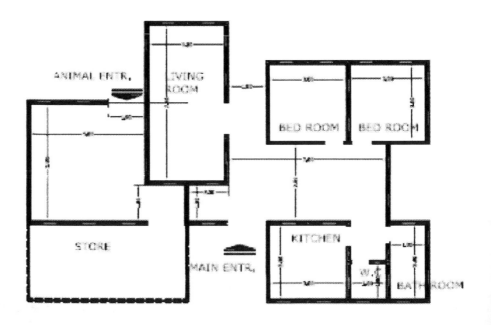

PLAN 3 UNIT LAYOUT

Figure 11.4 Flat roof units for larger settlements on dry land utilizing reed conglomerate panels.

but by that time most of the settlement would be over. It is very important to construct the island sufficiently higher than the designed level to allow for anticipated settlement of the fill. This additional fill will also provide some surcharge, i.e., a temporary load equal or in excess of that of the reed structure (maximum load of reed structure 250 kg./sq. m.), which will accelerate the rate of underlying primary consolidation and will eliminate most of the post-construction primary consolidation and part of the secondary consolidation.

It will also be very important to allow for a few months settling of the whole island, as during this period the level of the island would be substantially reduced unevenly. The large depressions due to settlement should be filled with humid earth excavated from the marsh bottom, and not in leveling the higher island sections to fill the lower ones. Once the leveling operation is over, the created island can be left for some time more for additional settling. The above procedure will help in island stabilization and is expected to reduce periodical maintenance to a large extent.

Modular Coordination of Housing Units

The proposed new technique for housing in the marshes made of panel modules 1.5 m. could be made any size and was well received and utilized by the inhabitants. The system lacks few important points. Lack of fixed joint between the panels. Joints should have lacing wire joining the edge running wires. The roofs are made of lightweight roofing materials. Insulation could be improved with a reed false roof under the roofing systems. Wall corners are exposed and without any protection. The reed could be fixed to the white metal wire. Construction members being used for storage and hanging. Cupboard storage should be provided and the interior lined to reduce fire-spread risk. Bathroom and service units without waterproof surface finish. Surface in all service units should have waterproof finish.

Stabilized Clay Bricks

With respect to earth materials, research was conducted to stabilize the soil with additives and compressing the blocks with compaction pressure of about 10 MN/m^2 initially using a manually operated press with hydraulic action so that the blocks produced are dense, more durable, strong in a green state, have better strength and better appearance (Samarai & Laquerbe, 1987).Different percentages of lime, cement and asphalt were mixed . A combination of more than one type was also tested. The best results in general were obtained from samples stabilized with cement then lime and then asphalt. However, results varied according to location of use and type of clay. Figure 11.6 shows the testing and manufacture of the stabilized soil bricks.

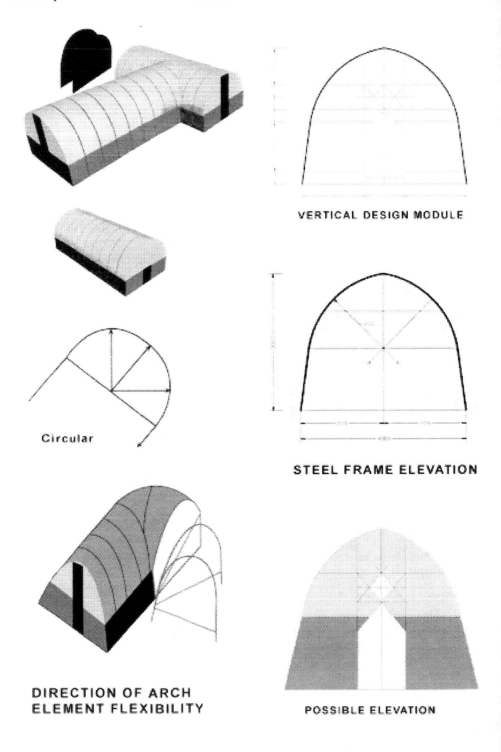

VERTICAL DESIGN MODULE

Circular

STEEL FRAME ELEVATION

DIRECTION OF ARCH
ELEMENT FLEXIBILITY

POSSIBLE ELEVATION

Figure 11. 5a. Erection of flexible arched elements.

Figure 11.5b Steel framed arched elements.

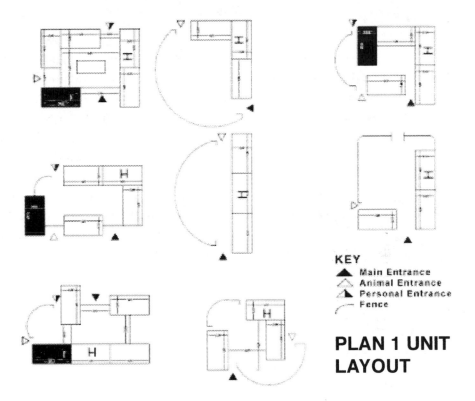

KEY
▲ Main Entrance
△ Animal Entrance
▲ Personal Entrance
⌒ Fence

PLAN 1 UNIT LAYOUT

Figure 11.6 Modular house units for different combinations of layout plans and roof types.

Figure 11.7 Testing and manufacture of stabilized soil bricks.

CONCLUSION

1. The main task in building low cost houses in the marshes is to find a simple structural frame which will make the house more durable and more functional. Wall and roof panels were produced using vegetable plants and their fibers after modifying them to be more fire-, insect- and moisture-proof. The proposed new technique for housing in the marshes made of panel modules 1.5 m. could be made any size and was well received and utilized by the inhabitants.

2. During the construction stage of the trial embankment, the settlement was increasing linearly with the increase of embankment height in both the reinforced section A and the unreinforced section B. At section A the rate of settlement increased markedly when the height exceeded 3.4 m. The settlement of unreinforced section B was almost twice that of the reinforced section A.

3. For the industrially prefabricated reed board it was observed that when using reed as raw material, with or without adding soft wood, board can be industrially prefabricated with glue and cement for use in partition walls. In this case there is also the possibility of using these prefabricated reed panels in superstructures outside the marsh area. A small production unit was built in the marshes where those panels were manufactured and different binding materials and reinforcing frames were tested.

4. The improvements and protections used for the roofs, floors and frames proved to be very efficient and effective. After one year of observation no deterioration or rotting was observed. This was not the case for the non-treated elements which showed some signs of defect after six months. For the framework, which was very durable, erection was rapid even with the non-skilled, non-trained builders directed by a craftsman, all from the occupants of the experimental village.

12

FUTURE OF THE MARSHLANDS –
A RETURN TO EDEN?

Jasim al-Asadi

GENERAL OVERVIEW

Since the beginning of history, humans have sought the secret of immortality. The Gilgamesh Epic (legendary king of Uruk – *c*.2700–2650 BC) is a prime example that reflects this maniacal craze in the search for everlasting life but in which the hero fails in all his attempts to find immortality. Nevertheless, in the final analysis they add to our wisdom and help us to understand the meaning of life and reconcile us to the inevitability of mortality. Similarly, the concepts of Eden and eternity go hand in hand and resemble twin brothers seeking infinite continuity and survival as portrayed according to the history of legends and religions. They share visions with different dimensions while at the same time they are close to one another in reality and understanding. The meaning of Eden to the Arab marsh dweller conjures images of a magnificent palace, with gardens full of song and mermaids and rivers flowing with wine and milk. But is this the Eden we are seeking to restore? Is this the paradise of the marsh dwellers – the reed burners, fishers and buffalo breeders?

The Eden which we seek here and which we are trying to regenerate in the Iraqi Marshland is essentially based on a way of life that permits the local inhabitants to live in harmony with their environment and microclimate. It is desired that the marsh dwellers be active culturally and in contact with the outside world in a manner that helps promote an understanding of different cultures and the active exchange of ideas and viewpoints. There are several factors that need to be considered to facilitate the implementation of the vision and aspirations of the local inhabitants and there are some necessary steps that are required to be taken to achieve them.

Initial steps that must be implemented if marsh regeneration objectives are to be achieved. These include:

- Preparation of a historical and current perspective of the wetlands.
- Evaluation of existing mechanisms.
- Limit trends and scenarios for reflooding and following developments.
- Translating and benefiting from previous experience – local participation and action of locals.
- Perceived constraints on improving the welfare of the local population.
- Provide guidance on the protection and wise use of the wetland ecosystems.
- Sustainability and consistency with other societal priorities.
- Acknowledge the human dimension in ecosystems and establish trust to gain full practical support of local population.

Consequently a restored Eden must be based on a different set of international and local visions and perceptions. These should include those of the executants, the beneficiaries and the experience of owners in social, technical or scientific fields. The ultimate goal for Eden should not consist of a mere rebirth; it should also include the necessary fundamentals for its continuous development in line with the social, spiritual and other basic aspirations of its people.

THE HUWAYZA MARSHES

The Huwayza Marshes are an integral part of the Iraqi marshlands complex and are located at the confluence of the Tigris and Euphrates Rivers. According to Ramsar , which is an intergovernmental treaty, "The effects of extensive drainage in the 1990s and warfare destruction, as well as dam-building activities upstream in Iraq, Iran, Syria, and Turkey, are seen as the chief potential threats to the site." It should be noted that the Huwayza Marsh is characterized by certain features that differentiate it from the Central and Hammar marshes such as:

- Huwayza is a combined marsh with Iran where the boundary lines between the two nations divide it into two dissymmetrical parts; the larger segment (75–80 per cent) is located within Iraq's borders and is estimated to be about 2350 sq. km., whereas the other (smaller) segment is located in Iran (and is known there as Hawr al-Azim) and is estimated to constitute about 1150 sq. km. The Huwayza Marshes are a complex of marshes and lakes on the plains to the southeast of the Little Zab River, a tributary of the Tigris, and straddle the Iraq–Iran

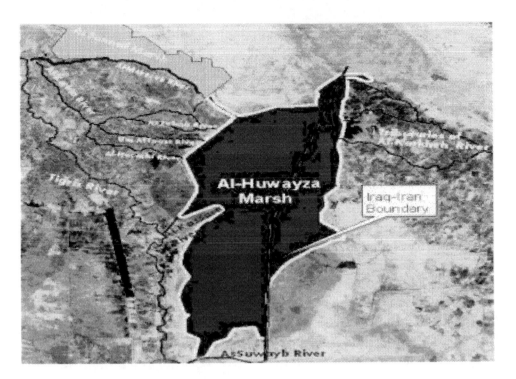

Figure 12.1 The Huwayza Marsh.

border (Figure 12.1) and extend approximately 80 kilometers from north to south, and 30 kilometers from east to west, covering an area of at least 3,000 square kilometers (Partow 2001). The marshes are located in the Maysan and Basra governorates.

- During the draining of the wetlands the Huwayza ecosystem reflected a slower and more gradual pattern of decline due mainly to the water inflow from the Iranian side. This is because the Huwayza Marsh depends for its feeding on the Tigris River in Iraq and the Karkheh River on the Iranian side (Figure 12.2). This strongly suggests an urgent need to create a united water policy between Iran and Iraq or a united environmental administration between the two countries.
- The marshlands had been directly involved in a devastating war during the 1980s (the war between Iraq and Iran), and to this day there remain thousands of unexploded mines and rockets which are proving lethal, killing many marsh dwellers and passengers on a regular basis.
- Even after the desiccation of the Central and Hammar Marshes, the Huwayza Marsh did not dry completely as an area of about 10 per cent of its land survived in spite of the cruelty of the Iraqi authorities at the time. The main difficulty facing the marshes is maintaining the water's quality and quantity.

The Huwayza Marshes represent the only significant area to have survived recent drainage actions and are considered to be the most intact part of the original Mesopotamian system which, according to Ramsar, "is of international importance as a staging and wintering area for at least 79 species of waterfowl and 9 species of birds of prey on their way between Western Siberia/Central Asia and eastern and southern Africa." The results of recent reflooding efforts have been inconsistent but encouraging, and some of the displaced Ma'dan and Marsh Arabs have started to return to their homeland to resume their traditional way of life (Figures 12.3, 12.4). The northern half of the Huwayza Marsh was never completely drained and is currently being used as a reference for monitoring the flora and fauna of the re-inundated southern sector. The continuous re-flooding of the Huwayza Marshes since 2003 has brought life to the marsh again and helped expand its borders with increased water levels, to become environmentally healthier than both the Central and Hammar Marshes. The Huwayza Marsh contains a wide variety of flora, birds, fauna and fish species as part of widely recognized ecosystem and thus decided to contract with the Ramsar Convention on the Wetlands treaty which came into effect on 17 February 2008. Contracting with Ramsar could offer many benefits to the Iraqi wetlands regeneration and protection program including:

- Providing an ecosystem icon and international acknowledgement of the importance of the Iraqi wetlands.
- Affords access to a wealth of experience in protection and management of the wetlands.

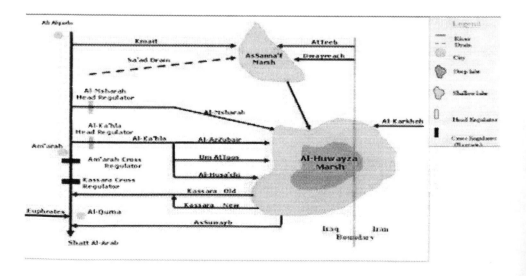

Figure 12.2 A Schematic Diagram of Main Water Resources of the Huwayza Marsh.

- Provides guidance on protection and wise use of wetland ecosystems.
- Provides guidance for international cooperation across borders and within river basins.

Historically, however, it has been shown that the Huwayza Marshes suffer from:

- Reduced discharges
- Suppression of traditional flood peak
- A complex network of canals, structures, and roads
- Elective changes taking place among human communities
- Inflow water with elevated levels of phosphates and nitrates through Iran inflows
- Iran has recently employed a 40-kilometer soil embankment to stop all inflow of water from the Iranian side to the Huwayza Marsh

For putting the Huwayza Marsh on the correct path to being restored we have to work hard in the following fields:

Hydraulics of the Huwayza Marsh

What should be noted regarding the Huwayza Marsh is that it currently gets its water from al-Kahlaa River, especially from the Zubair, Um Toss, a-Hissechey, and from one branch of al-Mishrah River which is also called Malih as the marsh is receiving minimal water inflow from the Karkheh River (Iranian side); likewise, it's feeding from seasonal rains is also very limited.

Irrigation developments on the Karkheh River Project in the Azadegan Plain (in Iran), as well as plains in the upstream reaches, would adversely impact the quality, quantity, timing and distribution of the water supplied to the marsh. Furthermore, regulators in the Karkheh Storage Dam, and releases according to the irrigation requirements, would change the natural characteristics of the river's flow. Building a dam on the Karkheh River with engineering works within the river and on the lands adjoining the river by the Iranians dramatically affects the amount and method of feeding of water entering the marsh from the Iranian side. On the other hand the presence of salts, phosphates and nitrates have a serious effect on agriculture and other activities further down the Karkheh River.

As the Iranian dams which are built along the borders (where the works still continue) and that separate Iran and Iraq, have greatly affected the movement of water and hydraulic activity as the water outlets through al-Kassrah and al-Sweyib Rivers towards the Tigris and Shatt al-Arab waterway respectively and remain unorganized and not having submitted to regulatory control. Moreover, its arbitrary draining depends on the water levels of the Huwayza Marsh. Thus in order to proceed to regenerate the marsh in the right direction from a hydraulic aspect, a number of corrective steps have to be taken such as putting in place engineering works and controls to monitor discharge times and volumes and keep water levels within acceptable limits.

Controlled Management

Recognizing that both "Natural In-Out" and "Semi-Natural" Management are no longer feasible or adequate in today's Iraq, although the last alternative appears to be the most appealing. We may refer to this strategy as "controlled", referring to a system where both inflows and outflows are fully regulated. The intended purpose of a "controlled" management system is to gain the necessary water inflow and monitor water level variations to allow the ecological system to thrive. From a hydraulic standpoint, "controlled" management will operate the marshes as if they were tanks that require filling and emptying through time. To do so, it is necessary to close or limit the outflows while the "tank" is filled and the water level is rising, and to limit inflows and outflows when a drop in water elevation is required. Although simple in principle, "controlled" management is the hardest to operate: scheduled flows must be ready when it is time to release water out of the marshes.

Figure 12.3 Woman and child in a *mashuf* showing partial restoration of the wetlands.

Figure 12.4 Marsh fisherman showing his catch.

"Controlled" management is not only feasible but is also the most water-saving and efficient strategy for the Iraqi marshlands, and was selected by the New Eden Team as the preferred management solution for the Iraqi wetlands. The following sections clarify the pros and cons of each alternative, first taking into consideration possible inflow strategies followed by possible outflow strategies.

Upstream Water Control

The previous sections discussed possible alternatives for overall marshland management and indicated that a "controlled" strategy allows for a level of flow control which makes it possible to achieve the recommended flow level of marshland restoration. "Controlled" management requires that a system of water regulators are in place both upstream and downstream of the marshes. Water control structures can be operated in a number of ways in order to meet the desired water flow-through and water level varieties inside the wetlands.

The following paragraphs present three alternative approaches for operation of the upstream water control structures:

1. Steady Inflow (SI): A first option for upstream water control consists of using available hydraulic structures to maintain an inflow to the marsh. This operation is simple and leaves all the responsibility for changing

water levels inside the marsh to the outflow water control structures. This operation will henceforth be referred to as "Steady Inflow" (SI).

2. Steady Inflow "On-Off" Option: The second option for the upstream water control is to use a hydraulic structure to maintain either a constant inflow or no inflow at all according to the period of the year; the management approach is basically similar to the SI system, the only difference being that inflows are switched off when not required. This On-Off system is quite simple to implement with hydraulic structures; the operations on the gate opening are less frequent during the year.

3. Optimized Inflow (OI): A third option for operation of the upstream water control structures is to continuously optimize the inflow necessary to obtain the required water level changes inside the marshes. The OI system is clearly more complex to operate and as an active management system is required at all times; operations relating to the gate's opening are quite frequent and changes must be made almost on a monthly basis.

Downstream Construction

Based on results of the New Eden Master Plan in 2006, the Iraq Ministry of Water of Resources agreed on the design of two water control structures to be built at the outlet of the Kassrah and Sweyib Rivers. These control structures are designed to regulate water levels inside Huwayza Marsh. As for the general functions of the proposed structures, Huwayza Marsh's high water losses are due to evaporation and by allowing only a limited amount of water to flow in and out of the wetland depending on the year in question and the marsh's hydrological condition at the time (dry, normal or flood years). Based on these considerations, the Ministry of Water Resources (MoWR) set the total peak inflow of water required for the Huwayza Marsh in the amount of 50 cu.m.\s.

The hydrological analyses prepared by the MoWR and subsequently verified by the New Eden Team also defined that prior to reaching the two outlets, the Kassarah and Swaib Rivers are where the flow comes out of the system. The Kassarah River is in the central part of the marsh and the Swaib River is in the southern part of the marsh. Such a flood wave would be reduced to half its size or approximately 100 cu.m.\s. Based on these results, the MoWR concluded that the Kassarah regulator should be designed to operate at 35 cu.m.\s and be able to pass a 100-year design flood of 125 cu.m.\s, whereas the Swaib regulator should be designed to operate at 65 cu.m.\s and be able to pass a100-year flood of 200 cu.m.\s. It should be noted that a marsh filled with water but lacking in outflows will be emptied in about a year, or near to the minimum water depth through evaporation alone.

Actions needed to achieve marsh regeneration:
1. Implement both the Kassarah and Swaib head water regulators according to the detailed design provided by the New Eden Team to the Ministry of Water Resources (December 2007).
2. Provide further evaluation on the impact of the internal roads and embankments to the general pattern of circulation inside the Huwayza Marsh.
3. Establish an infrastructure plan for opening and modifying roads and embankments in order to enhance water circulation inside the Huwayza Marsh.
4. Evaluate the possibility of removing\modifying the Iran–Iraq embankment in order to increase water exchange between Iraq and Iran.

Social and Settlement Position

During the last two decades many significant changes have taken place in the forms of settlements in the Huwayza Marsh, and when the marsh was drained during the early 1990s the marsh dwellers fled to neighboring Iran and major Iraqi towns and cities. It had thus become empty from permanent habitation as represented by the degradation of marsh villages; the deep marshes vanished and on its borders only small cottages made from cane remained. These were built by fishermen and buffalo breeders from where many of the residents of the near villages came. These were poor agricultural villages lacking in modern irrigation and draining and consisted of incomplete hydraulic systems. Also, the purchasing power of the local inhabitants was minimal. The social fabric of the local inhabitants has been decimated in spite of the fact they have lived in Huwayza Marsh and the land surrounding the marsh for many centuries and have learned to interact and to adapt to the existing environment.

Where there is interaction between factors of nature and the environment it is obvious that what is being supplied from these resources is water and plants (especially the bulrush, reed and papyrus, etc.). Finally, the native inhabitants have to determine whether suitable solutions can be reached using the available natural resources or whether they must adopt alternative building techniques. This interaction was to mitigate the negative impact of the environment and to facilitate and assist the inhabitants to try and create a suitable microclimate that befits the circumstances.

This relationship between humans and nature in the marshlands led to the creation of an organic environment consisting of three major forces: growth, change and decay. These forces affect nature's overall normal response – away from the central controls. It then creates a complete organic system through the control of the marshes and their surroundings. This is the dominant feature of these small settlements which may be called small villages and which normally have a population of about one thousand perople.

This clearly suggests that some parts of the marshes depend primarily in the first instance on fishing, bird hunting and breeding of cows and water buffalo. With the demise of the marshes, agriculture took on an increasingly important role. These activities include the cultivation of rice, wheat and barley. Other activities include the traditional handicraft industries which depend for raw materials on the presence of reed, etc., of which there is an abundance of in the area. These activities are not by their nature required in large urbanized centers containing high services because such centers like Basrah, Misan and Qlat Salah are near to it and can thus be supplied by it.

There are tens of villages in the Huwayza Marsh and in the area surrounding it forming a social fabric for the marshes. Typical villages include: Um Welha, al-Awana, Um Naaj, al-Mayil, Abo Khasaf, al-Raffai, Um-Warred, al-Akraa, Al-Triabah, Um-Nateeha ,Um-Aspeta, Al-Sakhrah, Bayt Helehil, Bayt Choban, Bayt Humood, Bayt Meri, Bayt Batah, Alboghnaam, Bayt Kishyaish, Bayt Battool, Bayt Khalif, Bayt Husan, Bayt Nagish, Marrbay, Albo Bokheett, Bayt Khoaaf, al-Baydhah, al-Zichayeih, etc.

Generally speaking, there are two main tribes that socially relate to them, these are the Albu Muhammad and the Swaaid tribes. The tribal impact on the social fabric of the population is considerable, making it difficult sometimes to apply the laws that help mitigate negative activities, whether relating to environmental or social aspects which are required to socially educate and put in place effective mechanical procedures to implement the laws. The role played by civil social organizations in Misan to improve the management of Huwayza remains very weak and ineffective and cannot be relied upon. Likewise, the governorate and municipality councils of Misan and surrounding cities of Huwayza have a limited role in this field too.

The regeneration process for the Huwayza Marsh should include:
1. The redistribution of population and human settlement by providing the necessary services in the form of infrastructure and land planning.
2. Appropriate use of water resources for economic development.
3. Developing the wealth of fish, birds and buffaloes and wildlife.
4. Providing adequate infrastructure to allow and facilitate distribution of human settlements.
5. Developing the environmental and constructional aspects through the use of traditional methods and materials to decrease the impact of pollution on the environment.

THE HAMMAR MARSHES

The Hammar wetlands (Arabic: *Hawr*) are among the more important of Iraq's wetlands because of their size and geographical location between two important governorates: Basrah and Thi Qar, and also due to the large number of marsh villages surrounding it and providing its economic diversity. Its importance is further enhanced by the proximity of ancient archaeological sites to the Hammar wetlands. They lie essentially to the south of the Euphrates River (which is currently the main water source of the marshes) and to the west of Shatt al-Arab. At Qarmat Ali, the water drains into the Shatt al-Arab which later flows into the Arabian Gulf (Persian Gulf).

The Hammar Marshes are the largest in terms of area of the three major marshes. However, scholars are not in agreement on when the wetlands were actually created or precisely how large they are. The scholar George Roux, for example, wrote in the Sumer journal in 1957 that the Hammar wetlands was a recent creation and that it did not exist during the years 1825–1827, whereas Dr Ahmed Sousa says that the Hammar Marshes is ancient and that many scholars and Arab historians refer to it by the name of 'Batiha al-Basrah' and 'Batiha al-Kufa'. Estimates of its size vary between 1,250 square kilometers and more than 5,000 square kilometers.

The American firm TAMS estimates (based on a survey it made in 1958) that the marshes, which draws its water mainly from the Euphrates River, is in normal times about 1,250 square kilometers. Dr Mohammed al-Taie estimates it to be 2,441 square kilometers and Dr Shakir Mustafa Salim estimates it to total approximately 3,900 square kilometers whereas Mr. Taha Al Hashimi puts it at about 5,000 square kilometers. Dr. Ahmed Sousa estimated it to be about 2,500 square kilometers. A primary reason for the wide difference between the various estimates is due to the lack of stability in the river levels which will also vary according to the season and year.

This area of the marsh is estimated to be about 3,000 square kilometers during normal circumstances of the season and before the drainage operations of the early 1990s; however, Hammar Lake from the hydraulic side is considered as a huge natural reservoir to control the flooding in the lower part of the Euphrates River and is also considered to be the largest extended depression for the waters on the right side of the same river.

The Euphrates River has many tributaries going out from it in the end of al-Nassiria City and many of these tributaries feed the Hammar Lake, but al-Galioon and al-Safha tributaries were the most significant supporters in feeding the Hammar Marsh which come from the Aakeka, Bani Hassan tributaries followed by other branches at the end of Suq al-Shuyukh (western Hammar) such as al-Hafar, Um Nakhla, Karmat Bani Saied. On these rivers there are some drainage systems which reach 150 cu.m./sec and 500 cu.m./sec and a total of 1,300 cu.m./sec.

The Hammar Marsh is also fed by the flooding of the Tigris River through the Qurna Marshes by bridges and pipes located at dykes along the Nasirya – Chubayish road which is parallel to the Euphrates River and which divides the Hammar Marshes which reach 500–600 cu.m./sec as a drainage system. When floods take place with a high water level, the water passes through the Central Marshes going to the Hammar Marsh over the embankments and travels upstream unless there is a dry season when the current will normally drift to the Central Marshes from the same barriers and pipes. The current of Hammar Marsh will continue to the Euphrates River and Karmat Ali River, Ashafi, al-Ghameeg, and Shat al-Arab; some of the water from Karmat Ali River goes to Khor al-Zubair and then the Arabian Gulf through Shat al-Basrah.

The Hammar Marsh forms a large lake during the flooding season, which in the dry season becomes many smaller shallow lakes having water levels of only 0.2– 0.5 meters deep. The length of the Hammar Marsh from the village of Hammar to the Karma River is estimated to be about 90 kilometers, and its width is estimated to be between 25 to 30 kilometers.

The highest recorded level for the water located in the northwest side is called *wana*, of the marsh named by al-Fihood and reaches 3.47 meters in the year 1969 while the depth of the stream on the west side is about 0.8m and on the east reaches 0.05 meters, the capacity of the stream in the flooding season is 5 billion cubic meters and it goes down to 0.18 billion cubic meters during the dry season.

Works and Projects Implemented in the Hammar Marshes after 1990
There was a major operation by the Saddam regime to drain the water from the Hammar Marsh and make it dry to the extent that it becomes uninhabitable and to allow the government to track political opponents and resistance and terminate them. At the same time, it was a good way to control the people using the official pretext of constructing agricultural projects for the people such as the numerous projects like the Malha, al-Shafi, Um Nakhla, al-Kirmashia, Ayman al-Furat and al-Mubzil al Qousi. The implementation of the Ayman al-Furat project in particular played a crucial role in the drainage of the Hammar Marsh. High dykes were constructed on both banks of the Euphrates to an approximate length of 94 km from the Haffar regulator to the point where the Euphrates River meets with the Tigris River at Qurna in addition to making other tributaries get together into the same flow to the Euphrates River in al-Fihood point and these tributaries to regulators of Suq al-Shuyukh as represented by the Giluoon, Akika and Bani Hasan Rivers.

To complete the dryness operation a newly constructed river called "Um al-Ma'arik" was constructed for the purpose of absorbing a large percentage of the water discharged from the Euphrates River at Nassariya and transferring it at a distance from the marshes so that it drains into a general area at Kilo 61 near the balancing basins. It should also be noted that the Basrah water project which is diverting the Garraf water to the city of Basrah intersects the Hammar Marsh and intersects the main basin; this creates a significant obstacle to the smooth flow of water inside the marsh.

The Hammar Marsh and its Reflooding

No appropriate planning procedures were taken to reflood the Hammar Marsh with water after April 2003 and furthermore no plan was put in place to feed water into these areas to an appropriate water level. To address this, the local people breached the al-Masahab dykes and flooded the southern part of the marsh in the opposite direction from the water of Karmat Ali tributaries in Basrah. The local Ma'dan also opened some other barriers in Karmat Bani Saied including the security barriers, to fill the lower parts from the north side of the Hammar Marsh after the fall of the Saddam regime.

However, it should be noted that this operation constitutes only partial flooding and has proved to be bad for the micro environment because during the summer months there are high concentrated levels of salt due to there being no outlet for the water in addition to the increased percentage of evaporation, especially during this period.

In the year 2007, due to the economic importance of the Hammar Marsh the native inhabitants of the surrounding villages decided to create three openings in the Ayman al-Furat dyke located opposite al-Muwajid area in Chubayish to flood a large area of the central part of the Hammar Marsh.

In order to create a healthy water environment in the Hammar Marsh that meets the general requirements of everyday living, we must first determine the total area to be flooded and to what depths, based on topographical documents, hydrological studies and mathematical models conducted during previous years. We also need to remove any barriers and barrages that restrict necessary flow of water to the marshes.

We also need to build a new feeding regulator system on the right side of the Euphrates barrage, south of al-Tar subdistrict (*nahiya*) in accordance with the Italian designs prepared at the beginning of 2008. In addition, reflooding of the marsh area located at the end of Um Nakhla and left of the Basrah water project up to the main Mubzil for the Malihha project by passing water from Um Nakhla through the opening of some regulators in the dykes of the Euphrates River on the south of the pumping station at al-Fihood area, and which forms a major part of the lower sections of the Hammar Marsh. The levels of Hammar Marsh range between 0.5–1.0 meters above sea level which requires 30 cu.m./ sec of water to keep the equal percentage between the water quantity and the evaporation level through summertime, also the same small connection with Um Nakhla River by watching the natural block will happen through the moving of the current, also by building some drainage system to regulate the water flowing into the main reservoir.

We can also join together the deepest canal of Hammar Marsh by keeping the dynamic hydraulic movement of the water from the north of the stream to Karmat Ali River with all the needs that are required to build control system and build vents and open the 135 ARAMCO vents under the North Rumaila road and Remove some of the upper sections of the Mabzil al-Malihha to succeed in joining the northern marsh with the southern marsh and to lower the pressure on the shoulder of the Basrah water project and the cultivated lands in al-Fihood area.

The Hammar Marsh Settlement Situation
The Hammar Marsh has great diversity in the types of settlements and their size and, because of the scarcity of suitable dry land area in the parts that were immersed with water, played an important role in the way that the scattered people in these areas lived. Moreover, due to the lack of any official interest from the government and other organizations, the marsh dwellers were deprived of necessary services to the area. Likewise, the Northwest areas surrounding the Hammar Marsh is excellent agricultural land suitable for settlement and for the production of rice and date trees except for the fact that there is no current plan in place or any future plans as part of a program or future vision for the region.

The social, economic and environmental circumstances that exist in the settlements of this area do not correspond to the naturally available wealth nor to the capital money being spent through dispersed development projects and scattered facilities because the existing standards of living, feeding, education, health, habitat and transportation were still at a primitive level in which little of the modern age had managed to permeate (Figures 12.5, 12.6).

The big change in Hammar Marsh came after the draining operations of the early 1990s, and then the partial reflooding after 2003 had a significant impact on the existing settlements in the area as more than forty villages which had populations of between 100 and 2,000 inhabitants completely disappeared. Many of the displaced villagers migrated to Iraqi towns on the middle Euphrates, like Najaf, Karbala, and southern towns and cities like Basrah and Nassiriya, in addition to districts like Suq al-Shuyukh, Chabayish and

Figure 12.5 Photo of two men in boat in north Hammar Marsh after gathering reed and transporting it to the village (Photo: Jasim al-Asadi).

Figure 12.6 Photo of *mushuf* in narrow canal in North Hammar Marsh.

Midayina, which have created a mixed heterogeneous group of towns that reflect negatively on the social fabric of the region due to the disparity in customs, education and traditions.

And to create from the Hammar Marsh a part of the legendary Eden, we need to create a suitable environment within the region that reflects the social aspirations and settlements that are characterized by an ancient culture.

THE CENTRAL MARSHES

The Central Marshes, also called the Qurna Marshes, lie upstream of the confluence of the Tigris and Euphrates and are bounded by the two rivers. These marshes are at the heart of the Mesopotamian wetland ecosystem. They are fed mainly by the Tigris distributaries and cover an area of approximately 300 square kilometers and it can absorb the floodwaters during the flood season which shrinks during the normal seasons. It is considered to be very diverse and is located within the boundaries of three governorates, Thi-Qar, Basrah and Missan. The Central Marshes prior to being drained in the 1990s was fed hydraulically by the end tributaries of the Tigris River in the area of Amarah and consisted of the river Butaira, the Areedh and the Majer al-Kabir up to the Euphrates River to the south between Suq al-Shuyukh and Qurna. The Central Marshes connect to the Hammar Marsh in the area between the Fihood and the Midayina. The Marshes form a continuous body spread between floating islands, settlements and reed houses reflecting their Sumerian heritage. But the major changes that have taken place over the last two decades have left their thumbprints on the fabric of the Central Marshes to the degree that it now requires concentrated efforts to revive them.

What happened to the Central Marshes?

After the early 1990s, the Central Marshes were completely drained and the marsh ecosystem completely desiccated. This was made possible through the use of military and political means against the local population. Some of these operations included engineering projects such as:

- Building of the glory River (Iz River) and diverting all the waters from the Tigris tributaries which flow into the Central Marshes to the Euphrates River south of Midayina City and from there into Shatt al-Arab.
- The construction of a dam east of the Euphrates River, blocking all the openings between the Central Marshes and the Euphrates River.
- Closing the openings for the Abu Lahya River which branches out of the Garraf River and preventing it from feeding the Central Marshes.

- Constructing a number of roads within the Marshes after they was dried to allow the military to seek out the rebels and anyone else against the regime that may be hiding in the marshes.
- The destruction and burning of the homes of local inhabitants and forcing them to flee their homes to neighboring countries and to other towns and cities within Iraq. This certainly is not the Iraq that the British author Gavin Young recalls and describes in his famous work *Return to the Marshes: Life with the Marsh Arabs of Iraq* in which he portrays the marshes as "another world".

The current hydraulics of the Central Marshes and what needs to be done

As was the case with the Hammar River, the pressing needs of the local population drove them to breach the barrages on the left flanks of the Euphrates and more specifically at Abu Saubat, Abu Alnarsi and Abu Jawaylana, which allowed the water to enter the Central Marshes in the middle of January 2004. This caused a reverse flow from the Euphrates River, which is characterized by high salinity, to an area that previously consisted of fresh water. This was followed by the creation of more openings on the same dyke by the Departments of Irrigation totaling more than seventeen openings. The amount of water entering the marshes normally depends on the Euphrates water levels at the time south of Karmat Bani Said and which is affected by the operation systems of the Haffar, Karmat Bani Hassan, Karmet Bani Said, Akeeka and Glyewain.

It is true that the density of biodiversity in the marshlands has increased substantially during the last few years since the commencement of reflooding, except that this type of diversity has been negatively impacted by the water's salinity and physio-chemical properties. It is also true that the hydraulic situation in the Central Marshes requires a number of topographical surveys and engineering work such as:

- Locate and record the water levels of the rivers and tributaries to the Central Marshes, including the estuaries of the Butaira, the Areedh and the Majer al-Kabeer and check the elevations of their embankments.
- Conduct a topographical survey of the wetlands and prepare drawings to an appropriate scale, accurately record all drainage systems and depth of water levels.
- Conduct a detailed hydraulic study to determine draining and water levels.
- Conduct a study to determine the possibility of breaching the upper section of the southern barrage of the Glory River in addition to constructing an observation post to monitor and regulate the water levels

at the confluence of the upper section with the vertical section. This will allow the diversion of all the water that will be accumulated from the Butaira, the Areedh and the Majar al-Kabeer Rivers to the marsh area through a canal or channel that can be built to connect the proposed opening to the nearest deep canal leading to the deep portions of the marshes.

- Construction of inlet regulator devices to allow the water to enter through the proposed openings using the required channels.
- Employment of inlet regulators upon existing openings on the way to the town of Chabayish in accordance with designs prepared by the New Eden Team with a study and putting in place of a lockdown regulator at the end of the Glory River (Iz River).

GENERAL OBJECTIVES

How can we regenerate the Iraqi marshes into the legendary Eden that once flourished, and what is the path to ensure that the human element harmonizes with the environment with all its biodiversity? Finding solutions to these questions allows us to put in place concepts for a visionary framework for creation of a healthy infrastructure for the building of a new Eden that is able to develop and flourish.

The initial priorities of these visions are the reflooding of the marshes using balanced policies that are in accord with the Tigris and Euphrates basins administration and which are based on mathematical examples, hydraulic calculations and the hydraulics implementation of all construction that pertains to controls, bridges and roads. It is also imperative to prepare complete structural designs for the Iraqi wetlands area as well as agricultural development plans for the areas adjacent to and surrounding the marshes, in addition to putting in place a marsh infrastructure that corresponds to the marsh area's importance and the magnitude of the marshes' desiccation using available resources.

DEVELOPING AND MODERNIZING THE TOURISM SECTOR

The tourism industry has become one of the fundamental sources that is impacting the global economy. And since Iraq has been endowed with so much natural beauty and great geographical diversity in addition to inheriting tremendous cultural heritage, it is only natural that an effective policy should be instigated to develop tourism, particularly in the southern marsh region. This region provides a prime tourist attraction because it extends to include a large area of the marshes that comprises a very diverse wildlife and ecosystem, including fauna, flora, mammals, fish and birds. And with the human factor and the other supplementary elements are the ingredients for successful Iraqi tourism. What is urgently needed is a study regarding the type of environmental tourism outlining the provision of necessary services which will offer suitable work opportunities that will help energize the economy and benefit and improve the sociological situation, which is why planners need to take into consideration the following factors when planning tourism in the marsh area:

1. Development of the marshes as a unique and rare region and placing it into a natural protected environment that benefits from the objectives of the New Eden Team project to provide government protection of the Central Marshes and to protect the environment and biodiversity in addition to the development of continuous activities and the preservation of its cultural heritage as shown in Figure 12.7.

2. Issuing laws to protect the region, the local inhabitants and society and also the issuance of laws to protect the physical environment and the organization of hunting.

3. Energize traditional crafts based on folklore as well as encouraging local industries, local social customs and traditions and the development of supplementary services.

4. Maintain the traditional way of life of the local inhabitants and maintain building traditions and preparing the local population to welcome visitors.

5. Particular attention to be paid to the formation of water passageways and transportation lanes that can benefit tourist tours using local means of transport which is mainly the *mushuf or tarada* (small and large canoes respectively) which provide excellent tourist attractions.

6. Finding local restaurants in the area that specialize in local menus and provide local food in an appropriate manner that relies on the vast wealth and variety of fish and bird.

7. Benefiting from the reed and bulrush for the building of the guest houses (*mudhif*) and local cafes or tourist chalets and forming a harmony between the local environment and tourism while maintaining the local identity of the region. Also implementing the building of villages facing the water and water villages as well as villages on dry land that were designed by the New Eden Team, especially those designed by the Venetian architects for the Iraqi marshlands in 2007.

8. Upon disposing of Saddam's regime, the Iraqi Ministry of Culture organized an architectural design competition consisting of a museum

and a research center in a town close to the regenerated marshes. The museum would reflect the biodiversity of the marshes and its indigenous fauna, flora, birds, fish and mammals. The center for research of the Iraqi Marshes can easily be located in a town such as al-Chabayish. Such a facility would essentially be a center of ecological research on the marshes and would offer community assistance to the native inhabitants of the area in terms of training and skill development in order to help create new jobs and invigorate economic development in the area (Figure 12.8).

9. Development of climatic and environmental monitoring centers in the marshlands.
10. Prepare a comprehensive plan for the archaeological areas in the marshes as well as areas adjacent to the marshes. Plans should be based on international procedures for its protection and maintenance.

The concepts and approaches required to develop the region necessitate total integrated political and practical support that is appropriate to the development of tourism in Iraq. Additionally, according to the United Nations Environment Program, (UNEP), the Mesopotamian marshlands might become a World Heritage Site in 2011. This initiative is funded by the government

Figure 12.7 Map of National Park Area.

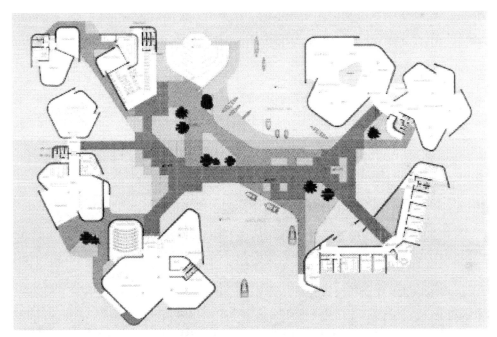

Figure 12.8a A proposed site plan for a museum and research center in the marshlands (Source: The RKBT Design Team).

Figure 12.8b A proposed museum and research center in the marshlands. The winning design of an architectural competition organized by the Iraqi Ministry of Culture, February 2005 (Source: The RKBT Design Team).

of Italy and aims to further the protection and conservation of the wetland, which has achieved global cultural, natural and environmental importance.

RECENT DEVELOPMENTS AND AGGRAVATING FACTORS AFFECTING MARSHLAND RESTORATION

Thanks to a combination of devestating drought, intensive dam construction and irrigation schemes upstream on the Tigris, Euphrates and other river systems, the ability to regenerate the wetlands has been greatly impaired.

In September 2009, Raheem Salman, an LA Times staff reporter, visited the town of Chibayish in the Iraqi marshlands, mainly to investigate the adverse impact the devastating drought has had on the region, particularly on its inhabitants, the marsh dwellers. In fact, what Salman found was that "Iraq's marshes are dying a second death. Vast lakes have shriveled. River beds have run dry. The animals are sick, the birds have flown elsewhere and an ancient way of life is facing a new threat to its existence. The fabled marshes of southern Iraq are dying again – only this time the forces of nature, not the hand of man, are to blame." The drought of the last couple of years has taken an unusually heavy toll on Iraq in general, but particularly on the wetlands. Salman says that today, the fish are dying once again, the buffaloes are sick, and the reeds on which they feed have disappeared. And thus, a proud people who have built their lives around this unique ecosystem for millennia, now find themselves helpless and no longer able to survive.

Although low rainfall is the primary factor in the marsh dwellers' current plight, the proliferation of massive dams, dykes and irrigation schemes along the headwaters of the two rivers (Figure 12.9) has stemmed a significant portion of the water supply, as well as much of the annual snowmelt floods which would not suffice even if Iraq's rain and snowfall exceeded normal levels. Much of this blame is placed on Iraq's immediate neighbors, Turkey, Syria and Iran. Representatives of the Iraqi government and those of its neighbors have been in ongoing negotiations for some time with no long-term prospects in sight. However, if the countries involved were able to mutually subscribe to proper water-sharing agreements and advanced management plans for water use, both upstream and in the marshes themselves, the future of the wetlands might be more promising. Moreover, the situation has deteriorated to such an extent that many tributaries have ceased to reach the sea, causing saltwater to seep into the marshes, rendering the waters undrinkable.

Additionally, Salman says that water that previously flowed freely now finds itself forming stagnant pools that breed harmful bacteria, so that, according to Salman, not only are the fish dying, but "Many marsh dwellers say their buffaloes are going blind, the female animals producing only a fraction of the milk they used to."

Moreover, many of the families that left the wetlands in the 1990s, and relocated again after Saddam was toppled, are once again either leaving, have already left, or are preparing to leave. This will be their second and perhaps final migration from the marshes. One can only hope that action taken by the authorities and international organizations ensures this does not happen.

Figure 12.9 Major water projects on the Tigris-Euphrates Rivers which are impeding the restoration of the wetlands (Source: After Amar Final Report – 2001, T. Naff & G. Hanna).

ABBREVIATIONS USED IN BIBLIOGRAPHY

A.A.	American Anthropologist.
A.A.S.O.R.	Annual of the American Schools of Oriental Research, New Haven.
A.J.	Antiquaries Journal, London.
A.J.A.	American Journal of Archaeology, Cambridge, Mass.
A.S.	Anatolian Studies, London.
B.A.S.O.R.	Bulletin of the American Schools of Oriental Research. Baltimore.
B.M.	Bibliotheca Mesopotamica.
C.A.H.	Cambridge Ancient History.
CIMI	Canada-Iraq Marshlands Initiative
GATE	German Appropriate Technology Exchange.
GTZ	German Agency for Technical Cooperation.
I.E.S.	Israel Exploration Journal.
I.L.N.	Illustrated London News.
I.I.M.A.S.	The International Institute for Mesopotamian Area Studies, California.
J.A.N.E.S.	The Journal of the Ancient Near Eastern Society of Columbia University.
J.A.O.S.	Journal of the American Oriental Society, New Haven.
J.A.S.	Journal of Archaeological Science.
J.F.A.	Journal of Field Archaeology.
J.N.E.S.	Journal of Near Eastern Studies, Chicago.
J.O.S.	Journal of Oman Studies, Muscat.
J.R.A.I.	Journal of the Royal Anthropological Institute.
J.R.A.S.	Journal of the Royal Asiatic Society, London.
NA	Nature Iraq
O.I.P.	Oriental Institute Publications.
P.E.Q.	Palestine Exploration Quarterly.
P.P.S.	Proceedings of the Prehistoric Society.
S.A.	Sovetskaja Arkheologija
S.A.O.C.	Oriental Institute of the University of Chicago, Studies in Ancient Oriental Civilization.
S.O.A.H.	State Organization of Antiquities and Heritage, Baghdad.
T.P.R.	Town Planning Review.
UNEP	United Nations Environmental Program
U.S.A.I.D	United States Agency for International Development
W.A.	World Archaeology.
W.V.D.O.-G.	Wissenschaftliche Veroffentlichung der Deutschen Orient-Gesellschaft, Leipzig.

BIBLIOGRAPHY

Abaychi, J.K. and Al- Saad, H.T.
1988   Trace elements in fish from the Arabian Gulf and the Shatt Al- Arab river, Iraq- Bull. Enuiron . Contam. Toxicol .,40: 226-232

Abdul Amir, Wasfi
2004   The Hammar Marshes, Unpublished research, Baghdad.

Abdulhasan NA, Salim MA
2008   Key Biodiversity Survey of Southern Iraq.

Abu Al-Soof, B.
Nd.   Use of Wood, Reed and Other Plants in Ancient Iraqi Architecture. Unpublished Manuscript.

Al-A'dami, K.A.
1968   Excavations at Tell es-Sawwan (Second Season). Sumer 24(1,2):53-94.

Ageel, S.G.
2004   Abundance and Distribution of zooplankton in some waters in southern region of Iraq. Marina Mesopotamica, 19 (1): 95-115.

Allouse, B.E.
1953a   Avifauna of Iraq. Al Tafyudh Press. Baghdad, Iraq.
1953b   The avifauna of Iraq. Iraq Nat. Hist. Mus. Publ. 3: 1-163.
1962   Birds of Iraq. Vol. III. Baghdad Ar-Rabitta Press. Baghdad.

Amiet, P.
1961   La Glyptique Mesopotamienne Archaique. CNRS, Paris.

Andrae, W.
1935   Die Jungeren Ischtar-Tempel in Assur. J.C.Hinrichs, W.V.D.O.-G.58, Leipzig.

Aqrawi, A.A.M.
2001   Stratigraphic signatures of climatic change during the Holocene evolution of the Tigris-Euphrates delta, lower Mesopotamia. Global and Planetary Change 28:267-283.

Aqrawi, A.A.M. and Evans, G.
1994   Sedimentation in the lakes and marshes (Ahwar) of the Tigris-Euphrates Delta, southern Mesopotamia. Sedimentology 41:755-776.

Azarpay, G.
1987   Proportional Guidelines in Ancient Near East Art. JNES 46, No.3

Baker, H.S.
1966   Furniture in the Ancient World - Origins & Evolution (3100-475 BC). The Connoisseur, London.

Banister, K.E.
1980   The fishes of the Tigris and Euphrates river. In: Rzoska, J. (ed.), Euphrates and Tigris Mesopotamian Ecology and Destiny; 95-108. J.W. Junk.

Barnett, R.D.
1957   A Catalogue of the Nimrud Ivories in the British Museum. London.

Beek, M.A.
1962   Atlas of Mesopotamia, A survey of the history and civilisation of Mesopotamia from the Stone Age to the fall of Babylon, translated by D.R. Welsh, edited by H.H.Rowley, London, Nelson.

British Museum
1969   Sumerian Art.   British Museum, London.

Bromehead, C.N.
1954   Mining and Quarrying, In A History of Technology, Singer, C. et al.,
                eds., Oxford University Press, New York & London:563.

Buller, H.
1983   Methodological Problems in the Microwear Analysis of Tools
                Selected from the Natufian Sites of El-Wad and Ain Mallaha.
                In Traces d'utilisation sur les outils ne'olethiques du Proche Orient,
                Travaux de la Maison de l'Orient no.5, GIS - Maison de l'Orient, Paris.

Buringh, P.
1957   Living Conditions in the Lower Mesopotamian Plain in Ancient Times.
                Sumer 13:30-57.

Butrus, Kheduri Butrus
2004   The Qurna Marshes, an unpublished research (Arabic), Baghdad.

Butzer, Karl W.
1965   Environment, Culture, and Human Evolution. American Scientist,
                Volume 65, Issue 5.
1976   Physical conditions in Eastern Europe, Western Asia and Egypt
                before the period of Agriculture and urban settlements. In Cambridge
                Ancient History, eds. Edwards, I.E.S., et al., Cambridge.

Carter, T.H. & Pagliero, R.
1966   Notes on Mud-Brick Preservation, Sumer 33(1,2):65-76.

Coad, W. B.
1991   Fishes of Tigris-Euphrates basin : A critical checklist. *Syllogeus* No.68.
2010.   Freshwater fishes of Iraq. Pensoft Publishers, Sofia, Moscow.

Daham, N.K.
1988   Development of fisheries in Marshes, Facts and Solutions. J. Al Kaleje
                Al Arabe, 20 (2): 85-97 (Arabic).

Davey, N.
1961   A History of Building Materials. Phoenix House, London.

Dawood, Radhi Mihsen
Nd.   Towards a general strategy to nurture the Economy of the Iraqi Marshes,
                Internet Site of the Imam Al Sheirazi for International Studies,
                Washington.

Delougaz, P., Hill, H.D., & Lloyd, S.
1967   Private Houses and Graves in the Diyala Region. O.I.P., Chicago.

Eaton-Francis, M.
1972   Mesopotamian building materials and techniques of the early dynastic
                period. Marsyas, 16.

Evans MI
1994   Important Bird Areas in the Middle East, BirdLife Conservation Series
                No. 2. Cambridge, United Kingdom: BirdLife International.
2001   The Ecosystem in Iraqi Marshlands: Prospects. Proceedings of a
                Conference of the AMAR International Charitable Foundation. London,
                United Kingdom.

Flandin, E.
?   Voyage Archeologique. ?

Flannery, K.V. & Wright, H.T.
1965   The ecology of early food production in Mesopotamia. Science 147: 1247-56.
1966   Faunal Remains from the 'Hut Sounding' at Eridu. Sumer 22: 61-63.

Forbes, R.J.
1964   Studies in Ancient Technology, Vol.I. E.J. Brill, Leiden.
1965   Studies in Ancient Technology, Vol. II, E.J. Brill, Leiden.

Forest, J.D.
1983a   Aux Origines de l'architecture Obedienne: Les Plans de Type Samarra. Akkadica 34 (Sept/Oct).
1983b   The Obeid 4 Architecture at Tell El'Oueili. Sumer, 39(1,2):20-30.
1983c   Kheit Qasim III - An Obeid Settlement, Sumer 40(1,2):85
1985-86   Tell El 'Oueili, Preliminary report on the 4th Season (1983), Stratigraphy and Architecture. Sumer 44:55-65.
1987   La Grande Architecture Obeidienne Sa Forme e't Sa Fonction, In Pre'histoire de La Mesopotamie, La Me'sopotamie pre'historique et l'exploration re'centge du djebel Hamrin. CNRS, Paris.

Frankfort, H.
1934   Iraq Excavations of the Oriental Institute 1932/33: Third Preliminary Report of the Iraq Expedition. University of Chicago Press,
1939   Cylinder Seals. Macmillan and Co., London.
1943   More Sculpture from the Diyala Region. University of Chicago Press, Oriental Institute Publications, Vol.LX, Chicago.
1970   The Art and Architecture of the Ancient Orient. Pelican History of Art, Penguin Books.

Fulanain (S. E. and M. G. Hedgecock)
1927   Haji Rikkan – Marsh Arab, Chatto & Windus, London, 1927

Gorelick, L. & Williams-Forte, E.
1983   Ancient Seals & the Bible. The International Institute for Mesopotamian Area Studies (IIMAS), California.

Guest, E. ed.
1966   Flora of Iraq in The vegetation of Iraq and adjacent regions, Ministry of Agriculture, Baghdad, Republic of Iraq.

Hall, E.T.
1959.   The Silent Language. Doubleday & Co., New York.
1969.   The Hidden Dimension. Doubleday & Co., New York

Hall, H.R. & Woolley, C.L.
1927   Ur Excavations I: Al-Ubaid, Vol.1, Oxford University Press, Oxford.

Hamdan, M. A., Asada, T., Hassan, F.M., Warner, B.G., Douabul, A.A., Al-Hilli, M. R. A. and Alwan. A. A.
2010   Vegetation response to re-flooding in the Mesopotamian wetlands, southern Iraq. Wetlands (in press)

Hammer, Joshua
2006   "Return to the marsh: the effort to restore the Marsh Arabs' traditional way of life in southern Iraq—virtually eradicated by Saddam Hussein—faces new threats." Smithsonian 37.7, p.46(10).

Hatt, R.T.
1959   The mammals of Iraq. Misc. Publ. Museum Zool. University of Michigan 106: pp. 1-113.

Al-Hilli, M.R.
1977   Studies on the plant ecology of the Ahwar region in southern Iraq. PhD. Thesis Faculty of Science, University of Cairo, Egypt.

Al-Hilli, M. R. A., Warner, B.G., Asada, T., and Douabul, A.A.
2009   An assessment of vegetation and environmental controls in the 1970s of the Mesopotamian wetlands of southern Iraq. Wetlands Ecology and Management 17:207–223.

Hinton, G.C.F., and Maulood, B.K.
1983   Check list of the algae from inland waters of Iraq. Journal of the University of Kuwait (Science) 10:191-264.

Hodges, H.W.M.
1970   Technology in the Ancient World. Alfred A. Knopf, New York.

Iraq Foundation
2004   The New Eden Project / Final Report

Iraqi Ministry of Culture
2004   Seminar on Iraqi Marshlands for construction of Museum and Research Center

Jacobsen, Th. & Adams, R.T.
1960   Salt and Silt in Ancient Mesopotamian Agriculture. Science, Vol.128: pp.1252-58.

Jasim, S.A.
1985   The Ubaid Period in Iraq, (1,2), BAR International Series 267(i), Oxford.

Jasim, S.A. & Oates, J.
1986   Early tokens and tablets in Mesopotamia: new information from Tell Abada and Tell Brak. In World Archaeology, Vol.17 No.3, Early writing systems: 348-362.

Joedet, Nada Shakir.
1980   Rural Settlement in the Marshes in the Governorate of Thi-Qar, Unpublished MA Thesis (Arabic), Baghdad

Al-Kaissi, B.
1984   Mural Paintings and Pigments in Iraq. Sumer. 43(1,2):168-174.

Keddy, P.A.
2000   Wetland ecology: Principles and conservation. Cambridge University Press, Cambridge, U.K. 614 pp.

Khalaf, K.E.
1961.   The Marine and Freshwater Fishes of Iraq. Baghdad: Ar-Rabitta Press.

Al Khayat, Hassan
1975   The Geography of the Marshes and the Swamps of Southern Iraq (Arabic), Baghdad.

Keeley, L.H.
1983   Neolithic Novelties: The view from ethnography and microwear analysis. In Traces d'utilisation sur les outils ne'olethiques du Proche Orient, Travaux de la Maison de l'Orient no.5, GIS-Maison de l'Orient, Paris:251-258.

Koldewey, R.
1914   The Excavations at Babylon. Macmillan, London.
Kubba, S.
1974   The Manufacture of Mesopotamian Furniture during the 2nd
                Millennium BC (in Arabic), Al Jamhooriya Newspaper Color
                Supplement. Feb. 16, 1974. Baghdad.
1987   Mesopotamian Architecture and Town Planning, from the Mesolithic
                (ca.10,000 BC) to the Proto-historic (ca.3500 BC). B.A.R., Oxford.
1990   Architecture and Linear Measurement During the Ubaid Period in
                Mesopotamia. B.A.R. International Series, Oxford.
2006   Mesopotamian Furniture, B.A.R., Oxford.
Al-Lami, A.A.
1986.   An ecological study on phytoplankton for some of marshes Southern
                Iraq. M. Sc. thesis. University of Basrah.
Lavers, G.M.
1983   The Strength Properties of Timber (3rd ed. revised by G.L. Moore).
                Building Research Establishment Report - HMSO.
Layard, Sir A.H.
1849   Nineveh and its Remains, Two Vols., London.
1853   Discoveries in the ruins of Nineveh & Babylon. John Murray, London.
1891   Nineveh and its Remains. John Murray, London.
Lee, G.M. & Falcon, N.R.
1952   The geographical history of the Mesopotamian plain. Geographical
                Journal, Vol.118. pp.36-38
Legrain, L.
1930   Terra-cottas from Nippur. University of Pennsylvania nPress,
                Philadelphia.
Lloyd, Seton
1954   Building in Stone. In A History of Technology. C. Singer, E.G. Holmyard,
                & A.R. Hall, eds., 457-489.
1985   The Archaeology of Mesopotamia from the Old Stone Age to the Persian
                Conquest, Thames and Hudson, London.
Loud, G.
1936   Excavations in the Palace and at a City Gate. O.I.P.38, Chicago.
Luckenbill, D.D.
1926-7   Ancient Records of Assyria & Babylonia. Chicago (pp. 287,300).
Mac Fadyen, W.A.
1966   The Geology of Iraq. In The Flora of Iraq, Vol.1, ed. E. Guest,
                Ministry of Agriculture, Iraq.
Mahdi, N.
1962   Fishes of Iraq. Ministry of Education, Baghdad.
Mallowan, M.E.L.
1951   Excavations at Nimrud, 1949-1950 (?). Iraq, Vol.XIII.
1957   (?)Ivories Newly Discovered in Nimrud's "Fort Shalmaneser". The
                Illustrated London News , London, Nov.23 & 30, 1957.
1976   Nimrud and its Remains, Vols.1 & 2. Collins, London.
1978   The Nimrud Ivories. A Colonnade Book, British Museum Publications,
                Ltd. London.

Maltby, Edward (ed.),
1994   An Environmental & Ecological Survey of the Marshlands of
                    Mesopotamia, draft consultative bulletin published by the AMAR
                    Appeal Trust, May.

2004   Towards Cooperation And Management of Shared Mesopotamian

                    Wetland.(unpublished lecture /Geneva).

Maulood BK, Hinton GCF, Kamees HS, Saleh FAK, Shaban AA, Al Shahwani SMH
1979   An ecological survey of some aquatic ecosystems in southern Iraq.
                    Tropical Ecology 20:27-40.

Maulood BK, Hinton GCF., Whitton, B.A., and al-Saadi, H.A.
1981   On the algal ecology of the lowland Iraqi marshes. Hydrobiologia
                    80:269-276.

Maxwell, G.
1998   A Reed Shaken by the Wind. Eland Publishers, London, UK.

Mayah, A.R.
1994   Aquatic plants of marshes of southern Iraq, 127- 143. In N.A. Hussain
                    (Ed.) Ahwar of Iraq Environmental approach. Marine Science Center,
                    pub. 18. Basrah University.

Mc Henry, P.G. Jr.
1984   Adobe and Rammed Earth Buildings. Wiley-Interscience, John Wiley &
                    Sons, New York.

Middleton, B.
1999   Wetland restoration: Flood pulsing and disturbance dynamics. J.
                    Wiley and Sons Inc., N.Y.

Ministry of Culture – Republic of Iraq
2004   Studies of the special conference on the Iraqi Marshes to create a
                    research center and museum.

Mohamed, A.R.M. and Ali, T.S.
1992   The biological importance of Iraqi marshes in fish growth (pp:205-215).
                    In: N. A. Hussain (ed.) Ahwar of Iraq environmental approach.

Moorey, P.R.S.
1971   The Loftus Hoard of Old Babylonian Tools from Tell Sifr in Iraq. Iraq,
                    33, 61ff.

1985   Materials and Manufacture in Ancient Mesopotamia: The evidence of
                    Archaeology and Art. BAR International Series 237, Oxford.

Moortgat, A.
1969   The Art of Ancient Mesopotamia. Phaidon, London & New York.

Morosova, G.S.
2005   A review of Holocene avulsions of the Tigris and Euphrates Rivers
                    and possible effects on the evolution of civilization in Lower
                    Mesopotamia. Geoarchaeology 20:401-423.

Moss, H.E.
1983   A Microwear Analysis of Burins and Points from Tell Abu Hureyra,
                    Syria. In Traces d'utilisation sur les outils ne'olethiques du Proche
                    Orient, Travaux de la Maison de l'Orient no.5, GIS - Maison de l'Orient,
                    Paris: 143-155.

Mould, A.E. & Shaaban, A.C.
1970   Analysis of Climatic Data, Building Research Centre, The Scientific Research Organisation, Iraq.

Nature Iraq Organization
2008   Management Plan for the Huwayza Marsh, Iraq

Nicholson, E. and Clark, P. (editors)
2002   The Iraqi marshlands: A human and environmental study. Politico's Publishing, London.

Nissen, H.J.
1986   The archaic texts from Uruk. World Archaeology, Vol.17, No.3 - Early writing systems:317-334.

Oates, D.
1973   Early vaulting in Mesopotamia, In Archaeological Theory and Practice, ed. Strong, D.E., London & New York, Seminar Press. p. 169.

Oates, J.
1969   Choga Mami, 1967-68: A Preliminary Report. Iraq, 31:115-152.
1972   Prehistoric Settlement Patterns in Mesopotamia. In Man, Settlement & Urbanism, Ucko, P., Tringham, R. & Dimbleby, G., eds., Duckworth, England, 299-309

Ochsenschlager, Edward, L.
2004   Iraq's MarshArabs in the Garden of Eden, University of Pennsylvania, Museum of Archeology and Anthropology, .Parrot, A.
1958   Le Palais, Mission Archeologique de Mari. Vol.II, Librairie Orientaliste Paul Geuthner, Paris.
1960   Sumer (translated by S. Gilbert and J. Emmons). Thames & Hudson, London.

Partow, H.
2001   The Mesopotamian Marshlands: Demise of an Ecosystem, Early Warning and Assessment Technical Report, UNEP/DEWA/TR.01-3 Rev. 1, Nairobi, Kenya.

Pearce, Fred
1993   Draining life from Iraq's marshes. New Scientist 17 April 1993: 11-12.

Perrot, G. & Chipiez, C.
1884   A History of Art in Chaldea & Assyria. Chapman & Hall, London.

Petrie, Sir W.M. Flinders
1897   Thebes – 1896, London.

Porada, E.
1947   Mesopotamian Art in Cylinder Seals of The Pierpont Morgan Library. The Pierpont Morgan Library, New York.

Porter RF, Christensen S, Schiermacker-Hansen P
1996   Field Guide to the Birds of the Middle East. Helm Field Guides. United Kingdom, A&C Black Publishers Ltd. London.

Porter, R.F. and D.A. Scott.
2005   *Report on the Environmental Training Programme for Iraqis and Birds Recorded in Syria – January 20-29, 2005.* Canada-Iraq Marshlands Initiative Technical Report No. 3. University of Waterloo. Waterloo. Canada.

Postgate, J.N.
1980   Palm-Trees, Reeds and Rushes in Iraq, Ancient and Modern. In
                Colleques internationaux du CNRS No.580 - L'Archeologie De L'Iraq.
                Paris.

Al-Rawi, F.N.H. & Roaf, M.
1984.   Ten Old Babylonian Mathematical Problems from Tell Haddad, Himrin.
                Sumer 43(1,2):175-218.

Rechinger, K.
1964   Flora of Lowland Iraq. Hafner Publishing Ltd., New York.

Richardson, C.J.
2008   An ecological approach for the restoration of the Everglades fen. In:
                The Everglades Experiment. Edited by: C.J. Richardson. Springer,
                N.Y. pp. 621-642.

Richardson C.J. and Hussain NA.
2006.   Restoring the Garden of Eden: an ecological assessment of the
                marshes of Iraq. BioScience 56: pp. 477-489

Richardson, C.J., Reiss P., Hussain N.A., Alwash A.J., and Pool D.J.
2005.   The restoration potential of the Mesopotamian marshes of Iraq.
                Science 307:1307-1311.

Roaf, M.
1976   Excavations at Al-Markh, Bahrain. Proceedings of Seminar for Arabian
                Studies 6:pp. 144-160.
1984a   Ubaid Houses and Temples, Sumer, 43 (1,2):80-90.
1984b   Tell Madhhur: A Summary Report on the Excavations, edited by Roaf,
                M., Sumer, 43 (1,2):108-167.
1987   The Ubaid Architecture of Tell Madhhur. In Pre'histoire de la
                Mesopotamie. La Me'sopotamie pre'historique et l'exploration
                re'cente du djebel Hamrin. CNRS, Paris. p. 426

Roux, G.
1985   Ancient Iraq. London.

Rzoska, J. (ed.)
1980   Euphrates and Tigris Mesopotamian Ecology and Destiny. J.W. Junk.

Saad, M.A.H. and Antoine,S.E.
1978   Data on transparency suspended matter , total residues and volatile
                matter in Tigris , Iraq . Bulletin of the College of Science vol. vii
                pp.15-45.

Safar, F., Mustafa, M.A. & Lloyd, S.
1981   Eridu, S.O.A.H., Baghdad.

Salim, S.M.
1962   Marsh Dwellers of the Euphrates Delta, University of London, The
                Athlone Press, London
1970   Ech-Chibayish- An Anthropological Study of A Marsh Village In Iraq.
                Ph.D thesis, 1955 - Al- Aani Press, Baghdad.

Salim MA
2004a   I: Field Observations on Birds at Abu-Zarag and Kirmashiya Wetlands,
                Southern Iraq, 30 June – 4 July 2004. Project Report. Baghdad, Iraq:
                Nature Iraq.

2004b   II: Field Observations on Birds in Abu-Zarag and Kirmashiyah Wetlands, Southern Iraq, 24 – 28 July 2004. Project Report. Baghdad, Iraq: Nature Iraq.

2004c   III: Field Observations on Birds in Iraq since 1990 Project Report. Baghdad, Iraq: Nature Iraq.

Salim, M Porter, R.F. Christensen, S Schiermaker-Hansen, P & Jbour, S.

2006   Birds of Iraq (in Arabic) Published by Nature Iraq & BirdLife International. Amman, Jordan.

Salim M, Porter R, Rubec C

2009   A summary of birds recorded in the marshes of southern Iraq, 2005–2008. In: Krupp F, Musselman LJ, Kotb MMA, Weidig I (Eds) Environment, Biodiversity and Conservation in the Middle East.

Samarai, M. A.

1986   "Kassir chemical Data and tests on reeds and reed products". International symposium on the use of vegetable plants and their fibers for buildings, 7-10 October, Baghdad, Iraq.

Samarai, M. and Azawi, A.

1997   "Use of Indigenous Building Materials in Ancient and Islamic Civilizations: Conference on Challenges that face the Islamic World in the Next Century. University of UAE. 20-22/12/1997. Al-Ain, UAE.

Samarai, M. A. and Laquerbe, M.

1987   "Cold Stabilized Bricks, SBFProcess". UNESCO publication. Expert group meeting on energy-efficient building materials for low-cost Housing, Amman, Jordan, 14-19 Nov. 1987.

Samarai, M. and Al-Taie, F.

1986   Mud houses in Iraq. NaC.C.L. publication 22.

Sanlaville, P.

2002   The Deltaic Complex of the Lower Mesopotamian Plain and its Evolution through Millennia. In The Iraqi Marshlands: A Human and Environmental Study, Nicholson E. and Clark P. (eds).

Schmidt, J.

1974   Zwei Tempel der Obed-Zeit in Uruk, Baghdader Mitteilungen. pp.173-187, Berlin.

1978   Tell Mismar, ein Prahistorischer fundort in Sudiraq, Baghdader Mitteilungen 9:10-17, Berlin.

Scott, D. A. (ed.)

1995   *A Directory of Wetlands in the Middle East.* IUCN, Gland, Switzerland and IWRB, Slimbridge, U.K.

Semenov, S.A.

1970   Prehistoric Technology. Bath: Adams & Dart.

Singer, C., Holmyard, E.J. & Hall, A.R.

1954   A History of Technology. Oxford University Press, New York & London.

Starr, R.F.S.

1939   Nuzi: report on the excavations at Yorghan Tepa near Kirkuk, Iraq 1927-1931, 2 vols., Harvard University Press, Cambridge.

Thesiger, Wilfred

1967   The Marsh Arabs, Penguin Books, Harmondsworth.

Thomas, Bertram
 1931   Alarms and Excursions in Arabia, George Allen & Unwin Ltd.
Townsend, C.C. & Guest, E.
 1980   Flora of Iraq, Vol.4. ed. E. Guest, Ministry of Agriculture, Baghdad.
United Nations Environmental Program (UNEP)
 2003, 2004, 2005, & 2006.   Iraqi Marshland Observation System (UNEP/IMOS)
 2004   Desk Study on the Environment in Iraq, Geneva, Switzerland.
USAID
 2004   USAID's Prime Contractor: Development Alternatives, Inc. The
                 Marshlands Restoration Program
 2006   Iraq Marshlands restoration program. Final report. Washington, D.C.
Van Zeist, W. & Waterbolk-Van Rooijen, W.
 1985   The Paleobotany of Tell Bouqras, Eastern Syria. Paleorient, Vol.11/
                 2:131-147.
Van Buren, E.D.
 1949   The fauna of ancient Mesopotamia. Orientalia, Vol.18.
Watkins, T.
 1987   Kharabeh Shattani: An Halaf Culture Exposure in Northern Iraq. In
                 Pre'histoire De La Me'sopotamie. CNRS, Paris. p. 225.
Watson, Philip J.
 1984   The Small Finds from Tell Madhhur, Sumer 43(1,2):159-163.
Woodbury, R.S.
 1963   The Origins of the Lathe. Scientific American no.208. 4. 1963, P.7056.
Woolley, Sir L.
 1934   Ur Excavations, Vol.II - The Royal Cemetery.   Publications of the joint
                 expedition of the British Museum and of the Museum of the University
                 of Pennsylvania to Mesopotamia.
 1982   Ur of the Chaldes. Revised by P.R.S. Moorey, Herbert Press, London.
 1963   Prehistory and the Beginnings of Civilization. Vol.1, Part 2 (co-author
                 with J. Hawkes). George Allen & Unwin, London.
 1956   Ur Excavations IV: The Early Periods. London & Philadelphia.
Woolley, Sir L. & Mallowan, Sir M.
 1976   Ur Excavations, The Old Babylonian Period, Vol.VII, British Museum
                 Publications, London.
Wootton, J.E.
                 A Sumerian Statue from Tell Aswad. ?
Wright, G.R.H.
 1985   Ancient Building in South Syria and Palestine, Vols.1,2, E.J.Brill, Leiden.
Wulff, H.E.
 1966   The traditional crafts of Persia. Cambridge, Mass.: M.I.T. Press.
Young, Gavin
 1977   Return to The Marshes: Life with the Marsh Arabs of Iraq, Collins,
                 London.
Al-Zubaidi, A.J.M, D.S. Abdullah, K.K. Houriabi, and M. Fawzi.
 2006.   Abundance and distribution of phytoplankton in Southern Iraqi
                 waters. *Marsh Bulletin* 1 (1):59-73

INDEX